Max Lake was f
Australian surgeo
successful vineyard and winery, Lake's Folly, and is in international demand as a wine judge and lecturer on tasting. He has written six standard books on wine.

Also by Max Lake

HUNTER, WINE
CLASSIC WINES OF AUSTRALIA
VINE & SCALPEL
THE FLAVOUR OF WINE
CABERNET
HUNTER WINEMAKERS
START TO TASTE: WINE
START TO TASTE: FOOD
START TO TASTE: PEOPLE
THE FRAGRANCE OF LOVE

SCENTS AND SENSUALITY

The Essence of Excitement

Max Lake

Futura

A Futura Book

First published in 1989 by
John Murray (Publishers) Ltd

This edition published by Futura Publications in 1991

Reproduced, printed and bound in Great Britain by
BPCC Hazell Books
Aylesbury, Bucks, England
Member of BPCC Ltd.

ISBN 0 7088 4753 6

Futura Publications
A Division of
Macdonald & Co (Publishers) Ltd
Orbit House
1 New Fetter Lane
London EC4A 1AR
A member of Maxwell Macmillan Pergamon Publishing Corporation

Freude, schöner Götterfunken,
Tochter aus Elysium,
Wir betreten feuertrunken,

Himmlischer, dein Heiligtum!

Joy, fair divine spark,
Daughter of Elysium,
Heavenly maiden, aflame with ardour,
We enter thy holy place.

Words: Friedrich von Schiller, *An die Freude*
Music: Ludwig van Beethoven, Choral Symphony

Contents

Part Three: Style, Taste and Flavour

Part Four: The Molecules of Attraction

Part Five: Until Now

Acknowledgements

Three people, more than any others, have readied me to write this book. Professor Emeritus Maynard Amerine of California, one of the world's leading wine scientists, has had a very special and continuing influence on his students and friends, none more appreciative than I although we live separated by the Pacific Ocean. He will probably be surprised to hear that much of this work has been written in anticipation of his criticisms. Not having read it, he is blameless. I would not have taken the path I have without the friendship and encouragement of the late Jack Shipton, food scientist at the Australian Council for Scientific and Industrial Research. More recently, Dr Tom Clark, psychiatrist and pheromone researcher, has been generous enough to give that part of the book that deals with his field much of its shape.

I hope that the people listed below recognise their contributions. They responded warmly to incessant questions, or provided specialist information or criticism, at times both of those, and more. I am most grateful to them, and to those people, including many children, all over the world, met socially or encountered in perfume departments and fruit markets who may have helped me without knowing the purpose of my enquiries: Jane Adams, Suzanne Arnell, Professor Richard Bandler, Dr Gaston Bauer, Oz Clarke, Alan

Cook, Alan Davidson, Ted Davis, Michael Edwards, John Elliott, Mogens Bay Esbensen, Yvonne Grant, Henrietta Green, Aileen Hall, John Hanley, Mark de Havilland, Professor Graham Johnston, Dr Morley Kare, George Kepper, Dr David Laing, Judy Lee, Dr Julian Lee, Paul Levy, Yvonne MacFarlane, Peter Madden, Dr Michael Mandl, Julian Marriott-Brittan, Warren Mason, Bruce Miller, Melanie Morningstar, the staff at *La Normandie* in Sydney, Tak Nishizawa, Garth Palamountain, the late Geraldine Pascall, Tony Phelan, Chris Pirie, Jim Quinlan, Jill Rivers, Professor Pascal Ribereau-Gayon, Cherry Ripe, Rupert Rosenblum, Giancarlo Rusti, Barbara Santich, Peter Scuddamore-Smith, Ray Shipton, Peter Max Sichel, Harry Skolnik, John Stanford, Dr Miriam Stoppard, the late David Sutherland-Smith, Judy Thompson, John Thorpe, the late Jean Troisgros, Dr Frank Whitfield, Dr Bill van Bronswijk and, not least, Liz Woods.

Only my family, and especially my wife Joy, know how much they have contributed to my work, by their enthusiasm, suggestions and criticism over nearly half a century. My wife's major contributions have been her unwavering patience and her support for a book which she has known from our earliest times together that I would have to write.

Chapter 4, 'Exciting Wines', is adapted from an address to the Oxford Symposium on Taste, 1987.

Scents and Sensuality has already been called a revolutionary book. I thank the publishers, John Murray, for their courage in commissioning it.

Introduction

> My first note-book was opened in July 1837. I worked on true Baconian principles, and without any theory collected facts on a wholesale scale, more especially with respect to domesticated productions, by printed enquiries, by conversation with skilful breeders and gardeners, and by extensive reading.
>
> Charles Darwin, *Autobiography*

This is a book about smell and taste, their pleasures and excitements, their attractions and repulsions. It spans food, wine, perfume, intimate odour, emotion, orgasm, and immune response. Our understanding of all these is undergoing a renaissance. It is a world into which I have been irresistibly propelled, and in this introduction I would like to touch on the journey. An American mother and Australian father gave me a flying start, and our home was one where asking questions was a virtue second only to getting answers. My father ran the Australian office of Metro Goldwyn Mayer in Sydney, so I and my brothers and sister met a constant stream of people from the film industry worldwide. At the same time we were encouraged to pursue our own interests – mine were music and chemistry – and to be as independent as we wished. I interpreted this a little too freely and, after a turbulent last year at school, my wise and tolerant father exiled me to a remote farm for the summer while I waited to start medical school. With hindsight, I see he could have done nothing better for me. Over those months I changed from a city boy to one familiar with the rhythms of life and death, the scents and mysteries of the growth and reproduction of plants and animals. I also discovered how to distil a clean and fragrant applejack.

This was 1941, and doctors were in short supply when I entered Sydney University Medical School at sixteen. The transition from unruly schoolboy to dedicated student took place against a background of war. That my schoolmates were dying overseas gave me a sense of obligation and responsibility, and by the time the war was over I had qualified. During that period I had the extraordinary good fortune to come under the influence of some of Australia's leading medical scientists in the fields of neurophysiology, anatomy and biochemistry. Among them were Sir John Eccles, and Professor A.A. Abbie, and later on in Melbourne, I was to learn from Sir Sydney Sunderland and other disciples of the great Frederick Wood Jones. In 1943 I had published a small paper on the hypothalamus, and I might have gone further in the field of neurophysiology. However, I surprised myself and everyone else by graduating top of my year in clinical surgery, and that propelled me into a surgical career, later as a specialist in the surgery of the hand.

My forty years in medicine were superbly fulfilling, but before I came to the end of them I had come to realise that they had interrupted a quest which began in my teens, when I was acquiring the grounding in the sciences which form the basis of this book. There were a number of reasons why I decided to quit surgery, but perhaps the most pressing was that my interest in wine and wine growing was increasing with every year – as was my fascination with flavour and fragrance generally.

Winegrowing in the Australia of my childhood was restricted to a few small groups in fertile valleys like the Hunter and the Barossa, and to some larger commercial companies, among them the descendants of concerns set up by doctors to produce wines for medicinal purposes. In Australia, as elsewhere, there has always been a strong link between medicine and the vine. It was rare to see wine in restaurants or in private houses. In the war, beer was diverted to the American and Australian troops in the Pacific, so I started to drink and study the excellent regional wines of the country. I became fascinated by wine and especially by comparative tasting, which I found as stimulating as a game of chess. With a lot of help from others, I reached the point where I could confidently judge wines. In 1959 I began, tentatively, to write about wine, and in 1964 published the first of my books on the subject.

There was a moment of truth in 1960 when I tasted a marvellous thirty-year-old cabernet. It was like nothing I had encountered before, and after six months' detective work I tracked it down to a long-abandoned vineyard about two hours' drive from Sydney. In due course I found a sixty-acre tract with similar geological and climatic conditions nearby. I called it Lake's Folly, and my family and I have been growing wine there ever since.

Within weeks of leaving my surgical practice, I was asked to chair the subcommittee set up to revise wine standards for the Food Standards Committee of the Australian National Health and Medical Research Council and I served on the latter for three years. That was a classic example of Lake's Luck, as I found myself in daily contact with some of the finest food, fragrance and health professionals in the country. There I was able to get answers to many of the questions which had been accumulating in my mind, and some idea of new worlds as yet uncharted. I now had time to think seriously about the scientific basis of the flavours of food, and the wider horizons of perfumes and human smells, especially those concerned with the reproductive cycle. Earlier, in 1968, the late Jack Shipton had asked me to address the Australian Institute for Food Science and Technology. *The Flavour of Wine* was the result. He also introduced me to R.H. Wright's *The Science of Smell*, perhaps the most illuminating book on the subject for the beginner. There was no going back.

I wrote *Wine*, the first of the 'Start to Taste' series, as a simple and clear response to thirty years of beginners' questions. *Food* followed, equally straightforward, then the third, *People*, represented a leap into the minefields of perfume and human pheromones. Had I taken an obsession too far? In truth I was already deep into questions which still continue to make some of us uneasy, in spite of the growing body of answers science has given to prove their importance in human behaviour. While I was writing that series, pioneer work into the nature and causes of drug addition was producing results which cast new light on the functioning of the normal brain. This picture of 'the brain as gland' was like a flare lighting my path. I was able to arrive at the synthesis that became this book.

It is a different and far more exciting world than the one I used to inhabit, with revelations and discoveries crowding in from every direction (none more surprising than the realisation that the key fragrances in some of my favourite wines have pheromonal, frankly sexual, characteristics). You could say that I came to my present state of grace through wine. Over the years my tasting and smelling abilities have improved from a less than average natural palate to one which can hold its own in the best company – though still not as good as your average dog's. I have become more sensitive, more sympathetic, and, with a dawning understanding of the feelings that woman derive from odour, perhaps even more feminine. Any reader can equal and better this. It takes a readiness to perceive and start communicating with those around, and to examine and analyse one's own reactions to flavour and fragrance. A lot of smell is about communication. Understanding of the former is improved by the latter. Every human being smells and tastes in subtly different ways. One can teach and learn through shared experience and mutual pleasure.

> Everything should be made as simple as possible, but not simpler.
>
> Albert Einstein

Taking this as a guideline, I have tried to share my own enthusiasm. Scientists may complain of over-simplification, others may occasionally find the going difficult. Be patient. There is much complex information, but you can skip and dip as your fancy takes you. Sometimes I start reading a book from the back. Use the bibliography, index and glossary at the end to take you further down any avenue you find inviting.

I hope my efforts will help you and those near you to increase shared pleasures by understanding hidden drives, as well as by training and tuning neglected senses. If you find it an exciting prospect to be welcomed to this new understanding of the chemistry of attraction (and repulsion) – then you and I have met at the right time. You *can* change. Fragrance and flavour can bring new adventures daily. Boredom and dullness are not virtues. Start now to make the most of the rest of your life.

Introduction to This Edition

The text, index, and glossary have been revised. 'The Flavour of Japan' (Chapter 17) is new. It is based on a paper given before the Oxford Food Symposium in 1989.

Anyone with the remotest interest in flavour and fragrance must be fascinated by the changes now occurring in one of the most influential countries of our time. From a rigidly structured and previously isolated population whose food, drink and personal habits were often in marked contrast to those of the West, a remarkable interaction is now occurring. It may well be that such changes as cheese in local 'delis', McDonald's hamburgers, Coca Cola, beer and wine challenging *sake*, are permanent – just as Western tables now enjoy raw seafood, new styles of noodles, and a novel array of fresh vegetables, with much more to come in both cultures. It is our privilege to be actually part of, to understand, and to enjoy, a microcosm in this century, which must be comparable to historic waves of people across the face of our planet. The voyages of Columbus and Marco Polo produced similar changes. These are further contributions to the theme I developed in 'The Essence of Excitement'.

1

THE ESSENCE OF EXCITEMENT

1

The Transfer of Excitement

Exposure to pheromones is the essence of sex.
Dr Winnifred Cutler

Without knowing it, people communicate sexual attraction to one another in greater or lesser degree by scent. That fact has been recognised since time immemorial, but the essential message waited until thirty years ago for a name. 'Pheromone', from the Greek for 'transfer' and 'excitement', describes the substance, usually volatile, produced by a male or female, that evokes a response in another. It is now realised that not all pheromones are sexual, and not all attract (plants for example may use them to repel insects) but those we are concerned with are and do.

In fact, from the instant of birth to the moment of death, the body is under the control of at least two systems of chemical messengers. Hormones are particles that hustle along inside the body, of which adrenalin and the various contraceptive pills are examples. Pheromones are molecules that travel by air to the sensors in the nose. These fire off to that part of the brain concerned with smell, later to be fine-tuned by the rest of the intelligent cortex. We hope. A lot goes on under the surface. PET scanning

X-rays may show activity in the odour-related areas of the brain of a person who categorically denies perceiving a particular scent or flavour.

Over the millennia of evolution the increasing importance of sight as animals stood up on two legs saw the downgrading of smell, so that today its importance in humans tends to be ignored. Of course, we run into the problems of the massive variation in the perception of smells – by up to 2,000 times from one person to another. And then there is the extraordinary difficulty of communicating about smell. We have to recognise the influence of smell on behaviour and emotion before we can give the subject the attention it demands.

Plants carry their scents in sacs attached to their 'skins' – their bark, leaves and petals. Humans do much the same with the odour-producing systems in their skins, and there can be as many as 300 components of male and female smells. There are some three million sweat glands in the two metres of skin of the average adult body, denser (about 600 per square centimetre) on the palms, soles and armpits. We produce two kinds of sweat, one from palms and feet, the other from all the remainder of the body. The former tends to be stress-induced, the latter arises from regulating body heat. Both smell. The odorants in fresh, healthy sweat are diet-oriented, and are not offensive on the average diet until resident skin bacteria have started to break the components down. Natural smells, in the main, are not powerful, probably because any strong odour can be disagreeable, and may make others aggressive. But the Western diet is high in saturated fatty acids, major constituents of milk and cheese, which are metabolised to produce sweat particularly offensive to the nose of races whose diet ordinarily lacks them.

We now know a good deal about the influences of odours on individuals. Less well understood are the factors that produce uniform behaviour by a group. When a single hawk turns a flight of starlings who have been virtually blackening part of the sky, or a snorkeller has the same effect on a shoal of fish, the movement is so uniform that the individuals seem part of a whole. Their movement is just like that of a snake except that there is no direct connecting nerve or membrane. Several kinds of sensory input govern crowd behaviour and odour could well play a part, albeit minor, in human groups. Who knows if androstenone-driven aggression boiled over the top in the Belgian Heyssel Stadium disaster, with male football fans, unable to make it to the lavatories, urinating at the back of the stand? Was there a similar role for the raised-arm Nazi salute with thousands of armpits fanning their pheromones among the already excited multitude? Do some people in the front rows want to get more than a good view? Having watched them at the high-kicking Rockettes in New York and Montmartre can-can dancers, one wonders how 'intimate' nightspots are. A wild flamenco in a bodega on a hot Spanish night, 'discos', and public underground transport systems at rush hour, offer plenty of opportunity to ponder the odours of stress and excitement.

The reader can only guess at the tolerance of the spouses of members of an annual celebration of garlic freaks; the naked bulb, plus an extraordinary amount of it in dips, roasts, curries and stews (though stopping short of the garlic milk shakes I know one girl used to enjoy). Anti-perspirants lessen the volume of sweat, and deodorants, local and space, do help; but time, thirty-six hours, is necessary to restore order after an orgy on *that* scale.

Bacteria are responsible for much of the body odour that assails the nostrils. Lactic organisms, so vital in other ways, tend to overdo fatty acid production if allowed to multiply unchecked, certainly for more than six hours on a hot day. The same applies to the bacteria that thrive on nitrogen in the cavities of the body, producing that double-edged broad-sword trimethylamine (TMA) – so important in both food and attraction, yet so repellent if more than just noticeable.

The most powerful body scents are produced by the apocrine gland system. They make a minute amount of milky secretion which is delivered by a tube into an adjacent hair follicle. The hair serves exactly as a wick from the source of scent, and to widen the area from which it evaporates. When a hair is pulled erect by its little muscle ('hair standing on end' or 'goose bumps'), secretion may actually be pumped to the hair. It is not an accident that nature has left humans with hair to store and waft the message from armpits, face and head, around the nipples, and last but certainly not least the genital area.

Frederick Wood Jones, the most original anatomist since John Hunter, listed the many attributes of pubic hair, for instance that it was short and curly and possessed a different cross section to other body hair, and that its free ends were all directed down towards the perineum. We all know the eagerness that the first sexual sprout engenders, the envy caused among their peers by earlier developing contemporaries. And the oddly different stink of the adult body, more perceptible by daughters, or at least by one who confided that her tomboy wrestles with her father ceased about the age of twelve when she became aware of his body odour. (He had been upset by her sudden and unexplained remoteness and their relationship had suffered. Twenty years later, I suggested she tell him the reason. She did so, and the rift was healed.)

The owner of a hairy armpit is continually reminded of its apocrine function. Women are more than aware of this, and in some cultures remove their own underarm hair partly, at least, to keep the sexual scent signal to an absolute minimum and avoid misunderstanding by the ever-receptive male. In some cultures, a hairy female armpit is considered positively sexy, especially in a sexual relationship. In others, less is more.

The male beard is the most obvious secondary sexual hair. Pheromone secretion is constant and can be a remarkable attractant to the other sex. Women have told me of the powerful effect of scent from their men's faces: sometimes from under the lip, sometimes the lower cheek, or cheekbone, or temple. I have heard some graphic descriptions of these effects! Rebecca West said the mustachioed H.G. Wells smelt of honey. After some preliminary careful explanation (without which things could get fairly awkward if I were to go up and start sniffing comparative strangers' beards), I have done a few field trials myself, to confirm their impressions.

Body smells in general and sweat in particular, have not always been criticised. Roy Bedichek attributes this saying to Mohammed:

> As I was taken up to heaven, some of my sweat fell to earth and from it sprang the rose, and whosoever would smell my scent, let him smell the rose.

Walt Whitman, with perhaps the schoolboy's insight about the delights of his own farts, self-described 'the scent of these armpits, aroma finer than prayer'. The blind Helen Keller, not alone in her feelings, was unrivalled in her eloquence when she said 'Masculine exhalations are, as a rule, stronger, more vivid, more widely differentiated than those of women. In the odour of young men there is something elemental, as of fire, storm and salt sea. It pulsates with buoyancy and desire. It suggests all things strong and beautiful and joyous, and gives me a sense of physical happiness.' She was, and others are, capable of entering a recently vacated room and stating whether the occupants had been happy, angry or fearful. The fictional contributions of contemporaries like Roald Dahl, Tom Robbins and Patrick Susskind correspond with Ms Keller's opinion.

The fresh scent of the skin glands is based on the hormones of the adrenals, testes and ovaries. The principal pheromone, androstenone, is a chemical cousin of the male sex hormone, testosterone, and the volume present directly relates to production of that (see 'the steroid miracle') in Chapter 24, 'Genesis'. Men who have been castrated do not produce any androstenone.

Though it is primarily the male sex hormone, testosterone occurs in females too, and is the raw fuel of the libido of both sexes. That further underlines the close relationship of hormones and pheromones. Testosterone rather dominates the pheromone system. Apart from its daily cycling (it peaks between sunrise and noon) of the libido and production of androstenone, it plays a part in tuning the sense of smell: in its absence, odour perception in a man falls away. It is in fact closely associated with loss of sexual drive in *both* sexes, and impotence in the male. Females produce more at the time of ovulation. Not only is this claimed to increase their sexual desire and receptivity, but there is an increase in their immune reponse also.

Of two hundred separate compounds distinguishable in normal body smells, androstenone, fatty acids, trimethylamine (TMA), and isobutyraldehyde (IBA) may be the important human pheromones. This discovery emerged from the finding that numbers of people are unable to smell one or other in various compounds, or at any rate show a serious loss of sensitivity to them. Androstenone (actually a group of closely related compounds which smell and act in a similar manner) is the male 'essential oil', in the perfume sense. It may suggest musk and sandalwood with the merest nuance of urine, unless you have selective loss of smell, when none or only one may be detected. Males secrete a lot of it, but a substantial proportion of them cannot pick it up themselves. In a recent survey by *National Geographic Magazine* and the Monell Chemical Senses Center in Philadelphia, 70.5 per cent of women and 62.8 per cent of men were able to smell it. Put another way, about a third of the population *can't* smell it.

There must be some kind of built-in natural buffer, because androstenone can provoke the most uncontrolled aggression. It is found naturally in sweat, tears, urine, beards and hair, and particularly in genital hair. Females also secrete this impressive pheromone, most of them in small or minute quantities. It adds an extra dimension to their attraction.

> Langorous, black, luxuriant locks
> Live pomander, incense burner
> Wafts her wild, musky fragrance
>
> Baudelaire

Veterinarians use 'Boarmate' (androstenone in spray cans, and under the patronage of Her Majesty Queen Elizabeth II) to identify female pigs ready to mate, and to prepare them for the event. Sows are biologically programmed to assume a rigid mating position when they smell the androstenone in the saliva of a male pig. The following event was reported in the *Sydney Morning Herald* in September 1985:

> LOVE PIGS FALL ON CURIOUS VET
>
> Taiwan, Friday: Two pigs, more than 300 kilograms in weight, fell on a veterinary worker as he was assisting them to mate last Wednesday

> on a farm in Southern Taiwan. The Chinese language newspaper, *China Daily News*, reported that Mr Su Cheng-Jen, who arranged the mating, was injured. Farm attendants had difficulty moving the pigs before Mr Su could be rescued.

No one could make this sort of thing up. There is more. One of the principle odours in the priceless truffle mimics androstenone; that is the reason that female pigs are used to search for the elusive fungus.

Musky scents are popular in all cultures. Much profit was expected twenty or so years ago from promoting musk as a natural aphrodisiac from the hippie wilds of Haight-Ashbury in San Francisco. Aphrodisiac to the female, that is. The trouble was that the early promotions were rather boring and one-dimensional, and failed to make use of many of the hundreds of other possible additions; the whole thing fell flat on its face. The perfume equivalent to the heavyweight androstenone is musk, which lives in the basement of perfume harmony due to its tenacity and ability to fix and mingle lighter fragrances.

Of the everyday foods and drinks that produce a musky result, besides the redoubtable truffle, the following are probably important. If it is not urgent, parsley is guaranteed to raise your aura several hours after you eat it. Any wine which has been aged in new small oak barrels, and especially wine made from the grape variety cabernet and its relatives, will perfume your whole body about six hours later. Just the other day I smelt a toadstool growing at the base of a stringybark tree. It was faintly scented by menthol and eucalyptus. That was a revelation! The fungus had taken up the tree aromatics as truffles must do at the roots of the oak tree. Oak barrels and cabernet, sandalwood and cedar, androstenone in great claret. How generous of nature! Chapter 4,

'Exciting Wines', develops this theme.

Boar meat is so high in androstenone that it can be a prohibited 'taint' in meat for import into some countries. I finally understood the popularity of certain little sausages after an educational session with Tom Clark on pheromone sniffing (including musk).

Some of the synthetic musks are remarkable in strength and staying power, and are widely used in perfumes, cosmetics, deodorants and even soft drinks. Think twice about raising the level of androstenone. Warders at a particular prison went on strike against conditions until it was realised that they and their charges were being stirred up by the odour of a new detergent used for washing the floors. They resumed work without complaint when it was changed. One officer volunteered that his own domestic relations had vastly improved afterwards.

It may work either way. Some years after a painful divorce, the contestants, meeting at a party, started to reminisce over their years together. He expressed continuing distress at the speed of their separation, which he still failed to understand, and they rambled on till she volunteered that she had first fallen in love with him because he smelt like her father, who used 'Old Spice' aftershave. He fell silent, and when she asked the reason: 'I stopped using that a short time before we split!'

The funniest androstenone story was told me by Tom Clark who had been at a three-day conference. Each day the participants resumed their same chairs. Early on the morning of the third day, the chairman's seat up on the dais was sprayed with 'Boarmate'. This chap was a rather pushy, dominant person, but he was later observed sitting quietly up the back of the conference room during the proceedings. When he was asked why, he replied that things were running quite smoothly now, thank you, and he was happy to take a back seat. There have also been tests where women selected only chairs, telephones and theatre seats which had been pre-sprayed with androstenone. Half of the human male population and about one in ten females are high secretors. The high secreting male group has the biggest divorce rate and fathers the most children.

John Amoore's studies led him to the concept of 'vestigial pheromones' but in view of the amount of detailed studies coming out since then, it is reasonable to drop the qualification 'vestigial'. Ours may not exert quite the power seen in animals, and our vomeronasal system and its alternatives may be less obvious than those of reptiles, but many people seem to be in green-and-go mode.

Both men and women produce 'fatty' acids. Full-blown, their odours vary from avid, sweaty and rancid buttery, to seriously unwashed goat, and, as we have seen, are produced by the activity of lactic and other bacteria. Nature's trick is to render all these smells rather attractive when they are just perceptible at, or just below, what we refer to as the threshold. Consider some of your favourite cheeses, the 'yeasty' note of Champagne or some chardonnay wines, even the 'sweaty' rieslings. It just does *not* do at a wine tasting to describe such a character as the smell of nubile underarm, freshly washed but with the piquancy of some added exertion.

Isovaleric acid (IVA) is found in the sweat of the palms, and the soles of the feet. In excess, it is fairly repulsive to most people, but a suggestion of it is the major incitement to coupling in the higher apes, when it and related fatty acids are sanctified by the term 'copulins'. They occur in the human female genitals, rising to a peak in mid-cycle when the ovum is at its readiest for fertilisation. Genital fatty acid odour is driven by oestrogens. Emily Jacobs has found that women on a progesterone-only Pill produce far less fatty acids. It is difficult to make a categorical statement of their general value in human attraction and reproduction, but there is not the slightest doubt that they play a role in some people. There has already been an application for a patent of a copulin mix for humans, but as half the human race possess an ample supply of the real thing at some time or other in their lives, it seems pointless except in cases of real sexual difficulty.

Trimethylamine (TMA) is another potent pheromone, which at full blast is redolent of decomposing seafood – perhaps rotten prawns even more than fish. This conjugated nitrogen may be among the most primitive smells we know, but when it is near threshold level it is one of the most popular flavour enhancers in the history of cooking, as several later chapters will show. TMA can be part of the odour of menstruation, and may also be found on the breath of both sexes with dental problems. The ritual post-menstrual bath of the Israelites still has much to commend it, not to mention daily oral hygiene. A teacher volunteered that one male student in her group became aggressive whenever she was menstruating. Could odour be disturbing any of the more rampant feminists and misogynists that pepper Western society? Do the women resent the influence of androstenone, and are the men fearful of the irresistible call of women's pheromones?

It is easy to make recommendations about simple cleanliness, but the manufacturers and their advertising agencies have established a deep feeling of inferiority and insecurity about body smells. This may be a part of race memory, but in the twentieth century it has far less justification with widespread use of water and simple soap. That this might not be universally applicable was brought home by the wit of Geneviève Edis in her book *Merde Encore!*

> The French themselves have revealed that the average Frog uses only 2.25 bars of soap a year. If you hear '*savon*' in a conversation it most likely has nothing to do with soap but with an unpleasant situation: '*passer un savon à quelqu'un*' means to give someone a real telling off, a real piece of one's mind. Now *that* '*savon*' gets used frequently, you can be sure!
>
> Worse than the news about soap is the revelation that toothbrushes are purchased at the rate of one for every three persons a year! Fifty per cent of them go to bed without brushing their teeth! They should exchange their ghastly bidets for an investment in showers, toothbrushes, toothpaste and deodorants. A *French* journalist wrote recently that many Frenchmen smell like kangaroos kept in cages. French kings' stink is well chronicled: one of the record holders was Henry IV whose odour nearly made his fiancée, Marie de Medici, faint on their first meeting.

Not everyone would agree. Many regard the bidet as among the great contributions to personal cleanliness, once they realise it is not just for washing socks and smalls.

IBA, isobutyraldehyde, is the malty milky smell that allows the baby to find the nipple of its mother, difficult with excess deodorant. There are other body odours with pheromonal properties. Esters of Para amino benzoic acid (PABA) are found in skin folds and creases and between the toes and are closely related to one of the principal vaginal odours of a bitch in season. The effect on domestic pets is well known. Pity and try to understand the confusion of a poor puppy who lacks the experience to know there is no fulfilment of his mating programme in the toes of your visitors, nor in or on shins basted with cosmetics or soaps containing a good deal of the lovely PABA.

About one person in six cannot pick up the odour of semen, pyrolline. It may also be found in the male pubic area and, combined with androstenone and a soupçon of the fatty acids, is a powerful stimulant to some women during the events of intercourse. Occasionally a woman may become enormously excited by the smell of a ripe, squishy persimmon, and conversely some males dislike it. There is always a big sign up saying WHY? when a strong preference or aversion is expressed. *Marrons glacés* or simple plain cooked chestnuts hint of this odour, as does corn on the cob. Caviar has a number of sexually suggestive notes. Why wouldn't it? The early fruit of the reproduction of two mighty fish, all those little eggs. It has something for both sexes, perhaps the sperm fragrance plus a fresh marine character. Body odours vary in other ways. The production of androstenone reaches a peak in the male in the thirties and slowly declines, but not steeply, till the end of life. The smaller output of the female has a peak, but virtually ceases at the menopause.

Diet is a powerful determinant of general body smell, mixing with ethnic and genetic influences. There is a classic clash between the body odours of East and West. This is due in part of the high fatty acid components of the Western diet, where the relative availability of land favours cattle (and milk) production. Chinese and Japanese traditionally don't take cheese as part of their ordinary diet and rarely drink milk after childhood. The diet of the Japanese until recently was based on fish, greens and rice; that with frequent vigorous bathing, leaves little if any body smell; indeed strong body odour used to be grounds for exclusion from the Japanese Army, and may still be. In the recent war in Vietnam, both sides used the difference in body odour as part of their strategy. The Americans devised sniffing machines to warn of Viet Cong, and the latter in turn were easily able to detect the odours of American culture, like aftershave, cigarettes, some candies, and the generally different body smell. Eskimos are said to smell 'fishy', blacks 'ammoniacal', and so on, but the rest of the world agrees that the 'European' smell in crowded areas is the most offensive.

Garlic is not offerable to the Hindu Lord Krishna. His devotees prefer *hing*, asafoetida, of which any quantity is nauseating to many. They also use the oily extract of butter, ghee, as their main cooking fat. The African bushman and Australian aborigine living in the bush are easily able to identify the origin and diet of most things and people they track. Experience and training help us understand this skill.

I wonder how many vegetarians avoid meat because of its pheromone content, rather than out of concern for our furry friends. Lady Dorothy Neville, during the siege of Paris in 1871 when some of the richer Parisians ate the zoo animals, wrote: 'Well, I rather enjoyed the donkey although it was a little dry, but I never partook of it further, it made me stink.'

Several metabolic states and diseases are detectable by their odour. The fruity aroma of the advanced diabetic state, the fishy urinous breath of kidney failure, are not all that rare. Diphtheria is sweetish, typhoid fever smells like 'baked bread', and the odour of gout is described as resembling a menagerie or petshop. In making any of these assessments, the smeller needs to compute his own exhaled breath against the new lot of goodies coming in on the tide. A diabetic gouty old physician (yes, there are some such) might have a problem.

Our knowledge of pheromones is embryonic. Evolution indicates that there are some that work at a distance and others that only exert their magic at close quarters. Worms depend totally on 'taste', but flying insects have the capacity to pick up airborne odour signals. The irresistible mating programme observed in moths has two components. Much has been learned since Henri Fabre recorded, in the last century, the eleven-kilometre flight of a male moth responding to the female's fragrance upwind. This is the distant pheromone in action. In some species, when the male homes in on the female attractant, he douses her with his equivalent from his abdominal or leg hairs. That renders her completely receptive to mating.

Despite the evolutionary distance, I believe humans demonstrate a survival of this programme. The female fragrances are lightweight and volatile, potentially distant pheromones, and the androstenone of the male, a far heavier molecule, corresponds to the close-up pheromone of the male moth. In humans, the rigidity of the programme has been softened by choice. There is a hint of the idea from our friend, the mighty Francis Bacon, who, three and a half centuries ago, divided the fragrances of flowers and plants into those 'which do best perfume the air' and the others which are only detectable close up. It even appears that the distant perfumes are naturally boosted by some mechanism, giving the 'lift' of wallflower, lime tree blossom, honeysuckle, evening primrose and others.

These stimulating odours have been classified by their effects into *releasers* and *primers.* The releaser effect is that seen when a specific message 'telephoned by' nerve impulses is immediately followed by some sort of activity. The primer effects are long-term, involving, for example, menstruation and pregnancy, and the molecules of odorant may actually travel along the freeway provided by the nerve sheath. The brain, with its dozens of internal hormones, the 'thinking gland', probably works in tandem with this extraordinary system.

There is a reciprocal relationship between stress

and pheromones. Certain smells with pheromonal potential can cause stress reactions, and stress is capable of wafting appreciable amounts of stimulating body smells about. Dogs are not the only ones to detect the fear smell. One particular office nearly had to lose a most efficient new secretary because of the strong body odour emitted whenever she was stressed. Matters settled down as she became more experienced and less agitated. And more attractive.

The substances I have just described are, in excess, mainly objectionable, so what makes an attractive body odour? Many of us have a wry recollection of the effects of highly successful advertising campaigns that pointedly drew attention to body odour and its capacity to offend. 'X takes the worry out of being close.' How many adolescents ended up smelling like a Listerian operating theatre after scrubbing themselves raw with carbolic soap? Do women still spend millions a year on sprays ensuring their vaginas smell of peaches, just one of the Madison Avenue excesses of the recent past?

We smell good when we are happy, fit and healthy. Odours depend on the tiny bacterial servants on our skin and body cavities and the degree of cultivation we permit in the gardens they inhabit. The attraction of subtlety is achieved by simple daily cleanliness, using the purest and least perfumed soap – at least until you learn the art of balancing resident and applied fragrances.

The food we eat smells of the things needed to produce it. We, in turn, smell of what we eat. A high androstenone meal, of boar meat (or beef with a truffled maderia glaze), parsley and parsnips, takes hours to declare itself. Great red wines make you smell nice. Garlic freaks enjoy each other, as do butter lovers ('butter lovers make better lovers').

Saffron, fresh ginger, cinnamon, pepper, betel nut, cardamom, nutmeg, perhaps with anise and cumin, make Indians pleasantly aromatic (one lady stayed with an Indian lover after she lost affection for him because of his body smell), but the most attractive body smell is probably derived from Thai cooking. The habitual Thai intake of mint, basil, lemon grass, peanut and coconut oils, green coriander and the little rosy-floral dynamite chillies, with a wealth of palm sugar and fresh fruit and green vegetables must surely be the most fragrant food in the world. I suspect the best-smelling members of the human race probably inhabited the East and West Indies and the South Seas, before the white man came. Garlands of tropical flowers as sweet as the frangipani, several daily swims in the warm ocean, fragrant oil rubs and a diet of tropical fruits, fresh fish, vegetables and occasionally feasts of barbecued pig; how close can you approach that idyll?

Finally, not the least important of all that has gone before, you need to feel good about yourself. A light added fragrance may be a happy choice, in every sense.

2

Marine Venus

> The breasts like lilies, 'til other leaves be shared
> Her nipples like young blossomed jessamine
> Such fragrant flowers to give most odours' smell
> But her sweet odour did them all excel.
>
> Edmund Spenser

We have already seen that the hormone testosterone identifies a man as such, but its pheromone, androstenone, plays a role in a woman that is truly astonishing. It sets her reproductive clock firmly on 'moon time'. It is the wellspring of raw sexual appetite and, even in the small amounts normally present in the body of an ovulating woman, it swells desire, improves her immune response, and makes her smell better to her partner. She best perceives the male 'musk' in mid-cycle and later, and this is also the time of her own usually small, but important androstenone peak. Dr Winnifred Cutler of the Monell Chemical Senses Center in Philadephia has some good news and some bad news. 'A man or his essence seems essential for an optimally fertile system.' It is his close physical presence that is necessary, but the act of coitus may not be.

Many women are uneasy about their body odour, particularly if they live in a culture where they are bombarded by conflicting social messages and 'hidden persuaders'. They may, in fact, sometimes genuinely not smell good, and if this is due to lack of cleanliness or temporary ill-health they should realise there is no serious problem, only solutions. No one knows how many men find the scent of a clean healthy female body attractive (and vice versa), but I suspect their numbers are considerable. Emily Jacobs of St Thomas's Hospital has shown that applications of vaginal secretions to the woman's chest quite definitely increase the frequency with which couples have intercourse. Other men prefer their partners either deodorised or artificially perfumed. We have already glimpsed what women like, in Chapter 1, 'The Transfer of Excitement'.

Women who are aware of their sexual odour may wish to conceal or minimise it in certain circumstances, for instance in order to separate their professional from their personal lives if they work in a male-dominated environment. (The same could well apply to sensitive men in female-dominated working situations.) For one reason or another the advertising wizards have been able to persuade people worldwide to spend billions of dollars to apply floral, animal or synthetic sexual secretions over the top of their own more eloquent ones.

I find that Botticelli's remarkable painting *The Birth of Venus* is the perfect catalogue of the ideal feminine fragrance – seen through Renaissance eyes, but just as valid today. It was painted in Florence during the years 1484–90, and now hangs in the Uffizi Gallery. The first time I went to Florence, in the spring of 1954, a black-and-white reproduction in a *pensione* bedroom did nothing to prepare me for the actual meeting. There she stood, one of the most beautiful women of all time, nude and upright in the centre of a large scallop shell, with a hank of her long hair held modestly over her *mons veneris*. There may be the dawn of a smile rising from the corners of her eyes and mouth and her clear eyes are riveting. In contrast, her attendant is fully clothed. Entwined winged figures blow fragrant roses towards her. The painting evokes the fresh marine smell of the morning tide, of flowers, of hair and the expression that comes from the knowledge that she carries the beginnings of creation. The odour is almost real, to stir lovers everywhere. No other painting of Venus seems to make this unique and comprehensive declaration. Why is this so? And why is it so much more moving than the explicit grotesqueries of Eastern art? There is a central focus on the vertical figure rising from the large fluted shell. The flowing tresses of hair with their pheromonal scent are held over the pubis which happens to be the exact centre of the painting. The symbolism is irresistible. All the ingredients of new life are there, so no wonder she is pensive.

Men who take an interest in that sort of thing find that the most alluring fragrance in a woman occurs at ovulation. Her breath produces a fairly clear signal, partly made up of dodecanol, an alcohol which smells somewhat 'soapy', and numbers of other odorants among which are pleasant but vague hints of some of the more questionable ones like DMS (attractive here, but like bad cabbage when strong) plus several fatty acids and even perhaps TMA. The apparent 'sweetness' of the breath at this time could be enhanced by the rise in blood sugar level which occurs at ovulation. If so, it is an impressive trick of nature because, as we see elsewhere, although sugar has no odour, sweetness lifts all fragrance, in this instance to increase attractiveness. A turned-on sniffer, especially if the woman is a familiar, may be able to pick the day of ovulation.

'Copulins', whose production is governed by the female hormone oestrogen, smell somewhat sweaty and acid, but are by no means offensive in clean and healthy people. In all primates, except women on the

Pill, they are said to increase at ovulation, but this is disputed. The TMA threshold varies by a factor of two thousand: that is, some people pick it up at one two-thousandth the concentration that others need to become aware of it. Some can't smell it at all. TMA over threshold, with its fishy smell, is not the fresh marine fragrance eulogised in pigment by Botticelli, but not everyone finds a trace of it repellant.

These different fragrances combine and intensify as sexual excitement grows and as the blood circulation in the pelvic area increases. At the height of stimulation they may well include the heavy molecules of androstenone, the musky note then continuing to assist the act of fertilisation *in vivo.*

It is important to know that some of the most telling research into human sexual odours has been carried out by women. They live far more in the world of smell than men and are both more realistic in their attitude to the effect of odour, and more sensitive to that of other women. Modern folklore is full of instances like that of the highly creative and volatile group in a big open office on a women's magazine. Their menstrual cycles had synchronised to the point where they all went through pre-menstrual tension about the same time and the atmosphere in that particular week could get very difficult. Anecdote gives way to scientific method in the research carried out by Martha McClintock with a group of 135 women sharing a Boston dormitory. Over a substantial part of a year she found that their menstrual cycles did come to correlate significantly. Furthermore, she noted that women who seldom if ever came into contact with the opposite sex had longer cycles than the average. Some years later, a female colleague of Michael Russell at Sonoma State Hospital in California told him of her own experience of the McClintock Effect, in particular that her own cycles appeared to cause others to synchronise with it. Russell collected her underarm sweat on sterile pads. Diluted with alcohol, it was applied to the upper lips of one group of women three times a week for four months, while a control group were dabbed with the alcohol without the sweat. At first there was little change, but at four to six months there was a remarkable convergence of the cycles of the first group.

Some of the most striking research emanates from Monell, whose investigators tackle questions no less critical than those of Kinsey or Masters and Johnson in the field of sexual research. Since 1968, Monell has tactfully approached problems which tend to be avoided in polite social discussion. Drs Winnifred Cutler and George Preti have for instance shown that regular heterosexual intercourse promotes normal menstrual cycles. It is also possible that there are better fertility rates and a milder menopause. The male pheromone, androstenone, is in the spotlight. I see no reason why the human female pheromones may not have an effect on male physiology. The results of such research should be worth waiting for.

Having now got some idea of the power of feminine fragrance, Marine Venus, love and creation – it is possible to understand the balance of nature's plan. Not all scientists in the field agree, but it seems that without oestrogen, the attraction of 'copulins' is lacking, and without the accompaniment of androstenone, the male fragrance, interest in the pleasures of sex, in the making of life itself, would be less; tuneless, grey and boring. Unproved? What do you think?

3

Aphrodisiac Foods

Even more than music, food is the food of love.

Peter Gay

Aphrodisiacs continue to lack credibility. The search for the ultimate stimulus is as old as history, but so much complete nonsense has been written on the subject that it is difficult for anyone to take it seriously. Truth is a stranger.

What are you looking for? To stimulate a partner's desire? To shift your own interest or performance into a higher gear? There are drugs, hormones and glandular extracts which will grant your wish and indeed Eli Lilly is now testing LY163502, a drug which mimics dopamine and which seems to be a true aphrodisiac. Dopamine is a neurotransmitter which could be promoted to Chapter 22, 'Highs and the Happy Hormones'. However, many products which have a positive response can be dangerous, because they are by definition powerful disturbers of metabolism, and may even kill the user before the desired result occurs. The most important aim of this book is to improve your enjoyment of life – not to ruin it; drugs should be avoided except under competent medical direction.

The sow in season stands rigid in the mating position when it gets a whiff of the boar's androstenone.

That conforms with one popular conception of an aphrodisiac. If you persist with such expectations after reading this chapter, you could be disappointed. One thing is certain. Humans are not pigs, any more than they are butterflies alerted by the presence of a mate far upwind. The safe, natural, potential human aphrodisiacs are less likely to have the direct genital effect which drugs can produce, and many social factors can interfere with their successful use. Having read this far, if you still think that any gain, even minor, could be worthwhile, then persevere. 'Aphrodisiac' foods are usually delicious, so whatever happens, it will not have been a total loss.

Several foods have flavours, textures and physical characteristics which hint of sexual pleasure, either at the time of eating or several hours later when they have been absorbed and appear in the body odour. Some foods suggest the male pheromone, androstenone. Parsley is one of the best (folklore has it that parsley only flourishes when the wife rules the house), and the character is also found in varying amounts in the seeds and leaves of celery, celeriac root, carrot tops and young parsnips.

> *Celery* Our conscience obliges us to warn shy people of this aphrodisiac property of celery that they might abstain from eating it, or at least use it prudently. It is enough to stress that it is not in any way a salad for bachelors.
>
> Quoted in *Grimod de la Reynière*
> by Giles MacDonogh

Among meats, male pig meat, whether from wild boar or from uncastrated domestic pigs, has a strong androstenone flavour and is sufficiently powerful to repel some people. But there are many enthusiastic supporters of a Balkan grill in Sydney which sells *cevapticci*, or skinless sausages made largely or pork and other meat. I wonder if their popularity may have something to do with the use of boar meat?

Below the ground, sometimes a handspan or more deep among the roots of a hospitable oak, lies the black truffle, irresistible to female pigs and parent of some of the higher flights of aphrodisiac fantasy in humans. Madame de Pompadour and the Emperor Claudius used them frequently, and Louis XIV is said to have eaten a pound a day. This sounds impossible, but I once succeeded in eating the kitchens of the Troisgros brothers at Roanne out of truffles – perhaps three-quarters of a kilo over three days. A major French exporter of truffles, M. Bizac, was there at the time, and was so impressed that he sent a large consignment of truffles to Sydney for my sixtieth birthday some months later.

To return to France, Napoleon's marshals made sure he had a constant supply for practical and patriotic reasons, and Honoré de Balzac wrote 'If a truffle falls on my plate ... it immediately hatches ten characters for my *Comédie Humaine*'. Few writers have described the search for the 'black pearl' better than Joseph Wechsberg, from whose *Blue Trout and Black Truffles* this account is adapted:

> There was a joyful grunt and a small cheerful-looking pig came running out ... the Widow Merlhiot formally introduced the pig to us with an elegant gesture ... 'down in the Lot they are using small hounds for their truffle-hunting and I'm told they have trained goats in Italy and Sardinia. A trained sow has a fine nose for truffles ...' There was a stretch of barren land with groups of oak trees, but no flowers or grass on the ground. I noticed that the pig was getting excited. Suddenly she stopped and rubbed her snout against the soil. The Veuve Merlhiot carefully scratched the ground away until she found a truffle as big as an apricot,

> which had been hidden a good ten inches down ... 'You've got to watch the pig or she'll dig the truffle up and eat it for herself. That's why you divert the animal's attention and give her a little maize or a chestnut as compensation.'

Truffles were eaten by the Babylonians four thousand years ago. The Romans appreciated them and the food scribes Apicius, Athenaeus, Pliny and Columella have much to say on the subject. The white truffle of Piedmont, considered superior by many, has a stronger musky note plus a whiff of garlic. Use of the black 'jewels of the poor soil', as Colette called them, reached its peak in Brillat-Savarin's time – the Revolutionary and Napoleonic era in France – though even then 'a truffled turkey was a luxury, found only on the tables of the greatest lords and kept women'. Many contemporary food writers avoid describing the flavour of truffle in specific terms. It is unique, in the same way as, for example, coffee or vanilla or a muscatel grape is, but if I were to try, I would single out a suggestion of its earthy origin, a dash of cooked (but not too pungent) garlic, that 'carnal' musky note already described, old Madeira, and a hint of mandarin. If your truffle does not possess these notes – and more which I may have missed – it is an inferior species, or has already been overcooked or otherwise 'mucked about'. If you can't afford genuine truffles, or don't have friends who can, you should try some of the stronger flavoured wild mushrooms – cèpes, chanterelles, morilles – or the dried chinese shitake mushrooms. These are a particularly good source of glutamate, whose importance will appear in Chapter 22, 'Highs and the Happy Hormones'. There are many aromatic fungi, but don't poison yourself in the search.

The mysterious fresh scent of the sea shore gives an evolutionary zing of some intensity to the palate ready for it. Oysters, with some justification on account of their smell, appearance and trace minerals, have long been regarded as a food of love. Caviar is prized on a level with truffles, and other fish eggs – in fact, probably to a lesser extent, all eggs – deserve their reputation for aphrodisiac qualities in the right context. Norman Douglas, in *Venus in the Kitchen*, recommends, only half jokingly, a caviar omelette. I fantasise with salmon caviar and a dab of low-fat yogurt in a scooped-out jacket potato. The salted eggs of salmon, whitefish, grey mullet and cod are all acceptable, especially as they are cheaper than caviar. Another favourite prelude to an *après-midi d'un faun* is Greek taramasalata spread on a slice of multi-grain wheatbased bread, topped with avocado, cracked black pepper and a splash of lime juice. It is also worth looking at the Chinese preoccupation with sharksfin soup and sea slug (*bêche-de-mer*) if only because a culture which has been using true musk for thousands of years must have discovered some truths about the sexual properties of foods.

TMA, highly diluted, is an essential characteristic of the flavour enhancer used in many cuisines, for example, the Roman garum, balachan, Bombay Duck, anchovy sauce of Europe, and the fish sauces of Asia. While not exactly aphrodisiac in the quantities in which they are used in cooking, they are certainly capable of heightening our enjoyment, and are also reminiscent of a key female pheromone.

A few people of both sexes adore the aroma of asparagus, especially the way in which it scents the urine. Some find that sexually suggestive, others loathe it. Most people are simply intrigued by it. If, however, I needed to plan an aphrodisiac meal, I would consider including asparagus, figs and mussels on the shell, for their evocative shapes as well as their flavours.

Green coriander (Chinese parsley, or *cilantro*) smells somewhat of musk and fresh sweat (not so different from the aromatic North Italian salad herbs like *rappa*), and arouses highly controversial reactions among people who encounter it in South-east Asian, Mexican and, increasingly, Western dishes. Another flavour which produces an extreme range of reaction is that of the durian. The interior is smooth and creamy: the skin has an unmistakable faecal note, sufficiently disgusting for it to be banned from confined spaces such as aircraft cabins and hotel bedrooms. For those who enjoy the indole base note it is the complete aphrodisiac: 'as the durians fall, the sarongs rise', or so they say. Among other erotic fruits are the mango and the persimmon where some varieties have semen-like overtones and a squashy texture that seems to be irresistible to the susceptible.

The vaguely sexual odours of certain cheeses may be pleasant to both men and women. Cheese hardly makes one rush away from the table or crawl under it, but there might well be a subtle boost. The 'cheesy' aroma of some Champagnes and the 'sweaty' character of some still wines can stimulate, and similar qualities are repeated in cheese like Brie. A French cheesemaker of the nineteenth century is said to have recognised the peak moment of ripeness of his Bries when they reminded him of his wife. Yeasty odours also get some people going. Fresh, yeasty bread, some Champagnes and still wines, all share this quality, perhaps analogous with and complementary to the smell of a clean body.

Chocolate is highly regarded as an aphrodisiac. There is some basis for this acclaim, discussed further in Chapter 10, 'Love and Orgasm'. Montezuma, Casanova and Madame Du Barry are among those who are said to have used it to fan their partners' fires, and many people become unsuspecting 'chocaholics' – though the advertising industry knows exactly why. Fermented, roasted and ground, with much of the cocoa butter removed, raw chocolate is used to make the products we know. Unblended, it is fragrant but exceedingly bitter, and the most bitter chocolate generally available is 70 per cent pure. Chocolate makes a surprisingly good combination cooked with chilli, and in both Spain and the New World is added to veal, game and chicken dishes.

Six millennia of use of hot culinary spices cannot be brushed aside lightly. Cantharides or Spanish Fly is to be avoided at all costs as a certain provoker of pelvic congestion and terminal irritation. But the capsaicin in chillis, and the pungency of classic curry spices are both controllable and highly acceptable, with the potential to stimulate even as they depart. Spices are marginally sexual. They are identical to some of the notes used in perfumes; for example, vanilla (Spanish, *vainillo* from the Latin, *vagina*) the lovely cinnamon, and nutmeg, mace, coriander seed, black pepper, clove, cumin, fenugreek, poppy seed – the list is endless. Even asafoetida, from the root of the 'stinking fennel', is irresistible to some if it is used only in minute quantities. And for those who can afford real saffron, its effect on a true bouillabaisse, a veal dish or a lamb curry, is well worth the effort and expense. Add it late, in fact just before serving, so that the flavour is not lost in cooking.

As we have seen with asparagus, the appearance of some foods is highly stimulating. Those who watched the eating scene in the film *Tom Jones* will know exactly what I mean. Albert Finney and Joyce Redman eat their food with the most explicit oral sexual cavortings, never taking their eyes off one another, still as yet avoiding physical contact. The Japanese noodle movie, *Tampopo*, remains a delightful memory for its visual specifics. The Italian slang for the female genitals is the same word as 'fig', and fresh figs eaten with Parma ham and melon may have more to do with the birth rate than meets the eye. Stuffed baked pig's uterus was known to the Romans and can still occasionally be found in rural Europe. Tomatoes were called 'love apples' partly because of their appearance when freshly cut. And how does one peel a banana politely in front of a potential sexual partner?

So there are foods which may be, or are thought to be, aphrodisiac. The cooking methods and presentation are very important. The principles of aphrodisiac cookery are lightness, intensified taste and unusual or frankly sexy flavours. If you have a little highly flavoured stock hidden away, trot it out for a flavour boost. Garlic enthusiasts know that it must be shared. Butter is an excellent cooking fat, but light cooking oils intrude less, during and afterwards. However good something is, don't overdo it.

I was recently at a dinner when I became aware of a smell immediately identifiable as androstenone. I didn't know where it came from – until several courses into the meal the source appeared. It was a perfectly cooked fillet of beef, served with a simple reduced pan juice with finely chopped truffles. The guests were well known to me, and I could see that they all became exceptionally stimulated as the meal progressed. The next twelve hours might have made an interesting survey.

An enormous investment of time and effort, not to mention money, has been expended on the search for aphrodisiac food and drugs. As we have seen, there are some that qualify, but most sensible people know that the truth lies somewhere in the middle, between the real or imagined qualities of the foods and the spirit and ambience in which they are used. People are the ultimate aphrodisiac, and a glass of wine, fresh crusty bread, tasty cheese, and a crunchy pear, shared with love, can be as potent as the richest meal. As Proverbs 15.17 has it: ‘Better a meal of herbs where love is, than a stalled ox and hatred therewith.’ Any great food or great wine can have an aphrodisiac effect in the right circumstances. The greatest meal can be ruined by the wrong companion, worry, or some perfectly trivial happening which breaks the spell. Any of the sexual pheromones, or anything that suggests them, may be aphrodisiac to males, to females, and sometimes to both. But nothing is ever 100 per cent effective. The timing may be wrong. ‘I tried it, and it didn’t work’. The answer to that is that it might well have worked some hours later – where were you?

The greatest love is the love of food
George Bernard Shaw

4

Exciting Wines

In flagrante delicious!

We have seen that the fragrances of flowers and fruits are irresistible to insects, birds and animals, and thereby become an intrinsic part of their reproduction and some of the most exciting notes in perfume. This book continually explores and develops the thesis that the pleasure and excitement of attractive smells are nature's lure and bonus for the continuation of life.

Have you ever smelt grape flowers? The scent of the grape vine in flower a month or so after bud burst is so delicious that to walk through the rows of vines on a still, warm day hints of swooning ecstasy, it is so poignant and of such breathtaking beauty. There is more. The haunting perfume you smell at this phase of the life of the grape, virtually its conception, is often recalled in the fragrance from a glass of the mature wine many years later, so aptly named 'the bouquet'.

Years ago, still innocent of many of the complexities and nuances of the excitement of wine, I read of the laboratory studies of Masters and Johnson, particularly their observations of neck blushing, pupil dilation and nipple erection, now known to a wider circle as some of the obvious signs of female sexual excitement. Soon after, I was astonished to notice just those three signs in a lovely lady conveniently wearing a thin silk shirt during the tasting of an excellent chardonnay, a '76 from memory. Scientists call this a random and uncontrolled observation. It nearly was. Since that time the reaction, in those capable of such responses, has been observed sufficiently frequently for it to be impressive. It is not just the alcohol and certainly, in all modesty, not the effect of the observer.

The very act of tasting a wine can start a cascade of sensations likely to trigger at least a dribble of happy hormones (see Chapter 22). The colour may excite, then the bouquet, the taste, even subliminal pain with the more potent wines, and, of course, finally the direct effect of absorbed alcohol in the brain. Small quantities of any wine are exciting, merely because of the alcohol lessening inhibition. 'Candy is dandy, but liquor is quicker' – the advice of the so-experienced Dorothy Parker. Substantial studies of this very point have been undertaken. The research techniques are most unusual, involving internal cameras for the ladies, pneumatic pump-up, pressure-measuring cuffs for the gentlemen, and some terminal pornography. Sober-sided science confirms what most people suspect, that the sexual response to alcohol in males tends to be influenced by their belief that they are drinking alcohol, but that females are more realistically and directly influenced by the amount of alcohol actually consumed. Of course we are talking only about very moderate use.

Teetotallers move in a world of total certainty about the evil effects of alcohol. At a certain college of Oxford University, a visitor, when offered port in the senior common room after dinner, claimed indignantly, 'Why, I would rather commit adultery than drink a glass of port.' The embarrassing silence was broken by the Master who said, 'And who wouldn't.'

One happy volunteer told of a new experience when, in the lag phase after vigorous lovemaking, she noticed a frankly sexual smell from a bottle of Champagne when the cork was popped. Severely censored, it goes something like this: 'It smells like you right now, darling.' 'Darling, I was just going to say the same thing about you!' That there was something in it for both is not always the rule with odours that make a clear sexual statement. At least one Champagne house seems to be aware of the relationship: 'We would like to describe the taste to you', its advertisements explain, 'but we don't know you well enough.' I wonder if the sexy odour of split yeast is an evolutionary reminder of prodigious and highly efficient cell reproduction.

This, of course, is much of the lure of Champagne. Champagne starts as a still wine, from black pinot and chardonnay grapes, one or several. Later a little sugar is added, plus some active yeast, the wine is corked tight, and the second ferment that results in the bottle makes the bubbles in Champagne. The yeast then settles to the bottom of the bottle as lees, to be removed before the sale of the wine one to ten years later. The time the wine lives on 'composting' yeast lees gives Champagne its characteristic flavour and now, it seems, much of its charm. Quite obviously, there is also a charge of excitement in the bubble-drive alcohol, one of the more striking benefits of the marriage of the art of the winemaker to the science of oenology.

Consider the smell of a container of bean sprouts, one component of which is called acetaldehyde. One of the important human pheromones is an odour known as IBA, and this happens to be a relative of the bean sprout odour. Great Champagne and sherries have many such aldehyde tones. There are also hints of fresh sweaty notes of the middle-range fatty acid smells, discussed in Chapter 24, 'Genesis and the

Seven Days of Flavour'. These attractants also occur in several of the world's most delicious and expensive cheeses. Will society ever get around to discussing the former as they do the latter?

There are other pheromones in wines. Some great rieslings and semillons occasionally have a 'sweaty' tone among the fragrances. Not a five-day unwashed labourer, rather the freshly bathed underarm of an excited and nubile female, or male, if you wish. Not everybody denies this attraction.

After that first chardonnay adventure, I started looking for a similar response to cabernet sauvignon. No really clearcut response, but the wine is usually served at table under conditions where a more complete observation is difficult. Englightenment came during the research of this book. Great cabernet wines develop from the early fragrance of blackcurrant into the beautiful essence redolent of cedar oil and cigar box. Cedar and its odour cousin sandalwood (the wood, its oil, and smoke for incense) have been part of religion and widely used to enhance physical attraction for seven thousand years. This knowledge readied me for an experience that changed what had begun as an olfactory joke to an idea that may well have a scientific basis. The day after I had been working with the booklet from the *National Geographic* Olfactory Survey, I was nosing a '66 Grand-Puy-Lacoste (a 75 per cent cabernet from Bordeaux – a reward for hard work) and was struck by the resemblance to the androstenone of the scratch-and-sniff box in the booklet. Comparing them side by side, to my palate they were almost identical, except the red wine had a more intense note!

Some cabernet wines have a hint of truffle aroma in amongst all the other goodies. The relationship of truffle, androstenone, and sows as truffle seekers is described in Chapter 3, as is the hilarious abandon in a wine and food group who had enjoyed a fabulous meal of beef with a generously truffled Madeira sauce married at the table to a great cabernet.

Time spent in new oak barrels silhouettes the cedar/sandalwood profile of the mature wine, and the lactone that does this (called the 'whisky' lactone because of its addition to some of them) gives, in my opinion, the wines of shiraz and pinot a pheromonal influence. This is distinct from that of oak mousse or moss, a lichen, that delivers a greenish woody note to certain perfumes and liqueurs.

Wines of ripe shiraz grapes sometimes have a fragrance of blackberries. Are you aware there is a musk note in ripe blackberry? I first picked it up after smelling the musky 'White Linen' perfume on a lady standing next to me at a smorgasbord. Having just tasted a blackberry wine from the Rhône valley, I noticed a clear resemblance, confirmed by independent parties, whom I call on wherever possible to lessen concern that I have gone round the bend.

Apart from the change produced by the bouquet of wine at the time of drinking it, the fragrance may appear in the body odour several hours later. A regular intake of cabernet wine seems to be the solution, but that advice is bound to be suspect from a cabernet wine-maker.

5

Knowing Perfume

> Fragrance may well be the signature of eternity.
>
> Tom Robbins

Scents are waste, the end-products of plant or animal metabolism, though as always in Nature there is more to them than that. The terpenes of the essential oils of plants, and some animal excretory odours, may be natural warnings to some of the creatures of their environment, such as parasites or competing males. Indole is a classic example, one of the more disgusting smells of faeces and putrefying animal tissue, as in a charnel house! Yet in high dilution it is widely used in perfumes. It is not surprising that jasmine, hyacinth, lily, jonquil, narcissus and others with high indole notes may be oppressive to some people in closed spaces, even causing headaches or nausea.

When the scents of flowers, fruit, and so forth, are attractive, you can be sure this will further their propagation, and borrowed for our perfumes they are truly seductive:

> Floral earth, the sexual planet ... Squeezed from the reproductive glands of plants and creatures, perfume is the smell of creation, a sign dramatically delivered to our senses of the Earth's

> regenerative powers – a message of hope and a message of pleasure ... the modern woman who dabs her body with expensive perfume is attempting to acquire the irresistible sexuality of flowers.
>
> Tom Robbins, *Jitterbug Perfume*

Flower petals are modified leaves. Mesnaud has studied the transformation of green chlorophyll of leaves into the pigments of flower petals and the production of essential oils, why flowers with green petals lack perfume, and why white petals tend to be the most fragrant. Finally, in flowers with the brightest colours, fragrance is often minimal or absent, though there are a few well-known exceptions. It is almost as if the natural design is to decide on either odour or colour as the reproductive signal. Exposure to sunlight and heat plays a role in aroma development. We start with aroma of unripe buds of lavender and end up with lemon, *via* rose. The chemical change is extremely slight, even though the effect is so marked.

We come now to some of the more interesting and important items of perfume construction. It is scarcely possible to read about perfume or body smells without encountering the word musk. Yet how many know what it is, or what it actually smells like? Some of the descriptions are confusing: unique and special, sandalwood, honey, urinous, stimulating, oppressive, repugnantly strong, animal, 'warm'; there is no end to the attempts. It is obviously unique and, like violet, clove, mint, truffles, muscat and raspberry, is itself used to convey an idea about the constituents of other complex scents. It is one of the most potent and persistent odours known. It has been recognised in the mortar of a mosque a thousand years after it was added during construction.

Tom Clark gave me the experience of smelling a

real musk pod in a jar. Open, at arm's length, an absolutely ravishing odour leaves one almost breathless, wanting more, much more! Closer, with elbow bent at right angle, the scent is heavy and tends to be tiring. Still rather wonderful, however. With the open jar held right under the nose, the smell is plain disgusting. There is no other word for it. The ultimate 'less is more'.

Musk is a milky secretion of the penile sheath of a small deer which inhabits the tree-line of the high mountains of Asia, where the alpine pasture begins. Himalayan musk is best known, but the highest quality comes from Tonquin in the province of Szechuan. As the animal ages, a pod of dried secretion accumulates near the navel, to reach golf ball, or slightly larger, size. It contains yellow to black-brown grains, not unlike coffee grains or dried blood, both of which have been used to adulterate the product for sale to novice buyers. When the grains are rubbed lightly on the palm, the additions remain in the creases. Well, if you are going to pay up to a thousand dollars for a pod, you want to know these things. Gold fluctuates, but on average, musk fetches one-third as much again per ounce. Why?

It has been used as a personal and space scent in China for perhaps five thousand years. It does not appear to have been known to the Egyptians. It was introduced to the Arabs by the Persians, to be added initially by them as a special character in the cooking of meat stew. It is still widely used as a flavouring in food and drink. As a child I used to enjoy penny 'musk' sticks, and look what happened! The sale of musk to Japan is a revelation. It takes 80 per cent of the world's supply. A universally advertised children's tonic there contains musk, ginseng root and deer horn. The children are certainly among the most beautiful-looking in the world.

I lived in Shinjuku, one of the lively towns that

make up Tokyo, for the best part of a month. Chemists' shops stayed open all night and they appeared to sell a lot of 'stamina' drinks (containing musk) to tired business men and a few ladies. It is not permitted to advertise anything as an aphrodisiac in Japan, despite the fact that research at Indian universities shows that musk produces an increase in the force of heart muscle contraction, without an increase in the rate, surely important in beginning and sustaining the act of love.

The mountain people who collect the musk pods wear them around their necks, possibly for the scent, possibly as an indication of wealth in the way others wear jewellery, or both. Courtesans of the nineteenth century wore musk amulets between their breasts. Napoleon, who bathed in cologne water, objected to the universal and overpowering use of musk by Josephine. You will recall he preferred her natural unwashed odour ... '*Je reviens*'.

Quite apart from its unique fragrance, musk has three special qualities that make it invaluable in the greatest perfumes. It blends all the notes, uniting them as nothing else can. Scents containing it radiate from the skin most effectively. And it lasts like no other aroma. A musk fragrance was first synthesised in 1888 and there are now over three hundred versions. We had better get used to the lack of 'warmth' of most synthetics, because there is now a ban on the taking of musk pods, and attempts at domesticating the animals for commercial production have not, to date, been wildly successful.

Making a perfume involves four considerations: the purpose; the structure of the product; the components; and their harmonic mix. For the first, I don't mean the acquisition of a fortune. Is it for male or female? Is it to last for a long or short period? Is it for morning or evening use? That sort of purpose.

It is necessary to understand the fabrication of the

structure, its foundation, girders, cladding, whether it is to be made at home (and there is every encouragement to do so – as a student I fluked a terrific aftershave from the citrus harmony of oil of bergamot obtained from a friendly pharmacist, and made up with half alcohol and water), or if it is to be the most significant fragrance ever produced.

An orchestral composition is a more exact analogy, and working models of a new fragrance are constructed on a framework of high, middle and low notes. They have other names both in English and French (*tête* or *départ*, *corps* or *coeur*, and *fond*) but the divisions are clear.

Top notes awaken and stimulate, and may be the most effective part of the perfume at a distance. The heart notes are delightful, and tend to be intoxicating and lessen inhibition; anyhow, the wearer has already made a statement in body language merely by the

The Notes of Fragrance

Top notes	*Citrus fruit, peel and leaves*, e.g. orange, tangerine, lime, bergamot; aldehydes, C_7 orange*; C_{10} also orange plus rose and lemon; C_{20} fruity, raspberry *Some flowers*, verbena, fruit blossoms
Middle notes (heart, body)	*Spices*, cinnamon, aniseed, mace *Herbs*, freshly cut grass; rosemary, fennel, thyme *Some flowers*, lavender, rose, violet
Bottom notes (base)	*Woods*, pine needles, cedar, sandalwood, oak moss, some nuts, vanilla *Some flowers*, jasmine, pachouli, iris root *Animal*, musk, amber (gris), civet, leather

*The numbers refer to the linked atoms of carbon.

wearing, and especially if it has been got right. How long the notes last will become important in the final blend. Imagine being left all musky quite early in the piece, when the desire was to be as subtly sexual as the freshest morning flower.

The Perfume Symphony

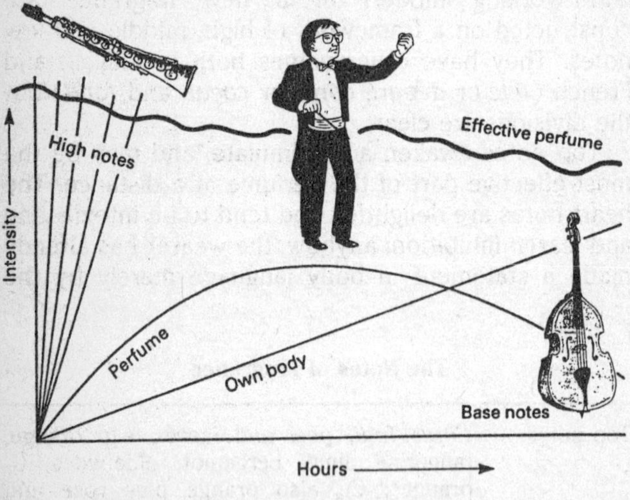

Top, middle and low note harmonies have been called 'vertical'. Others sustain the high notes all day (for example 'Poison', 'Chloe') and are, by contrast, called 'horizontal' (more professional jargon, not a tribute to *les grandes horizontales*, the best of last century's Parisian ladies of the night).

An understanding of chords and progressions is central. There are definite *octaves* (the jargon the profession uses); for example, heliotrope-vanilla-almond, or lime-lemon-bergamot. Elsewhere, the term *flavour spectrum* is applied because of the irregular intensities and distances between the components. There is much to consider; e.g., camphor has three times the odour intensity of attar of rose, and generally the latter far exceeds the strength of the aromas of the water-extracted and distilled compounds of that lovely flower.

Next time you catch a whiff of perfume, see if you can pick up an orange or lemon tone. Most commercial fragrances use one of the citrus notes. Be not discouraged. The composer has quite possibly sat before as many as five hundred separate little bottles, using cunning and skill to prevent you performing just that exercise. They have worked in a logical sequence. The top notes volatilise quickly so the base notes are next to be added to delay their departure. Fine oils and resins, for example olive and myrrh, were used for thousands of years, but the modern preference is for animal fixatives like musk or ambergris. Finally, the middle, or heart, is added.

This is the most difficult to balance. From here on each addition may disturb the previous carefully contrived tranquillity. Some unexpected synergism or antagonism may destroy. No wonder that the creation of a masterpiece can take a year or longer. In 1917, François Coty fashioned 'Chypre', which came to lend its name to a whole style of similar perfumes that followed. In 1921, Ernest Beaux introduced the first bright synthetic take-off to a perfume, in the form of several aldehydes (you may remember that they end in -al) and this also started a trend destined to become classic. Coty's 'Chypre' was inspired by a traditional scent from Cyprus, and contained rose, bergamot, oak moss, hide, amber, storax (a fragrant balsam from a tree resin) and, of course, musk. Beaux's masterpiece became 'Chanel No. 5' and is the subject of a separate note in Chapter 8, 'Queens of Fragrance'.

Eau de Cologne has never lost its popularity since it appeared in about 1709 and took off during the Seven Years' War, when it was adopted by the

French soldiers quartered in Cologne. It is associated with the name of Farina, but Frances Kennett holds the view that it took three countries to achieve this. Italy had the tradition, Germany an alcohol industry, and France the public to establish it.

Eau de Cologne
(16 drams per pound)

Rose oil	2 drams
Melissa oil	2 "
Neroli oil	5 "
Lavender oil	6 "
Geranium oil	8 "
Rosemary oil	9 "
Lime oil	1 ounce
Cedra oil	2 "
Petitgrain oil	2 "
Orange oil	2 "
Lemon oil	3 "
Bergamot oil	4 "
	1 lb

For full details of the volume of alcohol and water for the quantity, please refer to Erich Walter. You can wash yourself with bottles of it, should you wish, just as Napoleon did.

The Family Groups of Fragrance

Floral	Flower scent predominates. May be single, e.g. rose or gardenia
Green	Crushed leaf, freshly-cut grass
Aldehydic	Volatile, fruity, sharp floral
Chypre	Lively, some warmth or spice
Woody	Pine, cedar oil
Oriental	Warm and a little sweet
Animal	Leather, tarry, carnal, prolonged

All of these have subgroups, and, like so much of flavour and fragrance, the borders tend to blur a bit. Take lavender: both the flower and extract share floral, green and woody notes. The French use a further group clarification they choose to call *fougère*, the odour of fern.

The perfume composer is a threatened species. The Nose, *le Nez* (as distinct from *l'Olfactif*, anyone who has a fine appreciation of the nuances of perfume), is a person who has sufficient nasal dexterity and training to be employed creatively in the perfume industry. Such men have the skill to identify several hundred odours and of understanding compound smells. I have not been able to find if there are any women thus employed. Women wine judges are just appearing at wine shows. Currently, there are four French perfume houses employing in-house composers. The others contract outside specialists. Jacques Polge is *le Nez* at Chanel. He created 'Diva' for Ungaro, 'floral notes of Turkish rose, Florentine iris, narcissus, Egyptian jasmine, clustered over a deep amber base, and topped up by the heavenly fragrance of Indian tuberose'. Don't you wish you could do that?

We know that perfumes and natural fragrances arouse memories, as well as directly switching people on. Women tend to the more 'erotic' perfumes, showing in tests a preference for amber, jasmine, musk, tuberose, sandalwood and so on. Men seem to be ahead on pine, lilac, violet, carnation, verbena (some women can't stand it), leather; by and large the light florals. The more one learns about violet, the more fascinating it becomes. It cuts off quickly, yet leaves one wanting more. What does that remind you of? It has the ability to be perceived again in a few minutes or so. As it oxidises, the aroma shades off to cedar, and still later to something like a forest floor.

Straight vanilla can be most sensual to a number of people, particularly females. The dab of vanilla essence behind each ear had some reputation. Finally, some sexually aroused men and women reach escape velocity from the synergism of the partner's applied perfume and their own musky bottom (in the perfume sense) note.

6

A Rose is . . .

A rose is a rose is a rogue
Tom Robbins

The rose is old. Rock fossils of wild roses date back forty million years. The founder of Islam, the Emperor Nero, you and I, we all share the attraction of roses. They are at the core of the history and philosophy of perfume and flavour, making this chapter perhaps a paradigm of the whole book.

Even as I write, a small flash of 'Tea Rose' from the Perfume Workshop in America is open beside me. I got the idea from Guy de Maupassant, although he used something different. At other times I prefer tangerines or limes, which I am fortunate enough to grow. Tea rose, lime, tangerine . . .

I first encountered 'Tea Rose' during a memorable dinner in Paris. Scenting it on a beautiful guest as she passed to her table I sent, in time-honoured fashion, a card to ask what it was. Her amused response certainly seemed to provoke some tense questions from her companion. The occasion stays warmly in my memory and I hope it does in hers too.

At Cleopatra's first meeting with Mark Antony, Athenaeus records that the floors of her palace apartment were covered in rose petals to a depth of half a metre. So also were the sails of her royal barge drenched with rose water. Nero, among his other less charming attributes, was rose-obsessed. His expenditure on the importation of dried roses from Persia alone was enormous. Roy Bedichek reports that 'He breathed them, ate rose-flavoured food, drank rose wine, lay on them, walked over them, and slept on them. When ill, he even took medicine made from roses.'

The rose is also popular as an emblem among the warlike. At the height of the Persian kingdom's might, the warriors carried shields with a rose emblem. The red rose of Lancaster and the white rose of York gave their name to the English Wars of the Roses, and are still regional emblems to this day.

The rose is a shrub, a bush, a climbing or rambling plant of the family *Rosaceae*, and can form a thicket impenetrable enough to hide the Sleeping Beauty. It has survived by its ability to adapt to virtually the worst that soil and climate offer. Many members of its family, for instance the apple, the raspberry, the strawberry and the bramble, have flowers that look more like a wild rose than wild roses resemble their modern descendants.

Rose breeding probably began in China five thousand years ago, at much the same time as the Egyptians were using roses for domestic fragrance, adornment and religious ceremony. Everyone must regret that recent progressive breeding for size, colour and durability has been at the expense of scent. So few modern roses compare in fragrance to the roses of childhood. It sometimes seems that a conspiracy is afoot to breed the scent out of them. People can't handle odour, I used to think, in the same way that atonal music and abstract art shut out the verities of Bach or Rembrandt. Happily the facts are different.

Somewhere in the genetic pursuit of colour, durability and stem strength, fragrance got lost. It appears to be a recessive factor, and roses exhibit an incredible chromosomal mishmash. Breeding back to fragrance is slow work, almost hit-and-miss, and even with a promising new clone it takes something like seven years for it to be available for sale. But change is in the air, and at the US Patent Office, where new roses can be registered and a seventeen-year patent obtained, 'good smell' is coming back. In 1961, James Alexander Gamble of Maryland, USA, put us all in his eternal debt by endowing an annual award through the American Rose Society for outstanding fragrance in red roses.

There have been more than 20,000 varieties of roses, of which perhaps 7,000 of the choicest have endured. A favourite of mine is 'Crimson Glory' in which some people pick up a persisting note of clove. In case you find a clove character (eugenol) unusual in roses, you may be surprised to learn that eugenol is 21 per cent of the essential oil in *violets*! 'American Beauty', introduced in 1875 and classed as a hybrid perpetual, is another highly regarded for fragrance and form.

A wide range of rose scents have been described, quite comparable, for example, to those of grapes or apples. They range from rose, musk, apple, lemon, violet, clove, orris and cinnamon through to linseed oil and green. Some actually stink!

Among these may be the scent of 'tea', the name given to the Chinese roses which began to arrive in Europe in 1810, on the tea clippers. Western rose breeders were captivated by the ability of these roses to flower more than once a year, as well as by their strong red colour and their elegant shape. Napoleon's Josephine enthusiastically cultivated a library garden of about 250 varieties at Malmaison. Such was the international regard for the rose that British naval captains of the Napoleonic Wars sent on to Malmaison those roses destined for it which they found on captured ships.

A rose is one of the exceptions to the rule: bright colours, less perfume. Little sacs in the petals, actually visible to the unaided eye in some varieties, contain the precursors of the scents we enjoy, and their ability to function varies with the time of day, just as does the sniffer's. A rose is as responsive to sunrise as any bird. They smell at their best between 4.30 and 9.30 a.m. after which their oil content falls by as much as 40 per cent.

Long before Christ, Homer's *Iliad* describes how Aphrodite anointed Hector with oil of roses. Greece already had a catalogue of the best ones. Pliny preferred the wild roses of Capri, south of Rome, to all others. The pattern continues: contemporary Americans buy fifty million rose plants and six hundred and fifty million cut flowers every year, for one and a half billion US dollars.

Great civilisations treasured the rose, but it was the Bulgarian outpost of Islam which brought attar, or otto, the essential oil of roses, to Europe (the name derives from the Arabic word, *itr*, for perfume). Rose attar from present-day Bulgaria is said to bring top prices on the Paris market. The flowers of highest quality are picked early in the dewy morn. 'The best attar comes from wet skirts' says a Bulgarian proverb. It is preferred apparently even to the excellent product of Grasse in the South of France, where the fragrance made an unforgettable impression on two young fools in May 1954. The synthetic Attarose ABR 5000 is now being used in an attempt to replace the natural product.

To make attar, the petals are spread on to trays loaded with odourless fat (mutton fat and olive oil have both been used), and replaced every few days in the season till the fat is saturated. 'Concrete' is the term for the waxy mass left after the removal of the fat. Attar, the essential oil, is the result of a highly skilled steam distillation. Alternatively, an absolute can be dissolved with alcohol from the wax 'concrete'. That is preferred for flavouring, while the distilled oil remains the choice of classic perfume. One of the most interesting facts about a rose is that its principal odour can be effectively extracted with cold water if done carefully; hence rosewater, whose main character is phenylethyl alcohol, which is lacking in the steam distillate, attar. When this compound gets an amine tacked on it becomes PEA, part of the euphoric mix we call the 'highs' of love and discussed in Chapter 10, 'Love and Orgasm'.

One acre of commercial roses might be planted with seven thousand bushes. The yield in an average season could be five thousand pounds of petals, producing ten pounds of attar. This performance can be sustained for up to ten years.

Flavouring, you ask? Rosewater was a much-used flavour in medieval and later times. It was particularly popular in the Middle East, but was also used in Europe. The note can still be detected today in liqueurs, all manner of sweets, jellies and ices, biscuits and cakes. In blends that have citrus and spice notes, rose mellows and rounds off spikes and harshness. A curry freak, I have been puzzled at times by a rose note in Asian dishes, and have later found it to have one or other of the following as the source: turmeric, galangal (*laos*), lemon grass and the more fragrant of the small dynamite green chillies.

Romantics may be depressed to learn that little mystery remains about the constituents of rose fragrance.

Very few flowers have a single odour note, and a rose is no exception. Men and women both love the fragrance of rose, but it is *the* preferred scent of women. Many, perhaps most of the popular classic French perfumes, have a rose note. The American 'Tea Rose'

What Rose Fragrance is Made of
(Adapted from Giovanni Fenaroli, *Handbook of Flavour Ingredients*)

Ingredients	Parts by weight	Source
Geraniol	4.0	Geranium, lemon grass
Phenethyl alcohol	3.0	Rose
Linalool	1.25	Orange flowers, cinnamon, muscatel
Rhodinol	1.25	Geranium, oil of citronella
Citronellol	0.5	
Aldehyde C_9	0.05	
Citral	0.04	
Eugenol (M)	varies	Cloves
Nerol	varies	Orange peel, magnolia

is a fascinating and very successful effort to avoid some of the heavier base notes of the classics, pitched between them and the high tones, for example, of 'L'Air du Temps' of Nina Ricci. Roy Genders points out that 'Red Rose' is part of the fame of Floris of Jermyn Street, probably propelled to immortality by Edward VII's attraction to it on Rosa Lewis. Nothing really changes.

7

To Choose a Fragrance

Less is more
Mies van der Rohe

Why does anyone wish to change their odour, to unconsciously reveal what they aim to hide and, in the act, add to the thirty or so billion dollars a year spent for that purpose? Why add to your own essence, and especially why add the intimate secretions of male animals, mingled with the reproductive odour signals of flowers and fruits? Are you getting a message from thousands of years of human culture or, in Tom Robbins's phrase 'are you attempting to acquire the irresistible sexuality of flowers?' After all, you yourself just might have the most attractive and exciting personal fragrance in the whole of creation, to be tuned by a swim in the sea, or simply a shower.

When choosing perfume, different criteria apply for men and women. Another point: the net effect of your intimate scent, your mood, and the applied fragrance, is more clearly assessed by another. This is the only certain way to achieve the matchless delight of the right choice, which I am sorry to tell you is all too infrequent at present. Here are practical hints of which the first and most important is that ultimate guiding rule inviolable for all odour: LESS IS MORE.

Suggestion can be more powerful than a thump on the head. It is surprising how many intelligent people think that if a little is very good, a lot will be that much better. In our field, there may not be much neutral territory between delight and disgust. In the world of fragrance and flavour, in the kingdoms of the kitchen and the bedroom, a hint is intriguing, less is more, enough is enough, and more is much too much.

To take one of my earliest lessons: the components of blackcurrant juice were unravelled at a scientific meeting in 1968. At the end of a formidable list were two compounds in amounts so infinitesimal that one would have thought that they could not have exerted much influence on the final result. Even more puzzling, on their own they were well known to be quite disgusting to smell. What on earth were they doing there? Quite simply, without these ingredients, 'blackcurrant' does not taste 'natural'. This was my first introduction to positive and negative levels of the same flavour and the seed of the philosophy in this chapter, applicable to all human activities, as the architect Mies van der Rohe stated so economically about his field.

Smell is the most subtle sense, of that there cannot be any doubt. All smells in nature register at very low levels of intensity, and those who ignore this fact have no style. Big flavours and perfumes may make an instant appeal at one time or another, but they produce rapid fatigue, sometimes in seconds, to be followed by indifference, then aversion, then either a headache or nausea and disgust, and finally, if intense enough, even vomiting. The principal perfume bases have this potential, as do the pheromones of both sexes. One of the strongest odours of human faeces is indole, minute amounts of which are found in night-blooming jasmine and tuberose, two intoxicating floral scents. The attractions and revulsions of musk have been described. The same grading of response applies to IMP (iso-butyl methoxy pyrazine – the smell of freshly cut grass), almost the most powerful smell on earth.

Overkill with perfume, by manufacturer or user, is appallingly frequent. The user has a degree of protection, becoming refractory or temporarily 'blind' to it. Anyone downwind of the excess in a room or public space has to suffer, and the net result is the exact opposite of the wearer's intention. It is even worse if there is also a discordant body smell. The worst offenders today are men using totally inappropriate aftershave which suits neither their personality nor their own skin smells. I wish some of them would drink the stuff.

Never forget that it is the faint odour that evokes the most interest, something that has to be actively sniffed to be certain of its presence. Much of the resultant activity is taking place below the level of conscious awareness. All the sexual fragrances can be alluring at threshold levels, or possibly even below. Excess disgusts both sexes unless the whole environment is awash in similar odours. The most startling example of this is *balachan*. It has several spellings in English, but the stink of sun-dried rotting little prawns is the same TMA already discussed *ad nauseam*, transcending all barriers, in whatever language. In Chapter 12, 'Flavour Power', its use as a flavour booster will be followed throughout history and in vastly differing cultures. A little is lovely! It also is probably an evolutionary survival marker – that is, a hint from evolution to eat something critical to good health. A prisoner of war who escaped from the Japanese in the Second World War survived many years of privation of flavouring the dull jungle food he was able to find with *balachan*, the gift of friendly natives. He attributed his survival to it. Asafoetida is another good example of the principle.

Some religions use it as a substitute for garlic, and it makes a fascinating binder of curry flavour. Only a little too much and it becomes the most useful emetic in the pharmacopoeia and, in fact, still has a place in the immediate treatment of swallowed poison.

The minimal in architecture has already been mentioned. The simplest line drawing by masters like Picasso and Degas are entrancing. They invite the participation of the viewer, their own creative response to flesh out the spaces. The economical Francis Bacon is my own favourite essayist. The listener's greatest pleasure in the most elementary Baroque counterpoint comes from the silhouettes of harmony in the listener's own brain, a delight anticipated and encouraged by the composer. You have to learn to do this with fragrance and flavour, to permit another to insert their keystone in the arch.

Now back to choosing a perfume. You begin by selecting up to four personal preferences yourself. Then come the finals, accepting the decision of a trusted friend, the closer the better. The knowledge that you smell as attractively as you would like gives a confidence obtained in no other way. You need envy no one.

As a preliminary, have you made sure that your own personal contribution is as good as it can be? The average European has a rancid smell in the summer within a few hours of washing, and perhaps needs more bathing than is good for skin health. South-east Asians smell of lemon, sweetness and florals from the spices and fruits they take daily. The Japanese traditional diet produces a virtually neutral body odour. Southern Italy floats on fresh garlic – marvellous if you too are eating it. It is worth repeating that great benefits can follow the frequent use of parsley, celery, green carrot tops, parsnips, Italian salad herbs and specific table wines. Any aromatic foods, for example curry, will be part of your body smell during the following twenty-four hours at least. Remember that mood and personality, be it happy, angry or frightened, and extrovert, or introvert, contribute to the total scent you present.

Previously I adopted the perfumer's musical analogies of high and low notes, and hinted at divine harmonies. There is also a visual comparison, which will vary with the light of sun and moon, themselves strongly influencing body rhythms and mood.

In short, diet, health and personal hygiene produce the primary colours of your palette, and to these, in any twenty-four hours, you then add more subtle tones to round out the picture.

Some wish to carry a fragrance and a mood solely for their *own* enjoyment. The idea appeals, but the only certain way to be wholly acceptable to others is to keep such a fragrance away from your skin. A *boutonnière* or posy is fine. My father favoured a freesia in his lapel. I followed his example with carnations, and my operating theatre staff embroidered one on my surgeon's suits.

The tiniest drop of essence on a handkerchief or clothing is unlikely to cause problems, except that the latter may be difficult to alter or eliminate totally on another occasion. It is preferable to avoid the heavy bases, because they are so incredibly long-lasting. Aim for the explosive high light floral and green tones for this purpose.

Perfume, about 30 per cent of extract, persists long after eight hours. Splash cologne, less than a fifth of this intensity, lasts for a much shorter period. Eau de Cologne and aftershave are in between.

Some men and women who smoke aromatic tobacco have a motive other than their own enjoyment, of which they may not be aware. That is to produce an effect within their immediate sphere of influence beyond their body 'space'; perhaps, at times seeking an aphrodisiac response and, less commonly, achieving it. It can happen with the first fresh puff, but almost everyone is repelled by the tar-and-protein stink that develops later, unless precautions are taken to avoid it. I have been amazed to find some women are as 'switched on' by tobacco as by leather.

If you have sufficient insight to recognise that perfume is usually applied to be attractive to others, you will be appalled to learn how often the result is negative – a dismal, sometimes even disgusting, failure. To enter a lift, for example, where a heavy lingering perfume has failed to disguise the fact that its wearer has not washed for days, can be an inhibiting experience – the only choice to move to another lift or to walk up. There has been an improvement in the last ten years, but I still rate the really successful application of perfume at about one in five. How often have *you* been almost startled by the ravishing union of freshness, health, and the fruition of the perfumer's art? This is the essence of excitement and it really is easier to achieve than might appear.

Gifts of perfume, aftershave, soaps and the like can be expensive and counter-productive. I wonder how many unopened and part-used bottles clog the cupboards of the globe? You must have a clear idea of the result already discussed. How much more fun, if no surprise, to make a selection together to delight you both, giver and receiver. Really good chocolate or a bottle of fine wine could achieve a more reliable result, unless you are involved with a dieter or teetotaller. You should certainly never choose a heavy, clinging perfume unless you are certain it is their preference, and that it works. If you are buying scent or aftershave for someone you do not (yet) know well, go for the fresh, high notes and middle harmonies because nearly everyone likes them.

The most inappropriate fragrances can be bought

by one woman for another, and probably because they sense the problem, women seldom give perfume. It is sufficiently difficult to gauge another's taste in clothes with a gift in mind, let alone something as complex and personal as an appropriate scent. There is a different facet in the gift of an aftershave. 'Mandate', 'Antheus', and 'Jovan Musk', to name a few, include a strong musk note. Some men may find the intended message too difficult a puzzle to unravel.

When choosing a perfume or aftershave for yourself, you may already have an idea of the style that appeals to you. If you like it very much, there is a reasonable chance it will suit you, which does not really contradict the failure rate above. And if you don't like it, you quite obviously will not use it, whatever the advice or persuasion of another person.

A professional might start with a simple floral green classification. 'L'Air du Temps' (Nina Ricci) and 'Joy' (Jean Patou) are among the favourites. There are fuzzy borders with other fragrance neighbours, much as is demonstrated on pages 105–6 in the riesling-muscat-traminer spectrum. So when tuberose is added, as in 'Chloe' (Lagerfeld), the style is increasingly Oriental. There is a comparable transition from simple floral, to the supernatural synthetic explosiveness of 'Chanel No. 5' through 'Arpège' (Lanvin) to Estée Lauder's relatively recent 'White Linen', created in 1978.

In the Oriental group, Guerlain's 'Jicky' has the distinction of being the oldest survivor of the current century of perfume. It dates from 1889. The harmony moves through Schiaparelli's 'Shocking' in its Mae West bottle, to 'Opium' (Yves St Laurent) and the new 'Poison'. The leather-grassy-tobacco group is less widely used; more so by males, but as there is no absolute palate, so there is no absolute nose. I recall one male wine writer's attractive use of 'Jicky'.

Once opened, the perfume in the bottle begins a

slow change. Just as with wine and cheese, the maker has interrupted a natural cycle for our delectation. If it restarts, oxidation, evaporation and degradation will leave you with the building blocks strewn around instead of the promise you paid for. It is a good idea to keep it cold, stored inside a larger airtight vessel, to prevent leakage. All aromatics volatilise quickly if warm, more slowly if cold.

Talk to the trained staff of stores where a wide selection of fragrances is available; do not hesitate to ask questions, and for sample sniffs. If they have a supply of perfumer's strips, white blotting paper with their own little plastic envelopes, take some back to your lair for longer contemplation; try one drop on a corner of a fresh cotton handkerchief or odourless blotting paper. Not paper tissues, which usually smell woody or may even be perfumed themselves. Not silk and preferably not nylon, all of which give different results compared to cotton, which is the least likely to confuse. During your learning period, use the least concentrated essences and, as with all flavour testing, deal with light before heavy fragrances. The beginner would be well advised to avoid application to areas where pheromone production is high. A most attractive middle-aged lady and I were complaining about those who wear fragrance at serious wine tastings. I viewed her in a different light when she said 'I never have the problem, because I never apply perfume above the waist.'

This for two reasons: first the exquisite consideration she showed her tasting partners; second and more shockingly because the remark made me seriously consider whether she might be making the right perfume choice, should any be needed.

At last you have chosen up to four finalists, and you are ready for judgment day, your selector by your side. With knowledge, and the confidence born of another's warm opinion, in due course you can reach the ideal result. The time of day is important, both for the observed and the observer. As the clock turns, the intensity of the scent may be varied. Small hours, small scent. Many hours, big scent. One of Lake's Laws.

Where arteries are close to the skin, for instance the base of the neck, wrist (the pulse), elbow and knee creases, or behind the ears, are ideal sites to apply perfume. These pulse points pump fragrance into the air around, and they are also not pheromone production areas, thus avoiding potential confusion with body signals. That is the idea, anyhow.

You have four areas available if necessary – both wrists and both elbow creases. A suspicion of a dab, or spray, starts the exercise. An immediate assessment is performed. Each scent has its own particular emotional resonance. Later, after about an hour, assessment is repeated for the heart note, and finally, later that evening, again for the residual effect before going to bed. About six hours is a minimum period to reach a conclusion; no problem if you start before midday, when your nose is tuned to concert pitch (assuming you have not had a gigantic breakfast – which would negate that). Unless something has gone badly wrong, you should have a result at the end of the day. Your preferences and those of your assessor are very likely to lead to the right choice. Is it worth the effort? Most people think so.

> ... this scent would take on a gravity that no-one, man or woman, would be able to escape. People would be overwhelmed, disarmed, helpless before the magic ... And none of them will know that it is truly not how she looked that has captured them, not her reputed unblemished external beauty, but solely her incomparable splendid scent!
>
> Patrick Susskind, *Perfume*
> translated by John E. Woods

8

Queens of Fragrance

We come now to four of the most memorable individuals since Eden. Four women with a profound influence on our subject. Although their sex gave them a running start, it was their philosophy of fragrance, of the essence of excitement, and their application of it, that has enshrined them. Modern feminists might consider them to be among the ultimate career women. What secrets did they share, the Queen of Sheba, Cleopatra, Catherine de Medici and Gabrielle Chanel?

The Queen of Sheba

Sheba was the most beautiful, and perhaps the most remarkable, of the quartet. Her background provides a foil to the magnitude of her success. Despite the arid environment of her domain, or perhaps because of it, spice and fruit fragrances were used widely and formed a considerable part of the trade between nations. Spiced olive oil was widely employed for body rubbing and cleansing. The higher the standard of living, the rarer and more fragrant the ingredients. Personal hygiene preoccupied men and women of that era no less than today. In the year before marriage, custom involved two six-monthly regimes. The first initial purification was with oil of myrrh, to be followed in the lead-up to the ceremony by a mix of frankincense and other highly potent scents. After conjugal life began, sexual intercourse was forbidden during menstruation and the subsequent week. A special bath concluded the abstinence.

Women generally wore a small cloth bag suspended as a necklet between the breasts. The perfume of the myrrh and other fragrances that it contained was slowly released by body heat, for the edification of the wearer and those within sniffing distance. Myrrh had other uses. Added to wine it induced a pleasant trance-like effect. It also formed part of the most important incense burnt for ceremonial purposes. Today, in the wadis of the Sinai, part of the southern Araby of Sheba's time, there still grow more than sixty wild and often aromatic herbs – lavender, rosemary, sage, oregano, to name a few. Visitors report the pleasure of treading the paths where they flourish. Frankincense, a smooth-barked shrub, only grows there and in Somaliland. Myrrh is the gum of another shrub growing here, collected in fragments from the beards of the goats which nibble the leaves.

The mighty kingdom of Israel bestrode the trade routes from the Incense road to the east, to the Egyptian delta in the south, and west to Damascus. Solomon's Indian Ocean fleet of cedar ships was a large one, analogous to the bulk carriers of the huge international fleets of today's world. His vessels visited all the regions of the known earth. He was perhaps the first of the great industrialists, with an empire that controlled or had access to substantial reserves of iron and copper, and techniques developed to mine, extract and refine them. 'All kings of the earth' came to hear his wisdom, and naturally to discuss trade agreements. And now follows an adapted account of an episode from the Old Testament:

Sheba heard of the fame of Solomon and came to visit him at Jerusalem, with a very great company and camels laden with rare spices and fragrances, gold and precious stones. She came to prove him with some questions, communing with him of all that was in her heart. And Solomon answered all, hiding nothing.

When the Queen of Sheba had seen the wisdom of Solomon, and the house that he had built, and the meat at his table, the retinue and skill of his servants, and the attendance and clothes of his ministers, there was no more spirit in her; overcome she said: 'I did not believe it when I heard the reports of your greatness, your wisdom, your doings, but now I have witnessed them with mine own eyes, the reports only told the half of them.'

And she gave the king a hundred talents of gold, a great quantity of spices of the utmost rarity and fragrance, and precious stones. With these, the servants of both kingdoms carried gold from Ophir and the scented algum trees. These were planted in terraces to the temple of the Lord, and the king's palace and there were none such ever seen before in the land of Judah.

And King Solomon gave to the Queen of Sheba all her desire, whatsoever she asked, in addition to what had already been conveyed to the king. After that she and all her servants returned to her own land.

After II Chronicles, 9.1

Mission accomplished.

This spare account is merely a synopsis of one of the most memorable diplomatic triumphs in history. Some such are accomplished by the obvious political and geographical pressures exerted on the participants. Others are smoothed and speeded by the pleasures of shared wine and food at table, and some others are sealed by sexual delights, with their associated fragrances beforehand, and intimate confidences afterwards. Sheba's skills embraced the three. The remarkable Solomon was eagerly compliant, merely adding a courtesy towards a guest and her bodyservant to his everyday labours of love with his own wives and concubines. The mix of all these ingredients makes even a mind used to explicit modern novels whirl. How can one do justice to the spectacle conveyed by the music 'The Entrance of the Queen of Sheba' in Handel's oratorio *Solomon*? Or to the incredible determination of a woman brought up in luxury and who, like as not, had never travelled the vast distance across some of the most desolate country on the globe, to confront the most potent ruler of her day, and secure the trade routes of her small domain.

What follows is a very free adaptation from Ecclesiastes II. It is virtually a catalogue of all the spices and fragrances known to the Israelites of 1000 BC. The poem itself is lyrical, dramatic, candid, and its symbolism quite erotic to many, including myself. The simple act of adapting it from the original was a turn-on. It could have been written by King Solomon. It even seems a distinct possibility that the Queen of Sheba composed this love cycle for Solomon, or that they wrote it together. Who knows?

The male and female voices are marked separately for reading aloud to each other, perhaps late on a quiet morning, with Champagne and ripe mango or white peach to hand.

The Song of Songs

WOMAN Let him kiss me with the kisses of his mouth
for his love is more exciting than wine;
the king has brought me to his room
I will recall thy love more than wine.

My king is at table
my own perfume fills the air;
my lover has the scent of myrrh
he shall lie all night on my breasts.

Like an apple tree among the trees of a
grove
so is my beloved compared to other
men
I love to sit in its shadow
and its fruit is sweet to my taste.

He brought me to his festive hall
and raised the banner of love over me.
Stay me with flagons
and comfort me with apples
for I am faint with love.

His left hand is under my head
and his right hand caresses me.
O my sisters, disturb not my lover,
till he pleases.

O my dove, in the cleft of the rock
in the secret hiding of the stair.
My beloved is mine, I am his
he feeds among the lilies.

MAN Behold how fair thou art, my love
thy hair is of the balm of Gilead
thy teeth white as the fresh shorn sheep
thy lips are scarlet
thy speech charms all.

Thy breasts are as twin young roses
that thrive among the lilies.
Until daybreak and the shadows flee

I will visit the mountain of myrrh
the hill of frankincense.

Thou has ravished my heart, my
sweetheart, my bride
how much better is thy love than mine
and the smell of thy person than all the
spices
honey and milk are under thy tongue.

Thy garments are like the smell of cedar
thou art a garden enclosed, orchard of
pleasure
fruits, all the chief spices
a well of living waters.

There are threescore queens
and fourscore concubines
and virgins without number await.
My spotless dove is the one.

WOMAN Awake O north wind, blow on my
garden.
Fill the air with fragrance
let my lover come to his garden
and eat his fruit of delight.

MAN I have entered my garden, my
sweetheart, my bride
I am gathering my spices and myrrh.
I am eating my honey, I am drinking my
wine.
O beloved, drink copiously.

WOMAN I have already disrobed.
Why should I get dressed again?
Carefully bathed, shall I rise?
My lover put his hand to the doorhole
and my body thrilled and moved.

I rose up to my beloved
my hands dripped with myrrh
fingers of sweet myrrh grasped the
    handle

My lover is handsome and strong
he is chief in ten thousand.
His cheeks are as beds of herbs, spices
    and flowers.
His lips are like lilies wet with liquid
    fragrant myrrh.

MAN The curve and join of your thighs are as
    jewels
to be worked by a craftsman.
Thy navel is like a chalice, never empty
    of cordial
thy belly is like a sheaf of wheat set with
    lilies
thy breasts are as twin roses.
The delights of your love are without
    number.
You are as graceful as a palm tree;
I will clasp the boughs.
Your breasts are as clusters of grapes.
Your breath the fragrance of apples,
    and your mouth the finest wine.
Open to me, my sister, my love, my
    dove so spotless.

WOMAN My mother instructs me
have you drink the juice of my
    pomegranate,
Left hand under my head, right hand to
    caress me.
Quickly my love
be like a young stag on the mound of
    spice.

A fragrance catalogue from *The Song of Songs*, in alphabetical order, with frequency in brackets, follows: Aloes, apple (3), calamus, camphire (2), cedar (2), cinnamon, frankincense (2), honey (3), lilies (3), lily of the valley, mandrake, myrrh (8!), nuts, orchard fruits (3), rose of Sharon, saffron, spices in general (3), spikenard (2), wine and grapes (5).

The specific comparisons between the aromatics of spices and fruits and the scents of the male and female participants are far clearer to me now than they were when I first happened upon them in a fug of pubertal curiosity. And it is truly God-given that this masterpiece has survived the ministrations of celibate scholars, who often were brands plucked from the fire anyway.

Cleopatra

Cleopatra, daughter of Isis, Queen of Upper and Lower Egypt, Goddess of the Sun – these were the imposing self-bestowed titles of the young Greek woman who presided over the conclusion of the last elements of greatness of the kingdom of Egypt. She urgently needed the might of Imperial Rome to support her control of the throne of Egypt, while Rome used the wealth of her kingdom to pay its own legions.

Cleopatra and her brother were the children of the Macedonian general who bribed his way to the throne of Egypt after the death of Alexander the Great. The two offspring went through a form of marriage, as was the custom of the Pharaohs, but were soon split by the pursuit of absolute power. An appeal to Caesar, executor of the father's will, brought him to Alexandria. Cleopatra promptly seduced him. She was twenty-one and he fifty-two, the most powerful man in the world.

Cleopatra was striking if not beautiful. Her nose was long and hooked, the mouth large, but she had an excellent slim figure. Some years later in Rome, fearful of the local competition, she maintained it by strict diet, according to the gossiping Plutarch. She was mistress of the arts of cosmetics and perfumery. She followed the fashion of the period, applying henna leaves in powder form to cheeks, hands and buttocks, for that rosy blush; kohl, a kind of mascara, accentuated the eyeline, with complex perfumes like Kyphi applied in all the usual, and some unusual, places. Her hairdresser worked her long black tresses into many plaits and curls, set with perfumed oil massaged into the scalp. At times she wore a waist-length wig. In John Dryden's translations, Plutarch evokes her charisma thus:

> For her actual beauty, it is said, was not in itself so remarkable that none could be compared with her, or that no one could see her without being struck by it, but the contact of her presence, if you lived with her, was irresistible; the attraction of her person, joining with the charm of her conversation, and the character that attended all she said or did, was something bewitching. It was a pleasure merely to hear the sound of her voice, with which, like an instrument of many strings, she could pass from one language to another; so that there were few of the barbarian nations that she answered by an interpreter; to most of them she spoke herself, as to the Ethiopians, Troglodytes, Hebrews, Arabians, Syrians, Medes, Parthians, and many others, whose language she had learnt; which was all the more surprising because most of the kings, her predecessors, scarcely gave themselves the trouble to acquire the Egyptian tongue, and several of them quite abandoned the Macedonian.

The amatory skills of Cleopatra passed into legend while she lived. Apart from the rapid seduction of both Julius Caesar and Mark Antony, she is reported to have fellated one hundred Roman noblemen in a single evening. Her Greek nickname was *Meriochane*, 'she who parts wide for a thousand men'. Informed opinion suggests that such women are unlikely to reach orgasm, and thus have the stamina and endurance to give substance to the legend.

Mark Antony's welcome in Egypt, when the actual purpose of his visit was to question her about treachery to Rome, was the epitome of royal and fragrant style. Plutarch again:

> She received several letters, both from Antony and from his friends, to summon her, but she took no account of these orders; and at last, as if in mockery of them, she came sailing up the River Dynus in a barge with gilded stern and outspread sails of purple, while oars of silver beat time to music of flutes and fifes and harps. She herself lay all along under a canopy of cloth of gold, dressed as Venus in a picture, and beautiful young boys, like painted Cupids, stood on each side to fan her. Her maids were dressed like sea nymphs and graces, some steering at the rudder, some working at the ropes.

Shakespeare's description is almost palpable:

> the winds were lovesick ... From the barge a strangely invisible perfume hits the sense of the adjacent wharfs.

And Plutarch:

> The perfumes diffused themselves from the vessel to the shore, which was covered with multitudes,

> part following the galley up the river on either bank, part running out of the city to see the sight. The market-place was quite emptied, and Antony at last was left alone sitting upon the tribunal; while the word went through all the multitude, that Venus was come to feast with Bacchus, for the common good of Asia. On her arrival, Antony sent to invite her to supper. She thought it fitter he should come to her; so, willing to show his good humour and courtesy, he complied, and went. He found the preparations to receive him magnificent beyond expression, but nothing so admirable as the great number of lights; for on a sudden there was let down altogether so great a number of branches with lights in them so ingeniously disposed, some in squares, and some in circles, that the whole thing was a spectacle that has seldom been equalled for beauty.

Antony was completely captivated. Thus began the merry gallop that led to the neglect of his official duties and finally assured his downfall, defeat and suicide.

Cleopatra's table was unrivalled. Athenaeus has Socrates of Rhodes describing a banquet for Antony and his friends which extended over four days. The floors of the dining-rooms were strewn with roses knee-deep, and the walls were festooned with them.

Doctor Philostas told Plutarch that he 'was taken into the kitchen, where he admired the prodigious variety of all things; but particularly, seeing eight wild boars roasting whole, says he, "Surely you have a great number of guests." The cook laughed at his simplicity, and told him there were not above twelve to sup, but that every dish was to be served up just roasted to a turn, and if anything was but one minute ill-timed, it was spoiled; "And," said he, "maybe Antony will sup just now, maybe not this hour, maybe he will call for wine, or begin to talk, and will put it off. So that," he continued, "it is not one, but many suppers must be had in readiness, as it is impossible to guess at his hour."'

Antony and Cleopatra ran wild. They formed a private group called the 'inimitables' where members and their guests did pornographic turns as highlights of the orgies. During all the pursuit of pleasure this formidable lady managed to bear four sons, one to Caesar and three to Antony. Efficient contraception and abortion were available, so it is a fair presumption that the children were to cement the ties between Egypt and Rome. Soon after the birth of the son of Julius Caesar, the baby was put down before a multitude of his soldiers, in the knowledge that if he picked the child up, he acknowledged it, and it thereby became a citizen of Imperial Rome 'in the name of the Senate and the people of Rome, and by their will'; of course, he did so.

Cleopatra became very efficient in the use of poison. There are many reports of her proficiency, but the most charming is the description of a series of trials of various lethal agents on condemned prisoners, both for speed and minimal side-effects, like pain and spasms. With the certain knowledge of what fate she would meet in Rome on Antony's death, she decided on the bite of a small and very deadly snake, the asp. But we are getting ahead of events.

In the manner of the Pharaohs that preceded her, she had a mausoleum built adjoining the temple of Isis, to which she removed all her treasure, gold, jewels and cinnamon. On hearing of Antony's inevitable suicide, she repaired to her prepared chambers. She bathed, had herself made fragrant from head to foot by her two maidservants, and sat down to a sumptuous repast. This concluded with a basket of fine ripe figs in which the asp had been secreted. Her last request to her maidservants was to be buried beside Antony.

She had just died, and as the final adjustments were being made to her diadem by the now perishing Charmian, the Roman soldiers broke into the death chamber. One of them exclaimed angrily, 'Was this well done of your lady?' 'Extremely well', she answered, 'as befits the descendant of so many kings.'

Cleopatra lived for thirty-nine years. She reigned as queen for twenty-two, and was consort to Antony for fourteen of these. His statues were all thrown down, but those of Cleopatra were left untouched. Her death ended four thousand years of ancient Egyptian civilisation, with its unrivalled appreciation of beauty, fragrance and form.

Catherine de Medici

Daughter of a syphilitic father, and of a mother who died giving birth to her, Catherine de Medici was born in the year 1519. As head of the house of Medici, Pope Clement VIII arranged her marriage to a French prince, and she became the mother of three kings of France. It is widely held that she virtually transferred the flower of Florentine Renaissance culture to her new home, particularly that involving perfume and cooking. She inadvertently became a central figure in the savage religious conflict in France, and died on 5 January 1590, exhausted by the difficulties of her life, and disappointed by anxieties and personal frustrations.

Florentine perfumers of the day were versatile. Their specialities went beyond scent: they included 'hairdressing and care, face painting, correction of flaccid breasts, or of ill-scented armpits, narrowing of the matrix overwidened by childbirth, and restoration of virginity after deflowering', all described by Marinello in *The Ornamentation of Ladies.* They must have been well occupied, in view of the pockmarked faces, blackened and absent teeth, and general stench of their contemporaries.

Renaissance perfumers brought the art to its highest level since the civilisations of the eastern Mediterranean. Anne-Marie, Countess of Neroli, is one example of many to become traditionally associated with perfume, in this case oil of neroli, distilled with water from the bitter orange blossom, *bigarade.* We will note wide use of this in due course.

The powerful and illustrious Medici family made much of their fortune in the spice trade. Friction and competition between papal Rome and the civil state of Florence under Medici rule combined with the prodigality of the Tuscan countryside to create a peak in gastronomy and perfumery not surpassed before, nor in all probability since. It was from this city that 'little Catherine', as she was early called, brought her retinue of perfumers, cooks, bakers, confectioners, and a battery of cooking equipment which shocked and impressed the French court. It is reported that a different flavoured ice cream featured on each of the thirty-four days of wedding celebrations.

Catherine's first gift to the Dowager Queen of France was a pot of rouge 'to give colour to her lifeless complexion'. Italian perfumes and powders became the height of fashion. The vogue for these imports provoked a luxury trade with Italy that Sheba would have been delighted to acknowledge. One of Catherine's servants, René, opened a perfume house near the Pont Saint-Michel. The royal family repaired to Provence in the winter and a domestic industry for the production of floral fragrances began at Grasse, where the climate and soil helped roses, violets, jasmine and acacia to flourish. Signor Torabelli was dispatched to set up a laboratory there so that, in the following century, Grasse achieved the importance it still possesses.

It was in this period that the Guilds of Spicers and Apothecaries acquired separate identities. Cosimo Ruggieri prepared special creams and ointments to maintain Catherine's beauty. He was said to be an invaluable ally in the disposal of enemies, by virtue of his skill with poisons. A favoured device was the use of Spanish leather gloves impregnated with poison.

The reign of Catherine de Medici caused a revolution in the eating habits of her new country. Before her arrival, table manners had remained unchanged since the time of Charlemagne. He, giant of a man, had fathered fifty or more children by various wives and mistresses and had not considered them fit company at table. Meals before Catherine's time were gargantuan, and eaten off the point of a knife. Most food was spit-roasted and often poorly flavoured and tough. Prolonged drinking bouts began above, and finished under, the table. Catherine transformed all this into 'little Florence'. As Jay Jacobs puts it, 'the banquet became a coeducational affair and far less bibulous, at which her notorious squadron of high-born temptresses fragrantly displayed charms that must have grown increasingly convex as the ladies strove to follow the example of their epicurean queen'.

The foods of her native Florence became the inspiration for what the world of gastronomy now calls *haute cuisine*: milk-fed veal, piselli novelli (petit pois), broccoli, tournedos, carp, truffles, special preparations of kidneys and sweetbreads, and a marvellous range of fattening desserts, led by *zabaglione* (*sabayon*). Imagine the difference that the innovation of the fork made to etiquette (although centuries were to pass before its use became widespread).

Life at the court was not happy for Catherine. Despite her goodwill, intelligence and charm, she was less than popular. Called the 'Italian woman', she was identified with what were perceived as the Italian and especially Medici family traits of sexual excess, witchcraft and murder. One of the principal reasons for the union of the top families of France and Italy was to produce offspring who would unite the hostile factions. This ambition was nullified during the first ten years of the marriage by the absence of any children. Her husband, now King Henri II, was totally enthralled by his mistress, the ravishing Diane de Poitiers. Then, suddenly and surprisingly, Catherine successively gave birth to ten children. Diane was known to refer to Catherine as 'the tradesman's daughter', but this did not inhibit her from delivering the babies!

The exercise of regal power brought her nothing but hatred from both Catholic and Huguenot. She kept the Inquisition out of France, but any tolerance offered to the new religion was misunderstood by both sides. She never got over the massacre of two thousand Protestants on St Bartholomew's Day. Parisians called her Jezebel, although it may be with less reason than they had to treat Gabrielle Chanel the same way four hundred years later.

Her refuge and response was *excess*. A glutton, she became grossly obese in later life. Yet she may have been the worthiest of our quartet. By most accounts, an intelligent, innovative idealist, the world of flavour and fragrance owes her much.

Chanel

> The most mysterious, the most human thing, is smell.
>
> Coco Chanel

Gabrielle 'Coco' Chanel was born illegitimate in a poor-house in the Loire valley on 19 August 1883, and died in the best Paris hotel of its day, the Ritz, on

10 January 1971. In the first seven years of her life she endured the miseries of an orphanage. She rose above a lifelong fear of rejection to become head of the greatest fragrance business empire to be ruled by a woman since the Queen of Sheba. Bisexual, she died alone, except for her maid-companion, on a Sunday afternoon, the one day above all she hated. The funeral mass was celebrated at the Madeleine, amidst white flowers sent by her models, friends and former lovers. The models occupied the front pew at the service to say farewell to one who it is hard to imagine would ever have agreed to permit it.

Coco Chanel had the attractions of any ordinary young woman. Later her features took on an enigmatic cast. 'After you're fifty you have to deserve the face you've got.' Her face was quite sharp, with black hair and dark eyes full of interest and vulnerability; close-up she was almost cross-eyed. A contradictory broad nose set above the widest smile I have ever seen. From corner of mouth to corner, it split more than two-thirds of her face; quite extraordinary. She was slender rather than thin, with a fine natural breast line.

Her views on body cleanliness were strict. 'Ugliness may be forgiven, but negligence never. I make a speech to my models and give them a little present, soap first and scent after! And there could be negligence lower down than under the arms. Last night I was so tired I said to myself as I came upstairs: "I'll go to bed in my clothes and not bother to wash." But you know me ... if you're going to let yourself go you are lost. So I keep myself in order.'

With all this, she was quite modest about her own person. She lived by the logic of fragrance. Her father hated the smell of hair, any hair, and this coloured her adult views. Her choice of fragrances often involved those unknown in her childhood, which may explain how she fastened on to the high bright aldehydic notes, new and at first despised synthetics, in the perfume which made her rich. After its success, she became increasingly confident and dogmatic. 'If anyone speaks to you of perfume, it must be someone quite close to you.'

She had many lovers of variable durability. It was a source of some pain to her never to be able to bear a child, especially to those she truly loved. It has been reported how assiduously she cultivated her own legend, from the early times when she was a rich man's second-string mistress, *via* an incredible mix of lovers and high-achieving friends and acquaintances, to when she became empress of the Chanel empire. Anyone who would advance her interests or guard the business was courted, to the extent of her final favours. Cleopatra and Sheba could teach her nothing. The scope of her lovers is astonishing; they ranged from the British aristocracy to the Nazi conquerors of Paris. 'Women don't have friends. Either they're loved or they're not.'

Taste? She told another woman who, in her opinion, had taken a poor specimen for a lover. 'If you're dying of hunger you'll eat a rat.' She adored the Florentine ornaments of the Medici. Claude Baillen says her dresses were thronged with them. Sometimes she made some of her own jewellery. This hands-on approach stopped at fabric. Coco didn't sew, she cut. She got rid of corsets, she shortened hair and skirts and so much more. 'Simplicity doesn't mean poverty.'

Living in the *haute monde* of the twenties, she made certain that her general philosophy carried over to the pleasures of the table. Well-chilled Krug Champagne or a riesling sufficed for all occasions. Unsalted ham was a special favourite, and she abhorred floury sauces.

And what of *that* perfume? Fifteen million dollars' worth had been sold at her death, and no end is in sight. The simple facts are that Ernest Beaux, a Russian emigré, working from a laboratory at Grasse, presented her with some samples of a perfume he had been composing and tuning for some time. She made a choice and 'Chanel No. 5' was launched in 1921. The novelty was the use of a completely new, aldehydic, synthetic high note. The floral accompaniment (costly ylang ylang, jasmine and rose, plus an animal note) was abstract and rather indistinct, in comparison to the clear single florals of older perfumes. It initiated the most creative decade in the history of perfume and led a trend that has sustained its momentum ever since. A principal Chanel talent was in presentation. The ornate, complicated labels and bottles were replaced by a simple bottle and the stark harmony of a black name on a white label, unadorned except for her lucky number, 5. It went perfectly with the new post-war fashion for short dresses and simple, elegant suits. It continues today, a symbol of the institution she created. CHANEL.

She has been called treacherous, cruel, generous, repellent, magnetic, talkative, secretive. She changed forever the way women regard their appearance, and how fragrantly they present themselves.

Finale

Sheba, Cleopatra, Catherine and Coco make a quartet that have had a strong influence on perfume and flavour as we know them so far. They were truly feminine, in every nuance of the word. Their intuition was depthless. They were great opportunists and extremely ambitious, with absolute conviction of their various destinies – the rightness of their causes, if you wish. They did not loll about bewailing their misfortunes, of which they had their share.

Did you think about their own scent? With that kind of drive, I suspect three of them could well have been high androstenone secretors, which if balanced with other female essences can be supremely attractive. Dr Richard Gordon has remarked of Brigitte Bardot that 'her distinctive Parisian smell ... was indeed the smell of sex. I only ever smelled this overpowering muskiness before on women who shared Bardot's appetite for men.'

So what did they have in common, the crucial quality? Every woman who has towelled herself dry after bathing, and regarded the mirror, might guess the answer. *They wanted more.*

9

In the Mood

> He would now study perfumes, and the secrets of their manufacture, distilling heavily scented oils, and burning odorous gums from the East. He saw that there was no mood of the mind that had not its counterpart in the sensuous life, and set himself to discover their true relation, wondering what there was in frankincense that made one mystical, and in ambergris that stirred one's passions, and in violets that woke the memory of dead romance, and in musk that troubled the brain, and in champak that stained the imagination; and seeking often to elaborate a real psychology of perfumes, and to estimate the several influences of sweet-smelling roots, and scented pollen-laden flowers, or aromatic balms.
>
> Oscar Wilde, *The Picture of Dorian Gray*

Throughout this book I have sought to show where the burden is established fact, or when it is commonly held opinion, or when it is merely an idea that has arisen from observation. This chapter has plenty of facts, but the *terra* becomes less *firma* quite frequently. Judge for yourself.

We know much of the truth of smell and taste, but difficulties spring from the observations of people by people, rather than those involving machines and animals who can neither talk nor make 'free' choices. Everyone has blind spots in the perception of odour, due to diet, time of day, state of health, to name but a few of the factors that can skew things. Mood is that perpetual *bouillabaisse* of the old instinctive brain we have so proudly 'mastered'. The problems are now being addressed of how to measure, how to study objectively and record influences and their effects on our activities. Facts are few really, because humans are finally different from experimental animals. The areas of most concern inside our brain are also crucial to our survival, and few people these days consent to their invasion by scientists.

There is no doubt that odours are able to influence mood, the more so if we are open to perceive them. The individual personality tunes the response, even the reception. R.W. Moncrieff was one of the first to correlate the preferences of extroverts and introverts. Those with an outgoing personality share, with children, less fine tuning in their odour preferences. On the other hand those who are more reserved tend to be rather precise, hence the very intense 'teeth on edge' response they also have to the grating of chalk on a blackboard or a knife on a plate. Extroverts prefer lighter fragrances, introverts the heavier, so-called Oriental, scents.

Extroverts prefer a great degree of stimulation in music, colour and flavour. They are said to tolerate pain better. When they lose touch with reality, they swing in a cycle of high and low moods. Classic introverts are precisely the opposite. They don't swing. There is just one catch. Most people are a fair mix of the above qualities, and not easy to categorise.

Divinity lives in the uniqueness of the individual. Choice is a gift from on high. But there are dues to be paid; when the new thinking brain overrules the instinctive old one, we willingly pay our toll to travel this stressful route, otherwise we would live and die as animals in the wild. It may be difficult to accept the relationship of emotion, personality and odour. But odour can make you happy, hungry, angry, drowsy, depressed, frigid or impotent, or just plain sick, without the cause being very obvious. Each mood has an odour, and the more discriminating we become, the more information is available. Happiness is an odour improver. You can smell happy! And what about the pheromonal signal of the sexually aroused which can be picked up long before actual body contact?

Have you ever entered a strange, new vacant room and had positive or negatives 'vibes'? A hotel room, house, travel rest room, whatever. Some people can hazard a reasonably informed guess, on entering a recently emptied group-meeting room, whether it was successful or dismal. Helen Keller could do this, as we have seen. There seem to be subliminal odours analogous to those sound frequencies a dog perceives but which are inaudible to human ears. Blind people may develop various degrees of this faculty; in their natural state, Australian aborigines and African bushmen have it also. Often enough, those with it have to be asked because they rarely volunteer the information. Children tend to hide it because it can get them into trouble. I wonder how many 'difficult' children have odour-based problems.

Radiological scanning techniques confirm the brain registration of odours of which the subject claims not to be aware. The inhibition and denial may occur for emotional protection. Dogs can smell, and react to, our moods, without doubt. The fear scent can almost be touched, and dogs and wild animals may attack a frightened person for that reason alone. It works both ways. My Californian guru has not fairies, but rattle-snakes, at the bottom of his garden. The Napa valley abounds in them. At rest they smell of green melons; when disturbed and angry, like a wet dog.

The odour manipulators are on the march. The American fragrance industry alone has an annual turnover of many billions of dollars, of which only a fraction goes into the obvious use of perfume and cosmetics. Perfumers and flavourists can call up four thousand bottles of single odours, to produce 'fresh ground coffee', 'fish and chips', 'fresh baked bread', 'real leather' car upholstery, to name a few. Not satisfied with arranging air duct outlets at pavement level to waft mouth-watering smells of charcoal grilling to the passing throng, some restaurants actually add this and other aromas to the outflow. House agents use fresh, happy-family-type cooking smells when demonstrating the virtues of an empty house for sale. Linoleums and other floor coverings may have positive odours incorporated during manufacture. And, like Pavlov's dogs, what chance have we got?

Odour associations are intensively studied now. In the field of mental health they could be a tool to unlock early memories, associations between current problems perhaps originating at a time recalled by a particular odour. Pleasant scents may recall happy memories; upsetting smells could recall oppressive situations or even inflicted pain.

Garry Schwartz, in a biofeedback study, found spiced apples better than apples and better than spice alone, in relaxing stress; other strong scents can reduce hunger and ease pain. Incense based on soporific plants relieves insomnia. Peach alleviates pain!

The magazine *Omni* describes how International Flavours and Fragrances (IFF), among others in the private sector plus several academic centres, are deep into this study of the relation of fragrances and mind. IFF have patented a stress-reducing fragrance, and look to the time when this approach will be used to lower blood pressure and alleviate depression, and even perhaps schizophrenia; the latter patients often complain of the smell of their bodies, and some people attending to their care can in fact identify a characteristic odour of the illness.

Natural fragrances have been credited with influencing mood. Wild rose relieves depression, ylang ylang (in the tuberose-freesia range, if subtly used, only more ravishing) 'soothes frustrated anger'. Camphor and cinnamon are said to provoke vivid images in some, in others a feeling of relaxation.

Not a thousand or so years from the beginning of recorded history, the Egyptians were using cedar and sandalwood as relaxants in the form of both scent and incense. Today, the scent of a pine forest is often soothing to the city dweller. Europeans, especially in Germany, are desperately trying to save their forests from destruction by pollution. One can understand their emotional involvement, even though a few may not be aware of an odour basis as one reason for their concern.

Perfumes have been classified according to their perceived effect on mood.

Fruit and mints	Refreshing
Animal	Aphrodisiac
Wood and seeds	'Spicy'
Flowers	Intoxicating

This tallies somewhat with the thousand-year-old European conception that spicy and heavy animal scents are mysterious and 'Eastern', as opposed to the light-hearted, uplifting and often dazzling top notes considered to be the European mood.

Theophrastus, who lived from *c.* 372 to *c.* 287 BC, could have been the first aromatherapist, with his treatise *Concerning Odours.* In the Rome of Nero's time, there were over a thousand baths that specialised in fragrances, *unctuaria.* Early cultures treasured fragrance and its effects. There were the special fragrant rush floors of medieval times, and Elizabethan thyme paths, both to be crushed underfoot, when the mind 'turneth to happy thoughts'. The famous lawn at Buckingham Palace is said to be a low-growing chamomile, though for reasons of durability and maintenance rather than for its scent. Fragrance gardens are universal. There is a small one at Lake's Folly, several lavenders and geraniums, daphne, many roses, a bay tree, rosemary, and a triple grafted apple. Lime, tangerine and lemon trees compete with various eucalypts. I didn't know, years ago, why I chose them, but now I do.

The French School of Aromatherapy was led by the late Marguerite Maury, described by her pupils as a brilliant chemist with essential oils. Her Italian opposite number is Paolo Rovesti. Many centres in the United States are pursuing the concept. Steve van Toller and George Dodd have introduced the concept of osmotherapy, for actual treatment by odour, and they recently edited *Perfumery: the Psychology and Biology of Fragrance*, the book you should read if you wish to pursue the subject.

10

Love and Orgasm

Those who think that talking objectively about the art and science of love diminishes it should postpone reading this chapter or omit it altogether. There are no flowery tributes from warbling troubadours, nor are there eyes sparkling in the moonlight as ineffable tenderness overwhelms. Accepting this, you become a consenting adult. Read on.

The excitement of human love begins in babies within a few days of birth. Some actually tremble with the first whiff of milk, when the mother's breast is just within reach. From this earliest bud of love, that which exists between mother and baby, comes the ripe fruit of sexual love, glorious fusion of the spiritual and physical faces of love, which cannot exist in its natural perfection if the parties don't smell right – to each other.

How baffling to observe in others the irresistible attraction, the shattering effect, the bolt of lightning. Or to be dumbstuck and dizzy when we are ourselves on the receiving end. The converse is equally remarkable, the surprise of instant dislike, without rhyme or reason. How many such incidents are odour-based, with all concerned usually unaware of this?

What is a kiss? Of course there are kisses and kisses. We are here to discuss the serious application of four lips rather than the social brushing of lips to cheek or hand, even if these may hint of an overture. At the moment of the embrace the brain computer is on red alert, swamped with information. General body smell provides hints of recent diet, a suggestion of the health and age of the kisser, and their cleanliness. With luck, billions of dollars have not been wasted advertising social concern about dental hygiene and what to do to improve breath odour. A pleasant (to some) musky pheromone floats from the side of some men's faces, and in his book *Celebration of the Senses* Eric Rolls confessed to a preference for his wife's upper lip. There may be an attractive fragrance on the breath of a healthy woman, particularly at ovulation. Is that not the time of maximum desire? Nature's plan.

Pondering this close-up, there may be the intrusion of deodorants, soaps, lipstick, foundation, other creams, perfume or aftershave, up to twenty-seven scents a day which alter the basic natural box of tricks. Nor have we considered the saliva exchange should that be forthcoming. Leave it to the computer to come up with a stop/go answer.

'Falling in love' is a compulsive drive that ignores all reason. The highs and lows of adolescent attraction are an example, and the capacity lasts a lifetime in a few people. Those players in the human comedy may come to wish for less sensitivity and responsiveness. The tempest is powered by the adrenalin-like substances discussed in Chapter 22, 'Highs and the Happy Hormones'. Donald Klein and Michael Liebowitz have studied this phase of the tender emotion and consider that PEA (the alcohol form of which is the fragrance of rosewater) is an essential part of it. Diana Warburton calls it a mood-altering chemical that gives 'a feeling of post-coital bliss'. And what food is a well recognised source of PEA, some pheromonal shops specialise in like cheese, tobacco and liquor? Why chocolate of course. And don't some people become addicted!

In fiddling around with the formula of PEA (phenylethylamine), it struck me that not only was it closely related to rosewater but that its amine acid is known to slow the breakdown of beta-endorphin, one of the happiest of our hormones. So there we have a bevy of chemical relatives, roses, chocolate, euphoria and a quiver of Cupid's arrows. It has always been apparent that the boyfriend greeting his sweetheart with a rose and a box of chocolates was off to a flying start. Now we have an idea why.

Those widely experienced in love tell of three phases. Falling in love, infatuation, whatever it is, has been discussed. After this a calm period must follow. It is impossible to sustain the high, if the body is not to burn out attempting to fuel the flames.

Romantic love follows. Surely this is the most magical of all the human emotions. Both sexes float along on a stream of enkephalins. Other opioid effects include an increased capacity for illusion, and a lessening of the perception of pain.

The third phase is the long-established comfortable loving relationship, to which the brain responds by the release of more endorphins. These are soothing and habit-forming, in the same way that drug opiates are. The body is devastated by the sudden withdrawal of either. The 'broken heart' of the lover leads to a period in limbo until some sort of emotional balance is resumed. Human fascination with excitement increases as our knowledge continues to advance. We have already seen that many of the substances discussed are produced by the brain during physical exercise by a toned-up body, by listening to great music (anything *you* think is great), by the taking of fine food and wine, marvellous fragrances or wonderful visual experiences. Sometimes young people will describe a non-sexual experience as 'orgasmic', or an even bawdier equivalent, hinting at an instinctive understanding of brain function.

So what is ecstasy? Anyone who has experienced it knows, but it is almost impossible to define. As students, we paid rapt attention to our gynaecology lecturer when he defined it as the 'sensation of emptying a hollow organ', particularly as his current mistress was a student in our year and passed her exams effortlessly. Adolescents were extraordinarily naïve half a century ago. Ecstacy certainly is the name of the drug MDMA, an amphetamine synthesised from nutmeg in 1914. There appears to be sufficient in two nutmegs to be a threat to life, or at least a danger to your nerve cells. However, if you follow the philosophy in these pages, the happy highs should come naturally, without risk.

Describing the sensations of orgasm, the big 'O' of contemporary 'Do it yourself' manuals, is not simple. Richard Bergland says it is remarkable that the scientists who spend so much effort on it at night, do so little work on the subject during the day.

Those who have seen Bernini's masterpiece, the sculpture of St Teresa of Avila in the Santa Maria della Vittoria in Rome have gazed on a vision of timeless orgasm. Here is her own description (from her *Life* written in 1565) of her mystical union with Christ. 'The pain was so great that I screamed aloud; but simultaneously I felt such infinite sweetness that I wished it to last eternally. It was not bodily but psychic pain, although it affected to a certain extent also the body. It was the sweetest caressing of the soul by God.'

To many the physical aspects are secondary to the infinite delight. Whatever the duration. The feelings appear to be focused in the pelvis and are accompanied by blushing, heart racing, spasms and quicker breathing. There may be a total body response, even fainting, or merely a genital sneeze.

Breathing, as in the control exercised in some

Eastern disciplines, seems for some to be a pipeline to the central mysteries of the event. Judith Perera describes a fundamental Christian sect in Jamaica who hyperventilate to orgasm as they 'see the Lord'. As she so precisely puts it, 'an orgasm is impossible without a degree of panting to destabilise the autonomic nervous system'. And, may I add, let loose some striking hormones during the electronic discharge following.

The end result is relief of sexual tension. Sperm are released, and in some women, as in many animal species, an egg is made ready for fertilisation no matter what the time of the monthly cycle. For most people, the feelings are impossible to describe accurately or recall clearly. How clever of Nature to let us remember the intensity of the pleasure, rather than its actual quality. The design is to keep us at it, to ensure the continuation of life.

Those who achieve a clear-cut orgasm appear to be perpetually interested in learning more about it. Those who do not have been made to feel inadequate by popular writers. One book actually has carried the title *Seven Minutes*, said to be the time necessary for a woman to achieve 'it' from start to gO. Much the same as a little 'o' onion, which reaches its lachrymatory climax in about the same time. There is a further parallel. Some enjoy onion cut fresh; others prefer it very late. So do some women orgasm at a kiss, others only after a long time.

Recent findings on some of the brain hormones make it obvious that they are critical to the ecstasy of orgasm. Beta-endorphins cause contractions of the ejaculatory ducts in the male, and in addition may well have a specific effect in altering control of the blood brain barrier in both sexes, allowing the hormones across, like the momentary opening of the border between two countries.

And now a word on one of the most important of

them. Oxytocin is a hot topic, so to speak, since it was found to be released in substantial quantities into the male brain fluid during orgasm. Which may not have much impact on the reader unaware of the fact that it has been administered by injection for more than half a century to cause the uterus to contract to cope with a number of obstretric emergencies. More recently, it has been recognised as an intrinsic part of the feelings and activities of motherhood. It is a normal secretion of the posterior part of the pituitary gland which develops from and hangs below the hypothalamus. Keith Kendrick and his colleagues in Cambridge have found a rush of oxytocin in the brain fluid of the mother sheep at the time of birth, and even more striking, a large amount of it in the olfactory bulbs. This appears to be the basis of the importance of odour in the mother's response to the new-born lamb. Wonder builds on wonder. All this is triggered by the head of the baby stimulating the neck of the womb and the vagina and by the later act of suckling. We have been talking about sheep but why would this not have some human parallel? The uterine contractions of intense female orgasm could be the result of late and deep stimulation during intercourse. The delight some women experience during the simple act of suckling has a similar hormone background. Of course those who read a book (or would like to) during these events might need to increase their awareness, and train unsuspected latent gifts which still remain from evolution. Among the message in this book, perhaps the ultimate one is to learn to recognise that we have so much equipment of which for some reason we take no advantage.

One final thought on oxytocin. It is obviously orgasmically pleasurable in both sexes. A mothering hormone in the female, why not a fathering one in the male?

The big 'O' is odour-driven in some people, perhaps more than might be suspected. Anyone farming animals or having seen domestic pets in action is in no doubt about their pheromone-programmed responses. 'Unnoticed' smells of the human genitalia introduced into the air in the most minute quantities can initiate the phases of sexual excitement, including orgasm. Natural body odours may repulse those who are not sexually involved, but they are undoubtedly stimulating to many after sexual arousal, if not before. This is still disputed, but an informed guess is that it is very important to some and irrelevant to others, with all the variations in between.

Finally, there does not appear to be a clear connection between love and orgasm. Some are sufficiently blessed to know that each is better with the other. Come to your senses.

2

PHYSICAL FOOD

11

The Raw Truth

> It is certainly the case that a soil which has a taste of perfume will be the best soil. If we need an explanation as to what is the nature of this odour from such soil, it is that which often occurs even when the ground is not being turned up, just towards sunset, at the place where the ends of rainbows have come down to earth, and when the soil has been drenched with rain following a long period of drought. The earth then sends out that divine breath of hers, of quite incomparable sweetness, which she has conceived from the sun.
>
> Pliny, *Natural History*, Book XVII
> (translated by H. Rackham)

We prefer some foods raw, like seed sprouts and many fruits and vegetables. Others are inedible or indigestible without the conversions that take place during cooking. Wheat and potatoes need heat to make their starches available. Raw foods tend to be enjoyed for their crunch, sweetness, salt, pungency and so forth – primary tastes the depth of whose flavour increases with any aroma that happens to exist at the moment of eating. Many times in this book the opportunity is taken to point out how much fragrance is lifted by sweetness, even of synthetic origin. All flavour is similarly enhanced the nearer it is to body temperature. Hunting animals prefer their catch at this heat. For more than ten thousand years we have enjoyed the flavour from cooking, and have gone on improving methods whose modern equivalents are the vegetable or fish steamer, the microwave, claypot and foil-wrapped cooking, and the traditional frying, toasting and roasting.

Early food was far less varied. There was rarely enough grain to store it over the winter. By whatever method flesh was preserved, it did not keep all that well. Spices achieved much of their impact and value by their preservative, antibacterial abilities, in addition to the masking of off-flavours. By comparison with foodstuffs recorded in early documents and studies of middens and early campsites, the range of flavour available to the modern palate is vast.

We continue to seek out and enjoy increasing amounts of raw food. A crash course in the food of Japan convinced me that the enjoyment of texture was part of the core of enjoyment of their traditional diet, perhaps more than any other ethnic group.

Water and Milk

> Homer calls those waters which flow from rocks 'dark', meaning 'unfit for use'. He prefers to all others the water of springs and those which flow through fertile and rather deep soil, as Hesiod does also: 'A spring perpetual and ever flowing, which has not been fouled.' And Pindar says: 'Ambrosial water, honeyed delight, flows from the fair spring Tilphossa.'
>
> Athenaeus, *The Deipnosophists*
> (translated by C.B. Gulick)

Water tastes so differently in various parts of the globe that it should not be beyond a bright palate to do a Sherlock Holmes act on its origin. Who can forget the brisk near-sparkle of the limpid water of a clear mountain stream, or the recycled muck from a tap downstream of an industrialised great river. Some of the latter makes coffee and tea, for example, taste so peculiar that people are obliged to collect their own supply of rainwater or purchase decent water separately. Taste trials of a range of bottled waters are instructive. Use those with the mineral content specified on the label. Notice how flat distilled water tastes, and the flavour interest from sodium and other salts. Most 'soda water' has some added salt, unless there is a specific statement to the contrary. You may be certain that any water with a lift of flavour has something dissolved in it.

Everyone has drunk milk. In some societies, especially in Asia, people never touch it again after weaning. The flavours of milk and cheese vary a good deal: pastures differ; the bigger boned the animal, the more calcium; high energy users, like seals for example, living in icy waters, have high milk sugars. Milk fat levels may be quite different in breeds of one species. Among dairy cows, the Jersey, one of the smaller breeds, paradoxically has the highest milk fat, and makes a marvellously smooth ice cream. Cheeses vary in flavour accordingly.

Our Daily Bread

Give us this day our daily major energy source, and please make it taste good and support life. How fortunate to have our prayer answered with wheat, rice, corn, and other grains, and potatoes, taro, and so on. Wheat in bread and pasta tastes so good perhaps because it is good for you. In the West, bread is frequently accompanied by butter with its own thirteen or so flavours, or by other, cooked, fats.

Flat breads from ground grain, some without yeast, go back to prehistory. Carta musica of Sardinia, Matzo of Israel, Lavash of Iran, are some present-day relatives. Milk, eggs, malt and honey are among the innumerable additives to bread flavour, but to many nothing is needed to improve the flavour of simple, fresh, well-kneaded and properly baked hard-wheat bread. Read Elizabeth David on breadmaking.

> In some places bread is called after the dishes eaten with it, such as oyster-bread, in others from a special delicacy, as cake-bread, in others from the short time spent in making it, as hasty-bread, and also from the method of baking, as oven-bread or tin loaf or baking-pan bread.
>
> Columella (*c.* 4 BC–65 AD) *On Agriculture*
> (translated by Hamison Boyd Ash)

When crushed wheat is milled in the old-fashioned way, the flavour components that make wholemeal bread separate out on transverse cloth curtains that slope upwards from floor to tower. Pollard, the grain skeleton, comes off first, slightly sweetish. Bran is next, and it converts, when baked, to a delicious toasty flavour. Then comes the sweet and nutty wheat germ. Finally, at the top of the mill, there are the different grades of flour, coarse to fine, the latter residue making the finest textured white bread.

The great breads and wheaten pasta are made from hard high-gluten wheat. Chew to a pulp half a teaspoon of cracked or whole wheat which has been soaked in water for about thirty-six hours. It takes a while, and you will perceive an interesting range of flavours as you swallow the liquefied results. You are finally left with white 'chewing gum'. This is gluten, which gives leavened bread its lightness and elasticity. When soft wheats are used, even with added gluten, the bread is rarely as attractive. It is a strange exception to the 'natural' wisdom of the ages, how the preference for the highly refined product, as also happens with polished rice, has been a poor choice biologically. Even in the traditional Indian flat breads, 'roti' is refined from 'atta'.

The flàvours of wheat components after heating are fascinating. Try roasting raw bran – carefully, as it burns easily. It has far fewer calories than shelf brand, made-up, bran, and gives a flavour boost to anything to which it is added. Do children still compete for the bread end-crust at the family table?

Fruit and Vegetables

Several ripe fruits are exciting. Sweetness and fragrance increase as acidity fall. A few, for instance some varieties of persimmon (sharon fruit, kaki), may only be enjoyed overripe and close to decomposition. After a certain stage, many fruits continue to ripen after picking, while in others the ripening process stops at harvest. Avocadoes are weird. They will not ripen on the tree. They may be 'stored' by not picking them. A friend moved into an old house with a huge avocado tree in the garden. He waited for them to ripen over many crops, only to unlock the paradox when one ripened when put inside by mistake, having been picked hard as a rock. This opened the door to a bounteous supply of the semi-aphrodisiac delicacies that his neighbours could not cope with.

Many tropical and subtropical fruits, among them bananas, mango and tomato, picked just prior to ripeness, are said to develop their best colour and flavour after that. Actually that is an overstatement. With the exception of the avocado, nothing tastes better than tree-ripened fruit. I was so besotted with it as a youngster that, for the enjoyment of family and friends, there is now at Lake's Folly a continuous supply of peaches, apricots, plums, nectarines and so on, from late spring to late autumn, and several kinds of oranges, tangerines, mandarins, lemons, and limes during the winter. At vintage, we are awash in black and white squishy ripe figs, and many kinds of olives. The fragrance of some of the muscatel-influenced eating grapes is ravishing. Is it any wonder some fine palates have emerged in our group?

Some fruits that do continue to ripen away from the tree or vine (melons and oranges, for example, do not) give off ethylene gas, which accelerates maturity. This gas is used commercially to improve the appearance of fruit, and you can experiment for yourself by putting a ripe banana in a paper bag with other less ripe fruit for a few days.

Fruit is now bred, like roses, for appearance and shelf life. Tomatoes in city supermarkets today can be frustrating in their lack of flavour compared with home-grown ones. About twenty years ago, flavour seemed to depart, and certainly the sugar level dropped from about 6 per cent to 4 per cent or less in the new 'everlasting' varieties. When tomatoes first appeared in Europe from the New World, they were so intensely flavoured as to be named love apples. Speed their return, or grow your own, hydroponically if you are in an apartment. Let them get really ripe on the vine. Like wine, it is the *balance* of acid and sugar that hallmarks their flavour.

There is, incidentally, a peculiar geography in ripeness, varying with the fruit. Many ripen from the stem end. Pawpaw (papaya) is sweetest at the other end. The sweetest grapes tend to be at the bottom of the bunch, though complete ripening evens things up. Grape flavour is almost all in the skins. Most sorts of 'table' grapes look great but lack definite flavour, whereas 'wine' grapes make a strong varietal statement. Melons are sweeter next to the seeds, less so at the rind. Position on the tree is important to flavour. Oranges, in particular, are sweeter and more fragrant where direct sun can reach them.

'Farm fresh' in an urban supermarket can turn out to be another wry joke. You have to try something out of the garden within hours of picking to have any idea of the real flavour. If they are not *corpus delicti*, a partial solution is to rehydrate the vegetables in plain cold water (grandmothers inserted a knife blade in the water) for an hour or so.

The fascinations of flavour are endless. At the 1987 Symposium on Taste at Oxford, Alicia Rios discussed in detail the differences in the fruit and oil of many varieties of olive, an important staple of a substantial proportion of the world's population. Elsewhere the delights of the harvest pressing are described. *Primureggiu* is the first drippings of the press load before any weight is applied. It is very fine flavoured, turbid and absurdly expensive. From there down, the qualities are: extra virgin, virgin, superfine and fine. In one former existence I was a surgeon and well aware of the grades of plastic surgery exhibited in the restoration of virginity among the populace in consulting rooms behind the Imperial Hotel in downtown Shimbashi. *Extra virgin* did seem a little like gilding the lily, until, as W.C. Fields might have put it, I became aware of the oleaginous connotation. Less an anatomical description, the classification applies to the free oleic acid, 1 up to 4 per cent; the more acid the lower the temperature at which the oil will start to smoke. There is a flavour difference also: the first pressings are unrefined and taste of olive in a subtle way, while the heavier pressings develop a harshness and need to be refined.

The idea of a flavour spectrum occurred one day as I was perched before a long row of glasses of white wines, whose bouquets varied from carnation and cloves through rose/geranium to mango, passionfruit and lychee. They were made from three sorts of grape, traminer, muscat and riesling. Traminer from Alsace can smell so spicy that it merits the handle *gewurtz* (spice) *traminer.*

Riesling puts out a fragrance of tropical fruit and flowers, and muscat is its own dominant self; you might get near it with a mix of rose, geranium, honey and a tiny whiff of spice. The point of all this is that the separate wines could be set up so that there was only a minute difference between one glass and the adjoining one, the transition from one pole of heavy 'spice' to the other of complex 'tropical' being so gradual. I took to calling this the Muscat Spectrum, because the three varieties are direct descendants of an early muscat ancestor, and still share common fragrance notes.

Fiddling in the kitchen subsequently, I found the concept took flight. The difference between fennel seed and star anise is only a matter of degree, and the same might be said for fennel and dill. Star anise, caraway and cumin could be suitably spaced according to similarity. Have a look at the spectra of onion and of aniseed opposite; I speculated a further group in Japan, where chrysanthemum leaves and flowers, and oba are everyday food items.

Parsley is often misused. Except for the Lebanese *tabbouleh* or the occasional serving of fried parsley, it appears mainly as a garnish. At present, most of the parsley on American tables is thrown away! But it is a high source of available vitamins and minerals, and as we have seen, there is a potent suggestion of androstenone in its odour. So, also, with celery root, leaf, stalk and, to a lesser degree, seed. It might be a good idea to invest in parsley futures.

The traditional food of Japan is based on rice, fish and soya beans, and virtually anything edible that grows. Although modern Japan has adopted the ways of the West that suit it, and there is a case for arguing that the best French food in the world is served in Tokyo, the vast majority of the many tens of thousands of restaurants in the seven towns that make up the metropolis of Tokyo serve Japanese food to Japanese people. Ten thousand of these serve sushi alone. There is a connoisseur's choice of rice varieties. Soya beans support nutrition with the bland tofu, a white, set, beancurd; miso, a flavour-boosting bean paste; and a vast number of light to dark, thin to thick, soya sauces of varying sweetness, each with its followers. In many centres a tasting trial of several sauces is not too hard to set up.

Some visitors find the food bland. It is true there are fewer strong flavours in the traditional food of Japan, but on balance, there is a bewildering array of textures and colours available in all but the simplest meals; for example, a plate of five varieties of seaweed is an interesting and inexpensive start to a meal. If you compare the vast range of flavours available in the modern Western kitchen to the white light spectrum from red to violet, the traditional flavours of Japan lie largely in the yellow-green-blue segment. The texture contrasts complete the interest at table; the palate never tires, nor is there any feeling of repletion.

Simplicity and freshness of ingredients are paramount. Food is water-cooked, by steam or boiling. If oils are used, they are the lightest available. Anything battered has a coat of the airiest texture. Presentation is an art form, intrinsic to each day and all meals. Above all it is *the* essence of Japan at table.

For the *gaijin*, or foreigner, Japan is no exception to the excitement that new and foreign smells bring to the traveller. You meet the characteristic aroma in 'yeasty' *sake*, and some of the foods. Quite often it is in the air. Even local grape wines may suggest it.

The Concept of a Flavour Spectrum

1. Aniseed

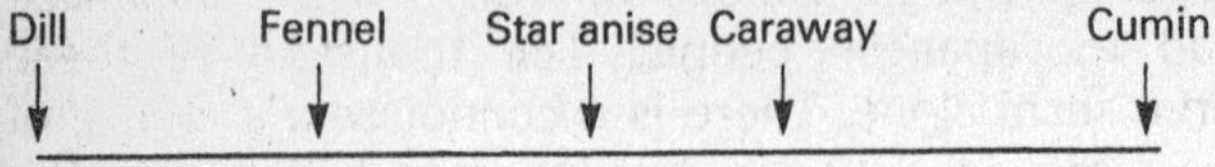

2. Onion

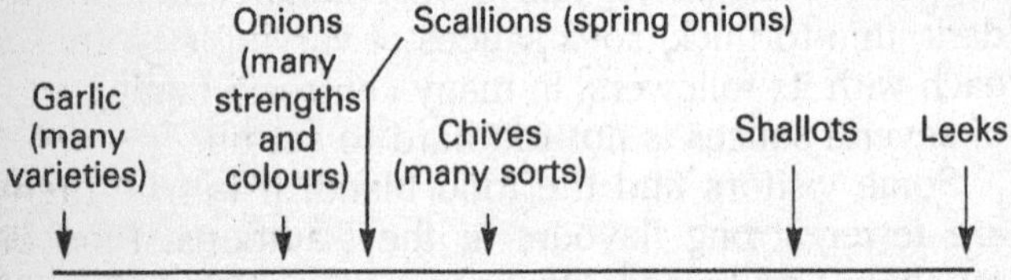

Fish

As a general rule, people buy food with their eyes. Ideally, they then consider their purchase further using their flavour experience. Fish is a good example. Just out of the water into the pan, it is far superior in flavour than anything eaten later, so much so that the Japanese use the time the fish has been out of the water as the criterion on which to decide the cooking use to which the fish is put. Fresh fish has a sheen, firm flesh, pink gills and, most important of all, the eyes are clear, not opaque or sunken. In some fishmarkets in the world it is an offence to spray the fish with water to make them glisten.

Flavour differences between the various species of fish are those of texture, colour, sweetness and oiliness, with occasional subtle overtones. Some of these differences depend on the time of the year and the diet and reproductive activities of the fish themselves. Salmon fast on their spawning run. A fresh deep-sea mullet is one of the really superior fish with its attractive 'sea' taste. An estuary fish of the identical breed may taste muddy and flat. Green-weed feeders tend to taste of that. If you like a brilliant 'marine' clarity of flavour with just a hint of iodine, the deep sea whiting off the Southern ocean of South Australia and Victoria is unsurpassed.

Meat

> The careful head of a household ought not to be content with the foods which the earth produces by its own nature, but, at the seasons of the year when the woods do not provide food, he ought to come to the help of the animals which he has confined with the fruits of the harvest which he has stored up, and feed them on barley or wheat-meal or beans, and especially, too, on grape-husks.
>
> Columella, *On Agriculture*

The things we eat taste of the things they eat. Meat is a prime example best seen in beef fed on special supplements. Over the past quarter of a century I have dined annually with a group of beef cattle breeders, tasting the meat of several breeds comparatively, and have not found any real difference attributable to the breed itself. The well-known and substantial differences occur from the pasture, finishing by lot-feeding with corn, for example, or beer and massage (the fabulous Kobe beef) and the differences a good butcher can produce in storage and handling. Fibre in muscle softens with 'hanging' at 40 degrees Fahrenheit for ten or more days. Bull meat is far tougher than heifer, so needs hanging longer. The more work a muscle does, the tougher it becomes, and indeed the more flavour it develops. That part of the beast less used in its daily activities, like the true fillet, is softer but lacks the flavour of the harder working muscles. You pay more for the scarcity and the shorter cooking times, as well as the tenderness. Beef buffs often prefer a rump steak or sirloin from a three-year cow 'matured' by a knowledgeable professional, who tends to favour the appreciative customers, so start talking to your butcher.

Light-coloured meat usually has less flavour than dark. Milk veal, with its own character, is a special example, and pork an exception though pork certainly shows the influence of diet on flavour. One of my farm tasks used to be to feed the pigs on pollard, plus leftover milk or the whey from the cheese factory; and, when they were ripe, small, unmarketable, but very sweet, little red apples which I fancied provided the magic of built-in apple sauce flavour. Peaches were also fabulous for the same reason. I particularly remember a great boar, Winfield Basil Balls (his registered name, and for the obvious reasons), whom I appreciated far more on the plate than was ever possible at the sty. *Vale et grazie* Basil! A similar happy interaction occurs in the Mediterranean, when the lambs graze on wild aromatic herbs on the slopes of the Maritime Alps, as do Sardinian sheep and goats.

It is not until one encounters the fourteen or more varieties of chicken available to Frenchmen that the discontent stirred by the flavourless battery-fed bird erupts. Who but the French would insist on appellation control of the best table poultry in France, probably in the world, at Bresse?

There are substantial differences in flavour and texture in different species and their parts. The Roman poet, Martial, a thousand years ago advised 'Let a duck be certainly served up whole, but it is tasty only in the breast and neck. The rest return to the cook.' (A foretaste of the fabulous *magret de canard* now available at any French *supermarché*.)

The British tend to carry on a bit about the virtues of their smaller game birds, of which the partridge is among the most favoured. The blackboard lists at the game counter at Harrods in the season are truly extraordinary. There are sometimes more than a dozen choices available. The hanging of grouse for weeks, until it is green and almost fluorescent enough to read by in the dark, and the whole mass falls off the bones, is not a universal delight. Martial may have hit upon it when he said 'whether woodcock or partridge, what does it matter if the flavour be the same? A partridge is dearer, and thus has better flavour.'

12

Flavour Power

You don't need a book to know that everything tastes better when you are hungry. Anything that improves appetite increases the excitement at table. Dry sherry, sparkling or still dry white wines, bitter aperitifs, deserve their traditional popularity. But for the life of me I can't understand the taste for the sickly sweet aperitifs one sees in Italy or France, whose sweetness is so intense as to banish appetite.

Some traditional flavour aids are prehistoric. Salt – sodium chloride – is used universally, and forms a surprising percentage of 'fast food', bread, and other products that are a central part of late twentieth-century urban living; it even appears in some canned baby food, truly a seduction of the palates of innocents. In ordinary cooking, more care in preparation, and the use of stocks and natural juices, avoids the salt overload that is increasingly seen as a health hazard. But where salt is needed, sophistication is possible; salt flavours vary. Some seafoods cooked in seawater taste better, especially crustaceans. Many chefs use their own particular choice of sea salt in all their cooking because they want more than NaCl to haunt the palate.

Sweetness boosts fragrance, and is widely used in South-east Asian food to lift the flavour of particular dishes. There are ethnic differences, from the imperceptible, for instance in certain Chinese provincial foods, to the very sweet, as in the 'heavenly beef' and some quail dishes of southern Thailand. Several types of sugar each add their own mysterious contribution to complexity. Brown palm sugar is completely different from ordinary refined white. Fruit sugars are the most deliciously complex: concentrated fruits like the Dutch *appelstroop* (reduced from countless contented ripe apples to a brown spoonful), or a similar reduction of quince or apricots used in the cuisine of parts of the Eastern Mediterranean, plus the pulp of tamarind, all contribute to a fruit-sweet lift of flavour, and in the last there is an additional strong, sour note. Apple sauce with rich goose or pork is a good example from European cuisine and I once saw a Texan smear his steak with orange marmalade! Since a recent visit to Hong Kong, I have been inspired to try small amounts of tangerine or lime marmalade in dry hotpot poultry cooking.

Sourness is highly valued in all cuisines. One important reason is that it cuts both sweetness, where this is out of balance, and fattinesss and oiliness, where these might be a problem. Lemon and lime juice are excellent. The natural new and aged vinegars (more than just acetic acid) of grape and plum wine, grain (rice, malt), apple cider, and so on, all have special flavours, regional uses and applications.

Great chefs know that there is no substitute for the slow, patient reduction of food flavour stocks over low heat. A fine cook described his early apprenticeship at a great hotel in London. His week began with his setting up two cauldrons of water and beef bones, nothing else. These were slowly boiled and skimmed on the Monday. Next day the bones were discarded, after which the fluid fitted into a single pot. Again, this was seethed and skimmed all day. On

Wednesday it went into a big stock pot on top of the stove and by Friday it had been reduced to a couple of quarts of thick, fragrant, fairly clear, brown stock. A spoonful of this was 'added to everything'. Alone or with additions like Madeira or truffles, as a glaze; or just as a base note, in much the same way as the perfumer works. This was his main job for the week, and the fruit of his labour was a small pot of intense stock, the basis of the dining-room's fine reputation. This approach, partly because it gave restaurant cuisine a certain similarity, and partly for reasons of time and space, has now largely disappeared. Modern stocks are much more quickly made and reduced from identifiably different bases, but the principles of flavour enhancement stand.

I remember a 'stock' that gave incredible depth and complexity. No one could identify it. Bets were made but we were all wrong. It was the clarified reduction of the pan drippings of hundreds of roast chickens prepared for a banquet the previous day. The great Chinese restaurants finish certain recipes with a ladleful of reduced chicken stock, often a cornerstone of their reputations. Fish stocks are the basis of many classical dishes. Vegetable stock is widely used, particularly in the Far East. The Japanese have a dried grainy powder, tekka, made from various vegetables, which gives a hefty punch to the flavour of any food to which it is added. Throughout the world, rural stoves that are kept going through the winter often have a big pot at the back of the hob, to which there are daily additions and subtractions, for a continuous supply of *la bonne soupe*.

The use of wine in cooking is almost a separate discipline. As a marinade, it softens the texture of fibre in meat (although it may toughen the actual muscle without the addition of some oil), much the same as happens in the South Pacific *poisson cru*, or the *ceviches* of Latin American cooking, when raw fish is marinaded in lime juice.

There are several old culinary tricks and fragments of kitchen knowledge which demonstrate taste modifications in the sweet/sour/salt/bitter area. A little salt increases the perception of sweetness. Coarse salt on the top of fast-roasted beef makes a good crust and heightens the flavour. Old timers added sugar to tomatoes to lessen the acidity, and claimed a pinch of salt would make an apple taste better. Country kids in Australia used to love brown sugar on bananas, and never drank homemade lemonade without a substantial sugar addition. Those people who take coffee as elevenses probably know that sugar and cake lessen its bitterness.

There is a great flavour boost when nature splits the protein atom. The *liquamen* of ancient Rome and the fish sauce *nam nuoc* of South-east Asia are probably identical. There is not a lot of difference between them and ordinary anchovy sauce, homemade, or in a bottle from the local delicatessen. They are all made from raw fish, salt and time. The oyster sauce of Chinese-influenced cuisines is made by packing a barrel with alternate layers of the shelled mollusc and salt, covering it and leaving the barrel a few months to ferment, after which the stench has subsided and the liquid can be poured off and bottled. All these are potent stimulants of flavour. Rotting prawns (*balachan*) are the peak of the crescendo. Powders, pastes and compressed blocks of this amazing confection are widely used throughout South-east Asia. It is the ultimate culinary example of the philosophy 'less is more'. The odour of TMA from *balachan* is repellent to most people at any but the least perceptible levels, but when skilfully used it is a subtle and exciting addition to stir-fries and curries.

Yeast residues after sake fermentation can be very tasty, like Marmite and Vegemite of the West, and are often used to flavour Japanese food. Fermentation of soya beans provides one of the most powerful non-specific flavour additions known. Soy or soya sauce is widely used in the East. The light ones are simply sources of *umami*, ('deliciousness' or 'savoury' – a quality the Western palate finds difficult to distinguish because we have no word for it) but the heavier types make rich, malty and complex contributions to a dish. In stir-frying, they seem to speed the Maillard browning taste conversion (more on this on page 123), but it may just be the brown colour contribution. Whichever is the case, the dish looks and tastes great.

Mature cheese is a flavour booster, either grated or in a sauce like pesto or mornay. The Swiss have converted it to an art form, as in the table sport they call *fondue*, a hot sauce dip in the centre of the table, made up in this instance of hard and soft cheeses with a dash of the cherry *eau de vie*, Kirsch. The ultimate cheese charge comes from aged Parmesan, but any really old good hard cheese works reasonably well. A friend, a cheese importer, gave me an unsaleable Edam red cannonball that had fallen unnoticed behind a storage rack. When we finally managed to break it up, there was nothing else to do with it but use it for cooking. The results were delicious. Gabrielle Kervella, a goatherdess from north of Perth, Western Australia, was kind enough to part with a treasured jar of old, hard, mouldy, grated (Nubian) goat cheese. A tiny quantity produced the most spectacular flavour boost. Glutamate, lactose and fatty acids, we salute you! All these things, used as sauces or as ingredients in cooking, reflect the perpetual search for flavour improvement of humble food in all cultures. The standard 'peasant' sauce for Italian pasta: Parmesan (1200 mgm of glutamate per 100 grammes) and tomato (fresh juice, 260) is another classic.

Athenaeus, in *The Deipnosophists*, recalls that:

> The following are listed as seasonings by Antiphanes: 'Raisins, salt, boiled musk, silphium, cheese, thyme, sesame seed, soda, cumin, cashew-nut, honey, marjoram, chopped acorns, vinegar, olives, capers, smoked fish, cress, fig leaves, rennet'.

Some modern synthetics derive from the protein reductions. Investigation of soya bean fermentation flavours led to the discovery of the potency of salts of the amino acid glutamic acid, in particular sodium glutamate, whose initials MSG have become part of the language. The addition of MSG increases the perception of the flavour of virtually anything, and will be discussed at length in Chapter 20, 'The Three R's'.

Two of the most highly regarded medical journals, *The New England Journal of Medicine* and *The Lancet*, carried a correspondence between 1968 and 1980 on the complaints of people affected by eating food containing MSG. They complained of any or all of the following (and more): nausea, vomiting, unusual perspiration, chest pain, dizziness, flushing sensation of the face or chest, headache, weakness, diarrhoea, abdominal cramps and heartburn. As most of these were experienced after eating Oriental food, the phenomenon acquired the formidable name of 'Chinese restaurant syndrome'. Before you are all converted into a lot of neurotics you should hear that these woes have been reproduced in test groups by placebos – that is, inert substances with no specific effects at all. Food 'behaviour' is highly idiosyncratic, with wide variation within any group, as is the case with taste and smell. The informed consensus at present (according to H.L. Meiseman in *Umami*) is that there is little support for the syndrome. So you can enjoy your Chinese meal without anxiety unless you turn out to be one of the few who react adversely to MSG, *or* if an excessive amount has been used. What is an excess? The Umami Information Centre, Tokyo, recommends less than half a teaspoon per pound of meat or six servings of vegetables. Once the right amount is added, more makes no further flavour contribution.

The puzzling pleasure of the pain from the pungency of chilli peppers leads one to philosophise on the paradox. Pungency – hotness – in food is pursued in most cultures. Does the congestion that results at the top and bottom of the digestive system help digestion and reproduction, or could it be an 'adrenalin' lift?

Mustard seed, peppercorns and horseradish go back a long way. Pepper from the Spice Islands was a Mediterranean import for much of its history. Chilli came to Europe from the Americas after Columbus, and from there was taken to the East by the Portuguese in the sixteenth century. There is wide variation in the pungency of chilli, from a mild heat that takes some seconds to register, to the blistering blaze of the tiny green varieties. I once found a pickle jar of these on a bistro table in what was then New Caledonia. Thinking they were a kind of aperitif, I ate one. It took the best part of a day for me to get over the burn, another before I could taste properly. And yet one sees people eating them for fun. The best varieties of the fresh ones have a marvellous 'rose' note in the flavour, with a bearable amount of heat. They are difficult to find, but 'worth a detour' for the subtle complexity, for example, of some Thai dishes. Most of the heat factor, capsaicin, is in the seeds and the lining ridges they are attached to, and if these are precisely removed with gloves (if you do it barehanded, do NOT touch your eyes or anything else delicate you value before washing thoroughly) the heat can be controlled. A dash of cayenne or Tabasco sauce gives the heat without the excitement or the fragrance of the fresh pod.

In temperate climates, mustard and horseradish served a similar function; both cause maximal stimulation of the pain fraction of taste. Pain and pleasure. The terminal incandescence of the green Japanese horseradish *wasabi* is the best example – and how well it illuminates that cuisine.

Some of the most exhilarating moments at the table come from the spicing of food. Chinese cookery uses star anise, fennel, Szechuan pepper, clove and cassia, mixed and powdered, as the 'spices of five fragrances'. If one bouquet can be said to personify the most fragrant of Chinese cuisine, this must be a leading contender.

Garam masala is another traditional spice group. Regions, even families, on the Indian subcontinent, make their individual mixes for curries. If added late, the result is high notes in general harmony. With early addition (the release of aromatics is accelerated by lightly frying them first), there is a sustained base, again like the bottom note of a perfume. All of them seem to contain cardamom, cinnamon and cloves. Some have peppercorns, nutmeg or mace, coriander seeds, black cumin and so on. Panch phora is a standard, made with seeds of black mustard, cumin, black cumin, fennel and fenugreek. If you wish to try a mix of your own devising, it may be an idea to freshen the aromatics by giving them a short time in a low oven, before cooling and grinding. Like coffee, they may be stored for months in the freezer without major aroma change.

National flavour preferences can be extreme, and seem to reflect what might be called the 'personality' of a country. Cold climates tend to less assertive flavours; hot climates prefer very definite, even spectacular food flavours (as they do colours); Korea and

Szechuan Province, both cold areas, are exceptions. The pickled cabbage with chilli, a staple of Korea, can be volcanic. The fresh and distinct flavours of Thai food contrast with the cumin/turmeric/brown onion-in-ghee sledgehammer of southern India, the fragrance of Kashmir, and the relative blandness (excepting *wasabi*) of traditional Japan. The world continues to shrink with the speed and ease of travel, ethnic cuisines challenge and mingle, and local food everywhere is becoming more exciting. One Sydney hamburger chain has offered four sauces, tomato, mustard, curry and sweet-and-sour since its billionth serving of burgers. *That* is progress.

Some ordinary foods contain extraordinary flavour stimulants and powerful odorants. Unpolished rice, food staple of a considerable proportion of the world's population, is an excellent source of vitamin B1, thiamin, which is said to be among the most powerful smells that exist. The fascinating thing about a mouthful of unpolished cooked rice is the way it seems to extend and etch the characters of the food that it accompanies.

Some smells stay at the same intensity. On the other hand, the intensity of the rancidity of stale butter increases as the amount of odorant rises. Because butter is such a common food, this may be another evolutionary marker – a hint from evolution of some good or bad health factor. The pungency of garlic and onion increases once they are cut, from enzyme activity initiated by exposure to air.

Experience shows the need for different levels of the same flavour, depending upon whether the food is to be eaten hot or cold. Fats, cream, butter and oils tend to become increasingly important aroma banks as time passes during cooking and storage. The principle will be demonstrated by the coffee tasting in Chapter 16, 'Start to Taste'. The net result may be an actual dampening of immediate flavour. Olfaction and taste work best at about body temperature and their efficiency falls progressively to nil at freezing point. Which is the reason why small children get such a charge from ice cream. There is the initial surprise of the cold, sweetness and smoothness, and then the bonus of warmed fragrances up behind the nose.

13

Fire, Smoke and Ice

> Mankind for the first seventy thousand years ate their meat raw, clawing or biting it from the living animal just as they do in Africa to this day. The art of Roasting was accidentally discovered ... Bo-Bo, the eldest son of Ho-ti the swineherd, was fond of playing with fire, and let some sparks escape. This reduced their poor mansion to ashes, in which was a fine litter of nine new farrowed pigs. He stopped to feel if there were any signs of life. He burnt his fingers and to cool them, he applied them to his mouth. For the first time in the life of the world, man tasted crackling. 'Oh father, the pig, the pig, do come and taste how nice the burnt pig eats.'
>
> It was soon observed Ho-ti's cottage was burnt down now more frequently; as often as the sow farrowed, so sure was the house of Ho-ti to be in a blaze. And Ho-ti himself, which was the more remarkable, instead of chastising his son, seemed to grow more indulgent to him than ever.
>
> Adapted from Charles Lamb's delightful essay on arson as a method of roasting pork in *Essays of Elia*

Have you ever wondered how it was and when that someone, not unlike us, first tasted the cooked meat in the charred remains of an animal caught in a bush fire? How long before campfire and cave cooking became routine? Apart from softening food for chewing, what does heat do to its flavour that is so attractive?

Ordinary cooking heat unites different arrangements of atoms in food to produce a large number of distinctive flavours. Research into exactly how this happens began with Arthur Ling, an English brewing scientist. But it really took off at the start of this century with Professor Louis-Camille Maillard. As a young physician, Maillard reported that sugars and protein acids heated to cooking temperatures, in the process of turning brown, produced some familiar aromas. The first patent for a synthetic flavour, based on what has come to be known as the Maillard reaction, was granted in 1948.

Heating sugar alone will produce caramel. The two reactions, Maillard and caramelisation, often occur in tandem, and mix quite satisfactorily. Refined sugar starts off as white or colourless. If it is heated when it is dry, it travels through yellow, amber and brown to charred black. After simple sweetness comes the ravishing caramel fragrance of more than a hundred different extra flavour molecules. Late-brown is bitter and it takes some experience for the cook to stop the process at the correct stage. The redoubtable Mrs Beeton described what happens during the boiling of sugar (scant kilo/2 lb to 450 ml/1 pint of water).

> Boil for a few minutes, wet thumb and forefinger and then dip the tips into the syrup. If, on immediately separating the finger and thumb, the syrup is drawn out into a fine thread which breaks at a short distance, the sugar is boiled *to the small thread* (100 degrees C/215 degrees F).

The style of description and technique, and temperatures reached, continues through *large thread, small pearl, large pearl, small blow, large blow or feather, small ball, large ball, small crack,* and *large crack,* and finally reaches *caramel,* the acquisition of colour, after 155 degrees C/315 degrees F. A touch of lemon makes barley sugar; butter and cream, butterscotch. Similar other miracles can be performed with golden syrup, treacle and molasses. Flavour additions like chocolate-coated almonds and fruit flavours make more fun for the children. The flavour and colour changes in our toffee foray are the direct result of heat restructures of the sugar molecules.

Now consider the bonus when the protein acids are added to the fire. Vanilla pods, cacao and coffee beans all need the Maillard browning effect to develop the delightful flavours we enjoy to the point of excitement. Bread crust, bakes and grills of all kinds, vegetables and meat, are everyday examples of our indebtedness. All the malted barley beverages, beer and whisky, pay homage. As chemical genius has produced a run of floral fragrances from serial additions to the carbon chain, so have a fascinating range of Maillard-type food flavours been synthesised. It would be hard to over-emphasise how widespread is the use of these flavours in the products on supermarket shelves.

The nearest kitchen is the best place to observe Maillard browning. Onion says it all. The study could be part of the single meal, perhaps with one day of a weekend set aside, or a dish a day; or merely check the flavours as they are encountered over a long period.

Most vegetable flavours are transformed by cooking, to produce attractive volatiles that do not exist in raw food. Consider the potato. There is nothing humble about it unless abundance and cheapness make it so in your eyes. It appeared in Europe in the sixteenth century, along with tomatoes,

Heat, Time and the Onion

How cooked	Colour	Flavour, depth	Use
Raw		Sweet, pungent, tear-jerker	Salad
Boiled	White	Flat	Stock, boiled vegetable
Sweated	Opaque, white transparent	Onion, not pungent	Light flavouring
Fried	Brown Hint of brown Opaque, hint of yellow	Strong, deep Delicate Perceptible	Meat stews Fish and white stews Delicate sauces, e.g. soubise
Refried	Deep brown	Rich, intense	Classic Indian Korma curry base note

chilli, maize, and many other startling influences. Raw potato is tasteless and lacks nourishment. Worse, the green tips of the plant are quite poisonous. There is a crescendo of flavour that develops successively with boiling, roasting (fat free), frying and refrying. Dr Ron Buttery points out there are seventy more flavour volatiles in fried potato chips than exist in the raw vegetable. Like peanuts, who can resist a second crisp yellow-brown potato chip (French fry) just out of the pan? There are at least two distinct textures in the potato family, each with different uses. The starchy, rather 'dry' sort can be used in most ways, particularly for roasting and mashing. The 'moist' waxy kind are my favourites. They taste almost as if they had a little oil or butter added, and the small ones, boiled and unpeeled with some cracked pepper, fresh dill, a smidgen of grated onion, and a splash of the best olive oil you can afford, one 'whacko!' as we say in my country.

I have chosen beef as the protein example of how various cooking methods influence flavours. There are several reasons for its popularity, including a genetic human preference, the position of cattle in history, and the billions of cattle that exist today. In Homer's Greece, a slave was worth four oxen, while twenty oxen bought a concubine.

> Thou shalt not covet thy neighbour's wife
> Thou shalt not covet thy neighbour's ox

Carving and tearing chunks of raw meat from a carcass and chomping grimly is frowned on today. One modern development is steak tartare, called so, it is said, because the Tartars of East Asia ate meat in this fashion. Chopped best cuts of steak should be as fat-free as possible; raw fat is disgusting to most people. The dish is usually served with a number of tasty additions to lift the rather bland flavour of the meat. Carpaccio, paper-thin sliced beef with olive oil and accompaniments, is an Italian raw meat presentation.

From this baseline, the first increase in flavour is to be seen at a barbecue, or in good steakhouses. There are two extremes of fire, the furious blast of a fresh wind-driven flame at one end, and the steady glow of coals at the other. The first blackens and seals the meat, the latter sets and cooks it through, during which the flavour, texture and colour change from soft and bloody to firm and grey. The degrees of done-ness vary from 'trembling', or blue, through rare (the French call this *saignant* – bloody), medium, well done, and 'ruined'. The complexity of the flavours, what we enjoy most, comes from the degree of browning and caramelisation that takes place. Pan frying will add flavour from fat changes, with yet further complexity from suet, lard, butter, olive oil, and so forth.

The ageing of beef vastly improves flavour; few apply this principle better than Vlado Gregory of Melbourne, one of Australia's national treasures. How would you like to go to a restaurant where a unique talent attends the fire, moved by the philosophy that the client is the designer of the final product? Vlado, the red meat specialist, starts from several basic elements which synergise finally on the plate. Fresh three-year-old steer beef, mostly grass-fed, some finished on grain, is stored on the bone at several degrees above freezing point for two to four weeks, resulting in unrivalled tenderness and flavour development. The fire merits almost as much of Vlado's attention. He uses charcoals from the dense eucalypt mallee root, making coals of uniform size which give a soft intense heat to penetrate slowly into the meat. Vlado describes the heat as almost 'wet' and he uses powdered ash on top of the coals to lessen heat intensity quickly.

In the final stage, he requires full instructions from the client, to be followed with precision. The cut of steak, the degree of done-ness – every individual meal is a separate operation from beginning to end. 'I can put a spirit into red meat.' In the realm of flavour, how do you set a value on the influence of such a man?

Patience Gray describes her philosophy in the following passage from *Honey from a Weed.*

> The nature of the fire determines the procedure; you make a fire with good draught, set between

stones and oriented according to the wind, and let it burn up fiercely, fanning if necessary. When the flames have died down and the heat is at its maximum, you throw some thyme and rosemary on the glowing embers and set down the loaded grill, the meat having been anointed with oil well beforehand. You fan again and seal the meat on either side. The fire dies down a bit, the roasting proceeds at a slower rate. The searing time is short, the subsequent cooking time, once the juices have been contained, varies with the nature of what is being grilled.

Large fishes are best left unscaled, brushed with wine vinegar and oil, and cooked on a much slower braise. The fish retains its succulence; the skin and scales are then removed entire.

Out of this procedure and greatly depending on the kind of wood employed comes the real fragrance. Apple, pear, plum, apricot woods have fragrance. So do pine branches and nut woods. Sweet chestnut makes a slow smoky fire; the wood is too sappy. Fig wood is poor. Tamarisk has an unpleasant smell. Olive wood makes the most incandescent braise, and ilex is nearly as good. Dry vine cuttings are excellent for small grills, their heat being of short duration.

The ultimate barbecue techniques and flavours were privileges of a Sydney group thirty years ago, of which Gerry Kearney was guru. He had an unparalleled knowledge of barbecue cooking, and as we progressed, his creativity took flight; there were three stages of the fire: flames, just right, and out. The coals were controlled with a fine spray of water, used when drips from the cooking food produced a flare-up. Later he developed a staged series of vertical metal boxes perched on one side of the iron grill over the coals, open at the bottom to let the heat pass through. Cuts of meat or seafood were grilled on the open grid. There are traditional Australian additions of aromatic eucalypt leaves to the 'barbie', and he had carefully selected varieties which were added to compartments of the multi-chambered chimney. With a precise idea of temperature of the small ovens at each height, various meats, seafood skewers, and vegetables and fruits were cooked at the different levels; so great was his skill that the meal proceeded with an uninterrupted crescendo of superbly cooked dishes *à point*, some 'smoked', some naturally flavoured. I have not seen anything quite like this achieved elsewhere, nor better use of the flavour principle of Professor Maillard and the food-smokers of pre-history; the challenge is richly rewarded if you wish to try.

These days specialists, the professional spit roasters, will turn a suckling pig, a lamb or a side of beef, on a motor-driven spit over a fire. They will bring their own paraphernalia so that you can relax and enjoy one of the best and oldest browning-flavour experiences. This is not a new phenomenon, of course; it was already a profession, the highest art of the King of France's kitchen, in 1248. The order, the Chaîne des Rotisseurs, was revived in 1950 by a group of whom Jean Valby of Paris is the eminent surviving and inspiring leader.

The tannins, and yellow and red pigments of table wine make a contribution to our cooking repertoires. The addition of wine during cooking is not as simple as it sounds. 'The better the wine, the better the flavour addition' is correct as far as it goes, but who can afford, or would wish, to 'waste' a really great wine for such a purpose? There are several approaches, each with a different result. Wine added to the pot early during the preparation of a dish on the stove for some hours will add to the depth of the general flavour mix, but does no more than hint of its origin. Added late to the dish, just before serving, the wine flavour can dominate. So it is overkill to use more than a half a glass or so at this stage. The trick is to cook the dish with any drinkable or leftover wine, and if you wish a final special touch, a splash of great wine becomes the exclamation point. Its alcohol must be eliminated by heating before serving. Confuse neither of these with a cold marinade containing wine, which then softens and flavours the ingredients in yet another way.

The stir-frying of Oriental cookery actually combines Maillard browning and superheated steaming. One method of wok cooking uses minimal quantities of oil, and a very high flame. At the point where the pieces of food are about to stick to the pan and char, a small amount of water or stock is added, keeping the food moving. The steam then generated actually pressure-cooks each morsel inside its seal, combining the Maillard flavours of chicken, beef and pork, garlic and onion, for example, with the texture pleasure of the fresh crunch and raw flavour of vegetables like celery, broccoli and bean sprouts.

Flaming with alcohol, particularly brandy, introduces a flavour unobtainable in any other way. The explosive conflagration on the surface of the food (whether duck, veal, strawberries or whatever) rearranges the molecules in the manner we have come to know and love. The enjoyment is heightened, I can assure you, if the restaurant wall catches fire, as it did on one memorable occasion. 'Adrenalin' also lifts flavour.

Parcel cooking, *en papillote*, food leaf-wrapped over hot stones (*luau*), in cooking parchment, foil, or in modern plastic oven-proof bags, retains many of the aromatics of the food otherwise lost to the cooking fluid, or to the air. Out in the bush, a large fish, wrapped in layers of wet newspaper, does as well. Discard the cooked skin.

Pot cooking came quite late in the progress of food flavour production. It had to await the technology of the container, of leather, clay, and then iron.

> Before they reached the lodge, preparations for the feast were evident in the delicious cooking smells that reached out with tantalising promise. Nezzie's stew was largely responsible. It was quietly bubbling in the large cooking hide ... In a large pothole that had been dug near a fireplace, hot coals were placed on top of ashes, accumulated from previous use, that lined the bottom. A layer of powdered, dried mammoth dung was poured on the coals, and on top of that was placed a large, thick piece of mammoth hide supported by a frame, and filled with water. The coals smouldering under the dung began to heat the water, but by the time the dung caught fire, enough of the fuel had been burned away that the hide no longer rested on it, but was supported by the frame. The liquid slowly seeping through the hide, though it had reached boiling, kept the leather from catching fire. When the fuel under the cooking hide was burned away, the stew was kept boiling by the addition of river stones that had been heated red hot in the fireplace, a chore some children were tending to.
>
> Jean Auel, *The Mammoth Hunters*

Taking the cooking temperature just to the boiling point of water (that of sugar syrup is substantially higher) gives an immediate moderate flavour enhancement, which then flattens to nothing quite quickly; and a 'nothing' flavour was the Continental idea of English cuisine, at least until recently. The first trip to Europe nearly forty years ago, then a pretty big event for an Australian, gave me a sharp feeling of anticipation, but unfortunately we had our first meal on the Riviera in a little hotel booked for us by our English travel agent. Eddies in the boiled-cabbage fug in the restaurant were created by several 'Fawlty Towers' types at the table, all speaking English. We had paid for set menu meals, and that is what we got. Boiled fish, boiled onions, boiled cabbage, stewed meat, all *à l'Anglaise.* Youth, and exuberant lack of experience can put up with a lot.

Cooking at the boiling point of water will not produce most of the browning flavours. They can be introduced to pot cooking by first frying onions, carrots, flour and oil, or whatever, and then continuing at a simmer, or less.

Lest anyone underrate boiled flavour here is Joseph Wechsberg's list of dishes on the menu of a Viennese restaurant:

> The restaurant was Meissl & Schadn, an eating-place of international reputation, and the boiled-beef specialities of the house were called Tafelspitz, Tafeldecket, Rieddeckel, Beinfleisch, Rippenfleisch, Kavalierspitz, Kruspelspitz, Hieferschwanzl, Schuterschwanzl, Shulterscherzl, Mageres Meisel (or Mauserl), Fettes Meisel, Zwerchried, Mittleres Kugerl, Dunnes Kugerl, Dickes Kugerl, Broselfleisch, Ausgelostes, Brustkern, Brustfleisch, Weisses Scherzl, Schwarzes Scherzl, Zapfen and Ortschwanzl.
>
> The terminology was bound to stump anybody who had not spent the first half of his adult life within the city limits of Vienna. It was concise and ambiguous at the same time, even Viennese patriarchs did not always agree exactly where the Weisses Scherzl ended and the Ortschwanzl began.
>
> from *Blue Trout and Black Truffles*

This abundance apparently depended on the

almost surgical skills of the old-time Viennese butchers, who were able to separate a beef carcass into thirty-two different cuts and four distinct qualities.There were many reasons for the excellence of the offerings; not least was the fact that the restaurant itself owned the cattle. The pampered beasts were housed inside a large sugar refinery and fed on molasses and sugarbeet mash, which partially explains the texture and flavour of the beef. The Japanese method of 'finishing' Kobe beef has elements in common, as has the American technique of stalling the animals in feed lots, to be corn fed. The boiled beef of those days in Vienna, Wechsberg says, was not a dish, but a way of life. Viennese travellers would take along Viennese cookery books, with an anatomical map of the cuts, numbered and subdivided, to try to ensure that they got their choice. Of course, they seldom succeeded.

The Viennese took a dim view of the French speciality, *boeuf saignant à la ficelle.* 'A piece of fillet is tightly wrapped around with string, roasted quickly in a very hot stove, and dipped for sixty seconds – not for fifty-eight or sixty-two, but for sixty – in boiling consommé just before it is served. The juice is kept inside the pinkish meat by the trick of quick roasting and boiling.' The best of Professor Maillard, and of pot cooking.

The two Viennese schools of boiling beef provide another example of flavour control. Those who wanted a pot of strong soup put the cut of beef into cold water and cooked it for hours over a slow fire, during which time celery, parsley, onions, carrots, and seasoning were added. Sometimes half an onion, fried brown, was added 'to give the soup a dark colour'. The other method, for those who had to have their beef juicy and tender, was to add it to boiling water, then let it simmer to 'close the pores of the meat and keep the juices inside'. Little of this genius survived the Second World War, but the lessons are indelible.

Steam cooking and poaching are excellent, low-fat methods of sustaining flavour, but demand a skill in timing that has to be learnt for each food. With steaming, a perforated container holds the food clear of the water boiling beneath. For many fish and green vegetables it is sufficient to bring the pot to the boil and turn the heat off at once. This provides enough steam to tenderise the food, yet sustain crunch and flavour.

Blanching, immersing vegetables for five seconds only in boiling water, moderates intense flavours. 'Refreshing', stopping the cooking process in its tracks, is yet another kitchen trick. Vegetables such as beans or peas are cooked almost to preferred texture by any method, then cooled at once under running water until quite cold. They can be stored in the refrigerator for a few days, plastic-wrapped, to be produced at will, then microwaved or steamed for a minute or so, and *voilà*, instant 'fresh' vegetables. Near enough.

Smoked food is widely enjoyed today for is aromatic flavour. This is a happy reminder of the prehistoric need to preserve meat and fish that could not be eaten at the time of the catch, to establish supplies for long barren winters, and also for light-weight food on journeys. Drying by the fire probably led to the technique of smoking and then to the realisation that the flavours from some wood smokes were more attractive, perhaps less resiny, than others. Not every culture has found wood resin too strong for food. It became part of the Greek wine flavour following the application of resin to waterproof clay vessels in which wine was stored. Under an azure Mediterranean sky, retsina is always enjoyable with fresh food, and is excellent for 'cutting' oiliness, but it somehow seems less attractive elsewhere.

Two methods of smoking are widely used. The historic form of 'hot smoking' drives much of the moisture from the food, and heavily impregnates the smoke flavour. It keeps reasonably well for a few weeks in cool temperatures. 'Cold smoking' is a more delicate cure, and is particularly used for the finer fish. Trout done this way can be ravishing, but will not keep.

Wood flavour in cooking has been developed into quite an art. Mesquite is all the rage for barbecues in parts of America. Australians have easy access to eucalypts. Hickory and oak smoking each have their devotees. Those lucky enough to have access to applewood or vine prunings don't talk too much about the result, lest we provoke serious envy. The smoked salmon trade acknowledges the superiority of Scotch smoked salmon, to the extent, it is said, that some fish caught elsewhere, for example off North America, is sent to Scotland for smoking because of the excellence of the wood flavour and smoking technique. Unhappily, you don't always get the genuine article. I had the best possible when I tried some that John Noble had smoked over the oak of old whisky barrels. Some of them were said to be made of American oak, and some had been used for sherry.

When I arrive at a new destination, I spend half a day investigating food stores and supermarkets to see what people eat. Back at the hotel, out on a towel if necessary, I spread out breads, cheeses, fruits and whatever else I have found. Only then do I begin to understand what the new place is about. In cities like London and New York where there are incredible food halls, I love to do a smoked salmon tasting. Many years ago, combining Harrods, Fortnum & Mason and Selfridges, I did a grand *dégustation* of seven different sorts. The rich softness, low salt, delicacy and aroma complexity of the Scotch was unforgettable. So was the price. Recently, Harrods had three selections of Scotch Salmon, not as good as I remember. If you don't run to this regally priced masterpiece you can have a similar experience with some of the mackerel, eel, herring, and other smoked fish, some as outstanding as they are inexpensive. One becomes expert at detecting food dipped in synthetic smoke-flavoured solutions. The smoke note is overwhelming, the flesh may be coarse and rather salty, and the colour odd.

All natural flavours derive from cells, and are best evaluated at body heat. Cooling to the point of ice formation quite simply eliminates flavour. The only positive virtues of very cold food or drink are texture, the novelty of 'cold' trauma, and the pleasure of the surprise assault of aromas as the mouthful warms up.

Fresh fruit and vegetables can be regarded as essentially water in fancy packages. Water loss 'cooks' flavour and texture. Any cell at a higher temperature than body heat for more than a short period suffers a breakdown of its membrane envelope. Flavour molecules can leak out, and the enzymes which have built up the flavours promptly go to work and break them down. Enzymes are truly ambivalent.

Below freezing point a comparable process lets cell water leak out. Slow freezing is a most efficient 'dryer' of food, unavoidably ruining texture and flavour when the food is rethawed. A worse form of chilling injury is caused by ice spicules penetrating the cell membrane, intensifying the fluid loss. Fats oxidise in the freezer, the more unsaturated they are, the more rancid will be the end result. Cold and ice flavour damage is the unnecessary penalty we pay for badly handled convenience foods. Some foods freeze better than others, and defrosting is an art in itself.

The faster the freezing process, the fewer the spicules. Liquid nitrogen is introduced in the tunnel-freezing process used commercially by large fishing trawlers and bulk frozen vegetable operators. It creates a frozen mush rather than ice daggers inside the cell, and if the food is cooked immediately on defrosting the result can be close to fresh in flavour. If after thawing it is refrozen again for later use, the food is a disaster.

The temperature at which wine should be served provokes much discussion and it is actually possible to buy thermometers with a wine type inscribed alongside what is considered to be the appropriate temperature. Even more emphatic is the inevitable appearance of the ice bucket beside the table at a trendy restaurant. I enjoy sparkling wines chilled, to sustain the bubbles, but as Stephen Lake and I are dedicated to sustaining all the flavour of a season's fruit in any wine we make at Lake's Folly, it is heart-breaking to see them served near frozen. All that effort, to have the result obscured by costly ice. The only benefit of chilling white wine is to make a refreshing drink on a hot day, or to hide faults. To enjoy the delights on offer, you should serve it cool, or even at indoor temperature. Please.

14

Blessed are the Cheesemakers

Ripe cheese, good bread, red wine and the crunch of apple or pear. Can you easily think of a more satisfying end to hunger? And for most of us, a simpler one? Of course, there are many marriages of breads, biscuits, cheeses, wines, fruits and salads. Some finish a meal with sweetness, to conclude appetite. The ancient Greeks ended with cheese, so they could continue drinking wine.

Cheese is an important, sometimes central article of diet in those cultures that drink the milk of animals. All mammals (from *mamma*, breast) start in the world with the milk of their mother. This is part of an educational programme, introduction to a lifetime of flavour pleasure which is itself a reward for good nutrition. Many continue to enjoy cheese throughout life, but such approval is not universal. Apart from individual variations, or reasons of health and preference, some ethnic groups avoid cheese, and often those who eat it as well.

Some years ago I was leaving Bordeaux, soon to visit a New York friend who was a devotee of goat cheese. There were fourteen different goat cheeses, young and old, named and bastard, in the Bordeaux market. I bought one of each, small differently shaped blocks and discs, and, lightly wrapped, they joined my clothes in the suitcase. About twenty-four hours later my host was delighted with the offering. We didn't, however, even manage to finish unwrapping them in the kitchen before we were ordered out of the house by his (till then) invariably charming wife. We completed our *dégustation des fromages* down in the far corner of the back garden. I like chèvres, but I was only at the half-way point on my trip, and the pong in the luggage was quite a problem for the rest of that particular voyage.

The Japanese, over the past half century, have moved a degree away from their traditional diet of seafood, rice and greens, but it is still rare to find cheese in an ordinary Japanese suburban supermarket away from foreign enclaves, and it is not seen at all in what correspond to 'corner stores' in the West. Japanese friends are politely interested in cheese, but I have yet to meet a cheese freak among them.

The nomadic peoples of central Asia are historic users of cheese, partly because it is a complete food, and partly because cheese is one-tenth the volume and weight of its milk source and is easily transported. It improves for years. Its constitution ensures its hygiene. No wonder it has played such an important role since before the first records.

Have you ever quietly pondered the *first* cheese, the *first* wine, from the chance action of airborne organisms on gathered milk and fruit, in a social group, somewhere? After its recorded use by many of the great civilisations of the ancient world, improved varieties of cheese, both fresh and ripened, became widely popular throughout the Roman Empire, and beyond. The principles of flavour demonstrated in cheese had become well known, and cheesemaking has been an established part of life in Europe and in lands settled by Europeans ever since.

We do know a great deal about the differences between the common animal milks – cow, sheep and goat – and what cheese flavours result. The effect of increasing amounts of the longer chain fatty acids is marked and, combined with the differences in sugar and protein of the milks of these animals, and the bacterial and mould activity, the flavours are very different. Goat cheese is far more piquant, for example, than the cheese of cow's milk. And, as a point of interest the five-carbon fatty acid that is one of the main flavours of cheese is a close relative of one of the mid-cycle vaginal pheromones. The pasture has some striking seasonal and other influences. Cheddar styles from the Darling Downs in Queensland and Gippsland in Victoria are as different as ... I cannot write 'chalk and cheese', because they are all fine cheddars, but they are different. The preferred Stiltons are made from summer milk, and start to come on sale in early autumn. This sort of variation happens everywhere where the animals' food sources may change. One only has to observe the feeding frenzy of cows or sheep on a paddock of new green shoots to know this will be reflected in the milk, to say nothing of the effect of flowering plants. Conversely the flavours of some weed flowers are unpleasant enough for a prudent farmer to keep his animals away from them.

The time of milking influences flavour, because if you think about it, morning and evening milk are different. Reblochon is a French cheese whose very name is a dialect implying second milking. This is rich end-milk, which was left in the cow till after the boss has tallied the day's production and gone home. The cowherd then stripped this fat-rich milk, making a superb strong cheese to be matured in the nearby caves of the Haute Savoie. It is a favourite of mine, perhaps a mite less attractive now that it is made legally.

There are at least two thousand named cheeses throughout the world. This is but a pale reflection of the past, when many households making their own product acquired a reputation for some special quality, beyond their own village and further afield.

Domestic efforts of small cheesemakers continue to surprise and delight the adventurous traveller. These tend to be mostly of the fresh variety made from natural souring of the milk, or curdled by heat, fig juice, the stomach content of a lamb, or whatever the cheesemaker chooses.

The French still make several hundred cheese styles, a fact which brought General de Gaulle publicly to despair at the prospect of trying to govern them. I think I tasted most of them at the *Foire Gastronomique* in Dijon in 1968. Twenty or so basic cheese types, however, make up the present-day pattern.

You will need some understanding of cheesemaking to grasp fully the flavour possibilities. It will do no harm, and you might be inspired to go further and experiment yourself. Cheesemaking is not difficult, just time-consuming. At the suburban domestic level it can be expensive because it uses a lot of relatively costly milk for not much cheese. On the other hand, if you have a milking animal ...

There are ten common stages in cheesemaking:

1 Milk is heated or pasteurised.
2 Lactic bacteria are added, to develop for one hour.
3 Rennet enzyme is added, producing curds and whey.
4 The curds are cut to small pieces ('cheddaring').
5 The mixture is held at blood heat for several hours (Cheddar only very briefly).
6 The whey is drained away.
7 The curd is cut into slabs or granules.
8 Under hard or light pressure, it is shaped to blocks or wheels.

9 Salt is added. Either it is rubbed on dry, or the curd is brine-soaked for seventy-two hours. (It may also be added after four.)

10 Specific micro-organisms are added to the coat, or injected into the cheese.

There is a continuing debate (see Raymond Sokolov, *Of Curds and Whey*), on the flavour of cheeses made of raw or pasteurised milk. The Europeans prefer unpasteurised milk, though that is frowned on by bureaucrats. Whichever it is made of, the cheese is then set aside for ripening at a set temperature and for specified times. It will be turned frequently. It may also be brushed, sprayed with water, rubbed with salt, coated with pepper, or left to compost in hay or grapeseeds; all methods which change flavour.

There is a scale of ripeness; at one end are the non-ripened cheeses – cream, for instance, or cottage, to be eaten fresh. Green cheeses (green as in unripe fruit, not as in mouldy) include ricotta, neufchâtel and mozzarella. They taste of milk alone, with little or no added salt. Ripening is a process of fermentation from this stage to complete maturity, and it increases quality magically over the months, sixty days or longer, depending on temperature and the texture of the cheese paste inside the rind. The longer the time of maturation the stronger the flavour – culminating in the aged *grana*, of Parmesan. The more heat at cheddaring, the nuttier and more caramel-like the flavour of the hard ripe cheese. From ripeness soft cheeses will go on to decomposition. Hard cheeses may dry out, but will retain their flavour for years in many cases, and are excellent for grating.

From Cantal and Cheshire and goats' milk cheese came a dull and muffled booming like a melody on the bass, against which the sudden little waves of the Neufchâtels, the Troyes and the Mont d'Ors raised their shrill cries. Then the smells began to run wild, mixing violently with one another, thickening with gusts of Port Salut, Limbourg, Gerome, Marseilles, Livarot, Pont l'Évêque, little by little merging and mingling, broadening out into a single explosion of smells.

Emile Zola, *Savage Paris*

Forty years ago I used to hand-milk eleven big cows an hour. That is good going. I became good buddies with the local cheesemakers, and discovered that one trick in making the marvellous, two-pound, cloth-covered cheeses we enjoyed was to turn them every day for a few months *after* they were sold as ripe. They dried and matured evenly, and better. Nothing like *that* flavour ever comes out of a plastic wrapping, which aborts the changes.

What Causes Cheese Characteristics?

Piquancy	Bacterial enzymes split fats to acids	
Sweetness	Milk sugars in small quantities	
Buttery	A second fermentation of lactic bacteria	
Peppery 'blue'	*P. Roqueforti*	specific bacteria
Pungent	*B. linens*, smelly, high	specific bacteria
Nutty	Heated, cooked curd	
Ammonia	Advanced bacterial activity on protein acids	
Salty	Too much added salt	
'Eyes'	Gas formers, particularly propionbacterium	
Soapiness	Immaturity of fatty components	
Rancidity	An excess of fatty acids	

Not many faulty cheeses get to the market-place. An excess of any of the characteristics in the list above is unacceptable. Odd and off flavours, rotten-egg gas, are cheesemaking disasters.

Ripe soft cheeses are sometimes called 'smellies' by connoisseurs who should know better. They have a different pong from 'stinkers', which is what professionals call off-odour rejects. Smellies get that way by the action of a type of bacteria on the fats and proteins in soft cheeses. These bacteria happen also to inhabit human skin clefts. In excess, the character can be off-putting, even disgusting, to some people.

Marie Harel, a widow of the village of Camembert in late eighteenth-century Normandy, did actually make fabulous little cheeses. They were inimitable, and her fame spread. Her secret, difficult to confirm or deny, was said to be that she formed and rolled the cheeses between her feet. There is a Rabelaisian suggestion that that is not the whole story. *Merci*, Marie!

Most men quite like the understated flavour of fresh Camembert, and women frequently seem to choose it first from a selection of cheeses. Perhaps, like Champagne, its pheromonal message is universal.

> Beware of young women who love neither wine, nor truffles, nor cheese, nor music.
>
> Colette, *Paysages et Portraits*

I don't mind Camembert, but there is a stage in its maturity at which my hedonistic rating is 'don't like'. This odour continues to develop without interruption in a sequence through Pont l'Évêque, to Munster and Limburger – concluding with an outpatients' clinic on an Australian summer afternoon.

Many do not like the smell of durian, but it is the most addictive fruit in South-east Asia, so who am I to complain? One man's cheese is another man's aversion. Sandy Carr refers to the American cheese, Brick (a washed rind cheese), as a cross between Limburger and Cheddar in flavour, 'obscurely described as the married man's Limburger'. How's that again?

I am not always on the side of the angels. For the better part of my life I have been privileged to enjoy the best Stilton cheese in the world, privately imported for one of Australia's better clubs for over a hundred years. This particular cheese is always a wondrous creamy yellow with the marvellous flavour of the blue-green penicillium mould. The savour is not the least of its sensual attractions. It is served wrapped in a 'dazzling white clawth', with a silver cheese scoop. Daniel Defoe recorded in 1728 the cheese 'brought to the table with the mites of maggots round it, so thick, that they bring a spoon with them for you to eat the mites with it, as you do the cheese'. Now, *that* doesn't bother me one bit. I've even watched them.

Stiltons do vary a lot. Some of the best commercial blues I have tasted have been from New Zealand, Gippsland and Norway. Danish blue is totally reliable and always good. Blue Castello is a double cream, cream of one milk added to another lot of milk. The very fat Gorgonzola achieves the highest flavour of all the blues, and a well-developed one may need to be tethered.

Salt, much more than is needed, is a problem in modern diet, and we are learning to take less of it. Like sulphur in winemaking, it is an essential part of the health of the developing cheese. The very fresh, non-salted cheeses tend to be rather insipid and are generally enjoyed with something strong-tasting, even a simple additive like crushed black pepper. The very heavily salted cheeses like Feta pickled in brine are slow to mature, and may even fail to do so if all the bugs have been killed off by the salt. It is not a bad idea to soak such a cheese in milk or warm water for a while, before using in salads or with olives.

Early in my pilgrim's progress, I met a surprising example of the influence of salt in flavour development. A particular Roquefort was different from and better than previous cheeses. Checking the provenance, I found that it had been destined for another, cooler continent but had been rerouted to Australia to fill an urgent order. In fact, the importer explained, different quantities of salt are added to different batches of the cheese, depending on their destination, as a preservative in warmer climates. Another surprise. How could there be different standards for a unique *appellation contrôlée* cheese? It was common knowledge, in fact French law, that the cheese had to be made from the milk of sheep in a statutory area, delivered to Roquefort village within eight days of making. The cylinders had then to be brushed with salt, and pricked twenty or so times with a needle. A penicillium culture had already to have been mixed in with the curd during the making. It had once been mouldy bread crumbs, but now a laboratory-made powder of dry spores was used. During the ripening over the next three or four months, an act of sorcery took place in the cool damp breeze of the caves and *voilà*! Roquefort.

Harold McGee considers that less than 20 per cent of the annual production of AC (*appellation d'origine contrôlée*) cheese genuinely qualifies. Since hearing that I have wondered less about the Roquefort variation.

The influence of bacteria on cheese is paramount. It is among the foods most heavily populated by micro-organisms. One or two billion bugs per gramme can be counted on the first day of cheesemaking and that is only the start. The process is generally safe enough because of the salt, the acidity produced by the fermentation of milk sugar, and the actual inhibition of harmful bacteria by other by-products. They unite to control the situation rather effectively.

Gas makes big holes or eyes in Emmanthal and little holes in Gruyère. The former is quite a difficult process to perfect, but the Swiss are not concerned about imitators. 'Anyone can make holes, only the Swiss can make the cheese.'

Some cheesemakers gild the lily. They add caraway seeds, sage herbs, fruits and nuts, cognac, no end to it. And not all at once! Some smoke their cheeses, a flavour I detest, although I like smoked meat. Milling cheese, then smoothing it out with emulsifiers is all right for children's lunches, but somehow it does not seem fair to foist them off with processed cheese when so many fine straight ones exist for their education and pleasure.

The best till last. Parmesan, Parmigiano – the 'heavyweight champion of the cheese world' (writes Sandy Carr in *Cheese*). The wheels can reach seventy pounds in weight and are very costly. I am with those Italians who eat it as a table cheese. A three-year-old *grana* with crusty, hard-wheat, stonebaked, fresh bread and a glass of young red wine has few rivals. A wheel of Parmesan is the archetypal salt-rubbed mature cheese. The rind becomes very hard and smooth, the cheese within has less salt and a far sweeter body. It also has less fat. Sbrinz, virtually its Swiss equivalent (the difference in flavour probably relates to pasture) is probably Pliny's *caseus helveticus*. It is difficult to find outside Switzerland.

Parmigiano Reggiano, named from the province of Parma in the region of Emilia Romagna, is the Parmesan prototype. *Grana* becomes the aged grating cheeses *vecchio*, extra old, *stravecchio*, finishing, *typico*, the last about five years of age.

At its peak, when cut, or rather broken, the surface is granular. On one occasion in Australia, when he had completed my order of wine barrels, a cooper took me to lunch round the corner at an Italian restaurant. It was a long lunch, and the restaurant had all but cleared. I was raving about Parmigiano and why was it not served as a table cheese; at which the proprietor disappeared. He was soon back, with a huge black rinded wedge of new split cheese, minute crystals glistened like sugar on the rim of a Daiquiri glass. We did it justice in taste talk till the sun set.

The area near Rome produces another famous hard cheese: Romana. Pecorino Romana is made of the milk from ewes, vacchino of cows, and caprino of goat. Pecorino Sardo is from Sardinia, which is another dimension. Despairing of surviving a *mistral* on a racing yacht off Sardinia, Joy and I mutinied and were cast ashore on the Costa Smeralda. For a whole week we had to put up with turquoise water and white sand; and incredibly strong Sardo, the large flat hard unleavened stonebaked *carta di musica* (so called because the cracks resemble staves on music paper), washed down with wine from grapes picked on Monday, bottled on Saturday, and thereafter copiously quaffed and not talked about. The wild honey smelt of the myrtle-covered hills, and was all but fed to us by curious bees which buzzed around our heads.

There is a geography of flavour, inside the cheese itself, which is not unlike that in some meats and fruits. This is very clear in the blues, and those with good manners cut a wedge rather than scoop the lovely blue centre out for themselves. The flavour of the cheese, rather than the mould flavour, is usually stronger near the rind. The organisms in soft cheese work inwards from the crust, hence the most development of flavour is there. Such cheeses, if too thick or too old, may develop an ammoniacal character on the centre, to the detriment of flavour. All the strong-smelling varieties show this character increasingly with age. To most palates, they are at their best about a few weeks old. This is a good argument for 'date of manufacture' on the box, rather than 'use by . . .'

They say little apples are sweet. The paradox of cheese is that the bigger cheeses tend to have a better flavour than the small. To many, the larger Brie has a flavour superior to the smaller Camembert, and yet they differ in manufacturing in no other way but size – another common cheese paradox. Small *makers*, on the other hand, generally make more subtle and complex flavoured cheeses than large companies. If a superb cheese comes from a large company, the odds are it is made by some artisan encouraged to work as an individual. So it is with wine.

Wine and cheese marriages are, like the other kind, made in heaven. Enjoy finding your own. There is room for all palates and persuasions. Here are some suggestions: Stilton with amontillado sherry or Madeira; Cheddar and Parmesan with anything; nutty flavoured cheeses, like Gruyère, with red Burgundy; Camembert with claret; old Cheddars, Edams, with white Burgundy or old dry white wines; Roquefort or other high-flavoured blues with Sauternes.

Old port trade experts got it right when they 'bought on apple and sold on cheese'. Apple sharpens wine appreciation, and cleanses the palate, cheese brings wines into harmony and balance.

Despite commercial pressures, cheesemaking, like that of its historical contemporaries wine and bread, continues to be an art. No matter what advantages science and technology, economy, uniformity and sanitation can achieve, art will prevail. Experience and skill give the human brain the ability to adapt to, and experiment with, biological variations, and that will never be replaced by any effort from a powdered box of chips. Remember we are interrupting natural cycles for our own advantage. During many great, shared bottles and cheeses, my old friend and mentor, Jack Shipton, used to say 'Nature always wins.'

15

The Flavour of Wine

Having considered the complexities of flavour generally, and how they come about, we now come to those aspects of wine, made from the fruit of the vine. The origin of the first wine is lost in antiquity. It may well have been made from dates.

Grapes are among the sweetest and most acidic fruits we have cultivated. Most of the acid converts to sugar late in ripening, and residual and complex acidity gives wine much of its flavour 'lift'. The perfume of the grape flowers in late spring is a heady, ravishing scent. The most extraordinary single moment in the evolution of the mature wine is the instant it casts the spell of its bouquet from the glass across the room. How unbelievable also to enjoy this bouquet at the moment of the wine's conception, so long before the wine itself is to appear in your glass!

There are over 400 flavour compounds in wine, mainly acids, and what a collection they make! The two violets, the vaginal pheromones, IVA and dodecanol, tsetse fly attractant (octanol and acetone), and several powerful fruit, flower and spice fragrances are on the list along with sugars, alcohols, colours and tannins. The last two, the colours and tannins, come from skins, pips and stalks. Whole grapes are fermented to make red wine but except in the case of a few curios, the skins of white wine-grapes are discarded after pressing the fresh fruit, and only the juice is made into wine. Red grapes are fermented on their skins, and the action of the alcohol, which rises as the yeast consumes the grape sugar, produces increasing strengths of colour and flavour. The structure of the wine reflects this. Many rosé wines are made by leaving the red skins in the vat for a very short time. White wines tend to have less depth of flavour and lack the coarseness that comes from the tannins. Tannins mask 'fruit', so that white wines and those reds made with fewer or no pressings often show a forward fruit flavour. Red wines overall tend to have more volume of flavour and 'thicken up' at the finish to the point of bitterness and astringency. Of course this differs from variety to variety and winemaker to winemaker, which is one of the many and endless fascinations of wine. Most of the other tipples that delight the heart lack the wherewithall to cause wonder and discussion of the contents of a glass or two through half the night.

All wines change at a much slower rate when bottled. The bigger the cask or bottle, the slower the rate of development. A half bottle will reach its peak of quality far more quickly than a magnum or double bottle. Age does not necessarily mean high quality. When Dorothy Parker heard of the death of President Coolidge she asked, 'How could they tell?'

The main wine styles are best explained by reference to European wines, because that is where it all began. Claret is made from red Bordeaux grapes, cabernet sauvignon and its cousins. Red Burgundy is made solely from the pinot noir. South-western Germany and Alsace produce riesling white wines, and white Burgundy derives from the chardonnay variety. Beaujolais is made of the gamay grape, and the Rhône Valley reds from syrah (Hermitage) and up to nine other varieties.

Sauternes is made south of Bordeaux, with a lot of sugar left unfermented in the wine. Champagne is made twice, the first time of pinot and chardonnay varieties, solo or mixed, from the Champagne region, with all the sugar fermented out 'dry'. This means all the sugar available for fermentation by yeast has been used up. In terms of flavour it is the opposite to sweet. (Alcohol and fruit flavour both impress the palate as 'sweet', but such wine may test 'dry', that is, with no available sugar.) Then, in the second process, this wine has sugar and yeast added, after which it is sealed in the bottle to undergo another ferment. The bottles are 'turned' constantly, and in due course sparkling Champagne is ready for our pleasure.

Some varieties of grapes have such characteristic flavour notes as to need special consideration. Two of them, muscat in white wines and cabernet in reds, are sufficiently dominant to sustain their individuality wherever they may be grown, and to be clearly picked up in small quantities in a wine blend. Muscat is unique; it justifies its own name as a flavour style, as have, for example, clove and musk. Nothing tastes precisely like them; they are inclined to be intense, and they cannot be truly duplicated by a mix of other natural flavours.

It is worth spending some time on the flavour of the cabernet grape and its wine. Many would agree that it is the most complex of all wines. (Another contender is the white wine grape, chardonnay, but it will be more illuminating to look at its wines later, in the context of climatic influences on flavour.) The illustrious reputation of the red wines of Bordeaux, 'the Englishman's claret' (and copiously imbibed by several queens and other ladies), rests squarely on cabernet sauvignon and its cousins. At its peak of development in bottle, its superlative flavour can reduce an admirer to silent awe.

When ripe enough to make great wine, in the so-called 'good years', the grapes of this variety are almost sticky sweet and taste of ripe blackcurrants. In lesser years or in cool conditions, the IMP, cut green grass smell, is apparent. Everyone likes the berry character, but if it is too obvious there is often doubt about the capsicum/bell pepper aroma that can arise. At the grape crusher, the stalks of the really ripe bunches give off a lovely almond character, the harbinger of outstanding potential.

Almost as soon as the wine has finished fermenting and is quiet in the vat, a special base note appears. It recalls the actual smell of a dusty country back road in midsummer. Some call it musty. It seems to merge with another occasional note, the aroma (not the pungency) of freshly cracked black pepper. I wonder if the musty, dusty note transcends to 'truffles', seen in the very great years. Other fruit flavours are sometimes apparent in cabernet wines. Ripe black cherry is fairly specific, but another plummy (as in ripe blood plums) character can be seen in very ripe fruit of this and other varieties.

The developed bouquet of the wine is the most complex of all reds. Remembering that one is unlikely to come across all the following in a single wine at one time, the most typical fragrance of cabernet sauvignon is that of the lovely cedar wood 'cigar-box' and its oil. It can extend to a sandalwood tone. I can be reasonably sure that it develops from the black-currant aroma of the baby wine, because on one particular occasion it was the cedar character which greeted my enquiring sniff of a can of opened black-currant juice that had got 'lost' at the back of a refrigerator shelf for rather a long time. In much the same way, it seems possible that the bell pepper aroma could develop into an attractive light peppermint that is occasionally found in this regal draught. The finest cabernets frequently carry the scent of small flowers, even the fragrance of violets. And truffles. Ah, truffles! Rarely comest thou, perfume of delight. Rare and so damnably expensive. The nose of the greatest wines can be ravishing. The various fragrances of the cabernet family are listed, with others, on the next page.

Climate in general and the season in particular have critical influences on wine flavour. Awakening from its winter sleep, the vine spends the next half year fulfilling the programme promised by its name. The seasons flavour the wine that follows, but it should never be forgotten that nature intends making vinegar, and that the winemaker interrupts this natural cycle with varying degrees of skill.

Let us now look at the wines of the chardonnay grape as we travel from the cool Champagne region southwards to more ardent climates. The taste of still wines of the chardonnay variety in this area is generally so meagre that it is scarcely recognisable. As we move south to Chablis, the characteristic flavours of the variety start to appear. There has been a quite definite change in the style of the wines of many of the best marques of Chablis since 1975. The classic Chablis was often made in difficult years and used to be somewhat understated in the volume of its flavour. It was characterised by a firmness, even hardness, of finish that the more dramatic writers called flinty. (Taste of sucked pebbles, smell of flint being struck, or what?) That is becoming less relevant now; with later picking and other modifications, the Chablis of today often tastes like a Meursault, between Corton and Montrachet in size – that is, in 'thickness' or volume of flavour on the palate.

Next stop in our flavour travelogue lies about an hour's drive south, to the hill of Corton. Chardonnay there hits one of its peaks of development, so that some see justification for the muted claim that it may be among the very best of its breed. The ripe melon

Typical Wine Flavours

These are memory hooks only. You may well perceive them differently. Not all occur at the one time.

	Aroma of the grape	*Bouquet of the wine*
White grapes		
Muscat	Typical, intense	Rose, geranium, spicy
Traminer	Carnation, clove	Spicy
Riesling	Tropical fruit, guava, lychee, and so on	Continues
Semillon	Ripe green-skinned small fruits, like gooseberry	Fresh straw, fruity, honey
Sauvignon blanc	Capsicum, bell pepper	Spicy, intense, honey
Chardonnay	Citrus peel, grapefruit, bergamot, lime, fig, melon	Peach, apricot, quince, hazelnut, butter, cinnamon, honey
Red Grapes		
Cabernet sauvignon*	Blackcurrant, bell pepper, capsicum, dusty-musty	Cedar oil, cigar-box, sandalwood, various small berries and flowers, mint, pepper (odour), truffles, cherry
Pinot noir	Ripe fruit	Strawberry, cooked beetroot, little flowers
Gamay	Raspberry	Persists
Shiraz, Hermitage	Blackberry	Ripe fruit, pepper (odour)

*and colleagues Cabernet Franc, Merlot, Malbec, Petit Verdot

Oak	
Limousin	Vanilla, chocolate
Nevers	Resinny, lemon
Memmel	Orange peel
American	Floral

(honeydew?) and fig flavour that chardonnay sometimes gives, even if understated, characterise the great years of Corton Charlemagne. They are among the longest living and slowest developing of the white Burgundies.

Moving south, just out of Beaune, reveals a further flavour dimension. In a few of the Meursaults and in Puligny and Chassagne Montrachet, one starts to see the richness of which chardonnay is capable, plus a new development. There is plenty of 'honey' in a wine of the right season, but now there is a stone fruit note, identifiable as peach or apricot, and often more than a hint of hazelnuts. There may be a citrus peel note also, ranging from grapefruit to lime. But it is in Macon, with its even more generous climate, that one encounters the upfront, generous chardonnays that chauvinist wine poets start to endow with the mammary dimensions of Hollywood legends. Rich and fruity, they can become quickly overblown with little potential for improvement. They tend to be 'drink-now' wines and are generally knockout value for money. In California, there is a further magnitude of ripeness, where the fruit in appropriate years is allowed almost to turn to raisins on the vine with the development of a sweetish mould ('noble rot'). These grapes make a luscious thick charmer of a wine. A similar and far more classic style is made from other varieties in Sauternes and the Rhine and Mosel valleys. Rare and often single berry selection, they can be understandably costly.

Water gets into the grape *via* natural rain or by the hand of man. At ripeness the grapes, unless they are tough-skinned cabernet, will surely split from too much of a good thing. The flavour dilutes as it distends and good wine cannot be made beyond a certain point. The production of grapes per acre is therefore controlled in the best areas, by law for the greedy, and by design by those who understand their fruit. The best intensity and balance of flavours comes from vines that produce in the low to medium range of their ability. However, the varietal characters of some grapes are so strong that good flavour is possible at a somewhat higher rate of production. But there is always a cut-off point. Cabernet sauvignon makes its best wine at about one and a half tons to the acre in many areas, but outstanding wines have been made at double this rate on occasion. Double this again and there is a phantom; a lot of it, but a phantom.

Yeasts flavour wine. They make alcohol, which gives its own sweetness and body to the wine. But there are many yeasts which make an individual contribution. Odours range from tropical fruit to bready. 'Yeasty' is its own specific character. Those with desirable qualities are cultivated by master technologists. Some are even given names that recall their breeding place, like Montrachet, Champagne and so on. Dial-a-yeast. The trouble is that yeasts reproduce so actively they miss their stroke and occasionally mutate to produce large amounts of volatile acetates and rotten-egg gas, to name but two of their less desirable metabolic products. The carpet of yeast *flor* (Spanish, 'flower') that floats on top of sherry in cask gives a lovely nutty note to finos.

Wooden barrels make two distinct contributions to wine flavour: the flavour of the timber itself, and a control of the oxidation in the wine by the passage of air in, and wine out, of the pores of the staves. Up to

15 per cent of the wine is lost yearly in this way. Controlled oxidation continues at a lesser rate in bottle for the entire life of the wine. All new oak storage imparts several flavours. Among them are vanilla, wood resin, a 'toasty' quality, sweetness, acidity, wood pigment and tannins. One of the principal flavours is the 'whisky' lactone, so called for its addition by dropper (not in Scotland!) in some countries, to heighten flavour. It provides a natural emphasis of the middle part of the flavour of the wines of cabernet sauvignon. Some of the greatest single variety wines in the world would be unremarkable without the Lautrec silhouette of their fruit provided by this oak lactone. And I include the great pinot noirs of Burgundy, merlot of Petrus, and even the occasional Medoc. Mind you, cabernet naturally has that note, easily verified in a wine that has not seen wood. The oak of different forests has different textures and flavours. In 1968, early in my winemaking career, putting wine from the same batch into barrels of twelve different oaks was a revelation. This is the best way to find the ideal marriage of wine and wood for a particular vineyard.

The development of wine is characterised by the change of the aroma of the fruit to the quite different bouquet of the wine that takes place by a process of limited oxidation. The word complexity is often used in the description of the flavour of better wines. Here, from Professor Vernon Singleton of the University of California at Davis, is the mathematics of it. Consider just the four main alcohols of which ethyl alcohol, what we know as 'alcohol', is the principal one. With age in bottle they slowly oxidise to aldehydes. Those in turn yield acids which combine or make esters, with some of the original alcohols resulting in numbers of these esters. As many as twenty-eight different flavours have sprung from the first four, and these are only a fraction of the 400 already identified.

Age, of course, is no guarantee of quality. Look at the people around you. It used to be thought that to go the distance and to improve on the journey a red wine had to be huge in size and hard as the hobs of hell. Not so, some of the greatest wines are eminently drinkable in their youth. Watch the progress of the relatively soft, fruity wines of the '82 Bordeaux. Vintage white wines develop on their acidity and red wines on their colour and tannins, but they also need acid to develop. Balance is the key to a good wine. Harmony between alcohol, acid, fruit and oak (if any) flavour and tannin, none predominating. Such a wine lasts and develops more flavour. Elegance in a wine implies a substantial fruit flavour in the company of only a moderate amount of alcohol. A high alcohol big-fruit wine may be balanced, but it is not elegant. Finesse is a function of the new intelligent brain. It is the perception of 'infinite' complexity that is understated. There is an implication of restraint in all the aspects of its greatness.

There is an intimidating range of off odours possible in wine, just as there is in any living thing. The most common one is the flattening of flavour by excessive oxidation and you can easily demonstrate this. See Chapter 16, 'Start to Taste'. A sharp vinegary taste is the prelude to complete conversion. So many great wines preferred at masked tastings have a touch of combined sulphur that there must be a variable acceptance of this flavour. The average threshold is 0.1–0.2 micrograms per litre. Anything above that is a problem. Any good book on winetasting (Michael Broadbent's is a classic) will tutor you on the others. And what in truth is a great wine? It is:

A wine that reeks of fruit before, during and after you drink it;
a wine that has improved and lasted;

a wine that is balanced;
a wine that delights you.

If it smells and tastes great, it is great. You don't need anyone to tell you.

16

Start to Taste, Training and Talk

There is no absolute palate

So many people
So many faces
So many palates
Oz Clarke, at the 'Cork & Bottle'

We have all come upon a flavour that was hauntingly familiar, and yet could not be named. Scarcely possible, without the correct memory tag. When you can put a word to a smell even once, you are unlikely to forget it. Taste is not a constant. Dr Morley Kare has observed that the salt threshold can change within six weeks. One of Dr Oliver Sacks's patients on a drug high suddenly developed extreme acuity of smell. This lasted for three weeks, then clicked back to 'normal'. Odour associations are learned, few are genetic.

This chapter aims to solve the enigma by an everyday, family and friends approach. Its purpose is to get people talking, to improve palates and communication by setting up a series of comparable flavours. If there seems to be an emphasis on coffee, it is because several sorts are usually easily available; the flavours tend to be subtle, yet distinct; and with milk or cream, an extraordinary flavour principle is demonstrated. If you don't appreciate coffee, tea works well, although the milk/tea interaction is far less interesting. The wine experiment is about wine flavour generally, and has another fundamental principle or two to impart. Honey is great to introduce children to thinking and talking about taste. Listen to them!

Among dozens of foods, and tens of thousands of wines, I have done tastings of oil (with pieces of bread), green salad herb tastings, apple tastings, water tastings, fish tastings, and so many others, and found in each something to learn and enjoy. Form or join a group of interested people if you have not already done so. Don't be too shy. Professionals do not always get it right, even to knowing whether they are tasting the same flavours as each other, let alone discussing them. We are at a developmental stage in this new science, and these activities will speed up our application of it.

Saying what you mean is one thing, but not having a clear idea of what you mean is another. On top of this are all sorts of factors one may not be aware of. When the *umami* taste was being investigated, there were major differences in the descriptions of this character by Japanese and Americans, depending on their cultural experience; for instance, 'salty', 'seaweed', 'indefinite', 'fishy', 'beef fat', and so on. You will notice a wide range of description in discussion of food flavour by those around you. In addition to cultural reasons, it will become obvious that people actually taste the same substance differently on different occasions. There may be odour blindness – for 'burnt', for example (15 per cent have that). Or you may have episodes of exceptional sensitivity. One can learn to adapt. The absolute palate does not exist except in machines. And those are not the last court of appeal.

When you are discussing tastes, don't waffle. If it is something you recognise, but can't put into words, say so and leave it at that until you can get someone to tell you what it is. It may be possible to state if there is a similarity from something you *are* able to describe, and you should express some preference or aversion.

Language may be part of the problem. People often fail to differentiate and communicate the sensation of taste which comes from the mouth, and that of smell, which comes from the nose. The confusion arises in the widespread use of the word 'taste' to mean 'flavour' (which precisely means taste *plus* smell). A mouthful of food or drink being chewed or sipped can be *smelt* as its odour passes up the back of the nose. Much of Chapter 20, 'The Three R's', elaborates all this. You do not have to accept completely the meaning of certain words you agree to share, provided you say so, and if possible, why. I don't know what astringent and bitter mean to some people, nor if there is any difference perceived by them; there seems to be a borderland where they are interchangeable at a particular intensity. There are some words peculiar (to put it mildly) to the trade or art concerned. It helps to know that these exist, even if you avoid them. For clarity, have a talk with a ten- or twelve-year-old. Children's comments on flavour, or any other complex subject for that matter, are absolutely fascinating. Listen and you will learn. Learn, teach and share.

You may find one particular professional technique helpful. It is called flavour profiling, and is exactly that. The characters of a particular food or drink you wish to assess are set out as if around a clockface. The centre of the clock is the zero point, the radius ten points. You end up, after rating the components, with a kind of starburst.

The children could tick their own preferences at a

Flavour Profile of Two Coffees

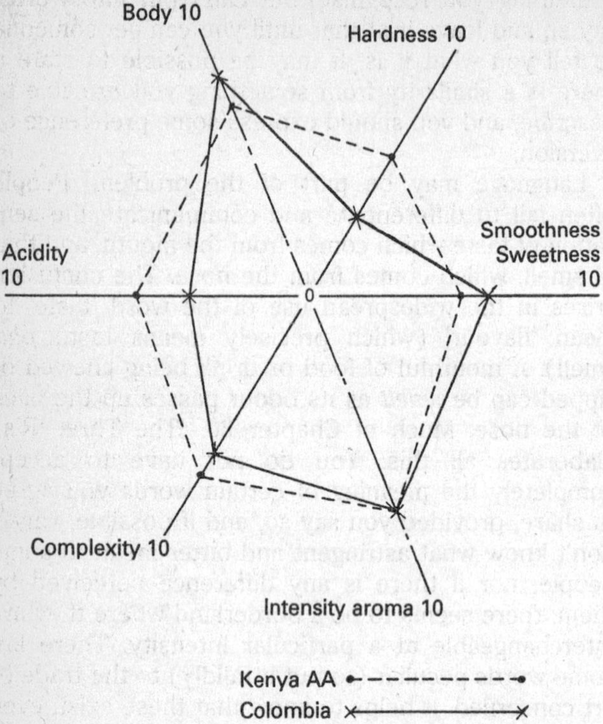

simpler level (see next page).

There are many variations of this technique, even three-dimensional ones, as far beyond me as three-dimension chess is. They do have the value of leaving a permanent visual record. The method is applicable to any food, and it does show up personal differences.

Don't feel crushed by the apparent difficulties confronting you. 'Oh, I could never do that!' You are likely to feel suddenly and unexpectedly at home in the new world. Everyone who learns a new skill finds

Flavour Statement for Children

this. The greatest jazz pianist I know has had the same experience with music. My own initiation progressed slowly over years of wine judging, but I reached a peak one day sitting before forty 'identical' barrel samples of the new vintage at Lake's Folly. I sniffed back and forth along the line of glasses of wine, then tasted each. They were difficult to separate. About half an hour had passed when suddenly they started to fit into place. Exposure to air had opened them up, no doubt, but my discrimination had also clicked into a new phase. I never had the same kind of difficulty again. So stick at it, the rewards are unbelievable.

Wine

Wine flavour was detailed in the previous chapter. What follows is a more general tasting approach.

For a start, the beginner might care to remember three important preliminaries. First, good air – no perfume or tobacco (though as an international wine judge who was a smoker, I believe that smoking only seriously affects the judgment of nearby non-smokers), furniture polish, or other intrusive smell. Second, good light – daylight or white light – to see through the wine and check its colour. Third, good glasses – clear, clean and colourless, with the rim narrower than the waist to concentrate the bouquet.

When you start to taste, begin with a look. Inspect the colour and clarity. Then smell. Sniff with concentration, repeating the process until you really know what the wine smells like. Swirl the glass, even shake the wine up, to release the volatiles. Finally, taste. First get a general feel of the wine, and then suck air in with your mouth slightly open to swirl the mouthful. (This sounds risky, but you will only choke the first few times.) This method gets the wine fragrance to the top of the back of the nose, where it counts. Finally, spit it out, if you don't want to intoxicate yourself with a series of wines. It is socially OK world-wide to spit carefully into waste vessels at formal tastings. You should keep going back to wines you have already tasted, particularly the reds, as they change character fairly rapidly in the open glass. Talk about them. Communicate. Be as precise as you can.

Ask yourself two quick questions to assess quality and longevity. First, how long does the bouquet haunt the empty glass? That of ordinary wines doesn't last long. Second, assess its future. Keep trying the quality, for as long as twenty-four hours if necessary. The longer the wine stays good in the glass, the longer will its life be in bottle.

We can now set up a test tasting for a few single wine components, to learn how they influence the perception of flavour. The list can be expanded when you have more experience. Sip plain water between each, to clear the palate and to assist the contrast of flavour. Sometimes there is not much in it, and the plain water helps to make a clear separation between two similar tastes.

Start with alcohol, ethyl alcohol, SVR from a pharmacy or scientific supplies merchant. Make a solution of 10 or 12 per cent in water, that is about one part absolute alcohol to eight or nine of water. If alcohol is impossible to obtain, neutral vodka will do;

make it up to a similar strength, after checking the percentage of alcohol on the label. First, smell the mix. It smells sweet, even fruity. Taste it. It tastes sweeter, and 'thicker' than plain water. This is much of the 'body' of a wine. And above 11 or 12 per cent, delicate palates will start to get a feeling of warmth in the mouth. There is little or no aftertaste.

Tartaric acid, the main wine acid, can be bought from big supermarkets, health-food shops or home-brewing suppliers. Mix and stir to dissolve with hot water, using enough acid crystals to cover a small coin in 500 ml (about 1 pint) of water. This should make a solution of no more than 0.4 per cent. Taste it. There is a harsh acidity (dilute it with water if it is too strong), and the taste finishes with a hard sensation.

Palate Length

When do you feel Malic and Tartaric Acids in your mouth?

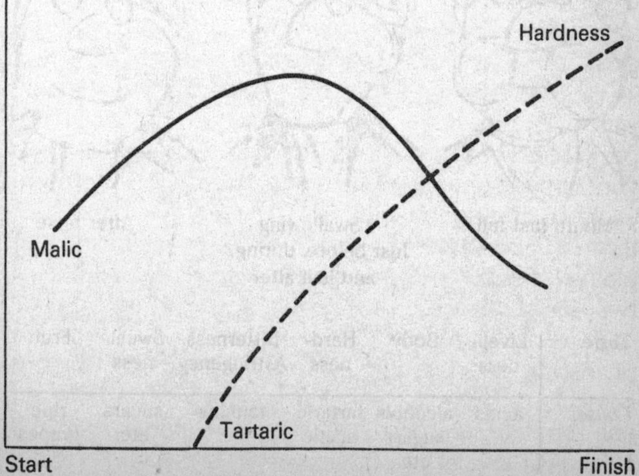

Malic acid is available from the same sources, or from scientific supplies merchants. Mix and stir to dissolve in hot water, using enough crystals to half cover the coin in 500 ml (about 1 pint) of water. This is 0.2 per cent or less. There may be a slight apple smell with some batches of malic acid. It has a pleasant acid flavour, filling the mouth early on, and it does not linger, at least in the strengths in which it exists in wine.

Now take one or two teaspoons of vinegar in a cup of water, dilute with more water if too strong. Smell it; there is a strong characteristic odour. Tasted, there is a sharp acidity, a lift of flavour, and then a hard finish to the flavour, even harder than that of tartaric acid. Finally, there is a lingering aftertaste, when the mouth is empty.

Where Do the Tastes in Wine Arise?

Mouth just full | Swallowing Just before, during, and just after | After taste

Taste:	Liveliness	Body	Hardness	Bitterness Astringency	Sweetness	Fruit
Cause:	acids	alcohols sugars etc.	tartaric acetic	tannins	sugars etc.	ripe grapes

Cut a few slices of apple and orange, leave uncovered for twelve hours, and then compare with fresh-cut slices. Apart from the browning effect of oxidation on the surface of the old apple slice, there is a remarkable change in fruit flavour. There is a flat taste and a different odour quality. This is caused by oxidation. Now try a glass of good wine, perhaps with some fruit or cheese, as a reward. *Bon appetit.* The day moves on.

That is the beginning. Wine is so many things. If it wasn't so complex we wouldn't talk about it so much, and would just pour it down, like beer or ardent spirits.

Honey

Honey is the saliva of the stars
Pliny

The ancients related the gift of honey to the early morning activity of bees. It is a syrup, a fragrant essence of flowers, collected by worker bees, and cured and ripened to honey as we know it, in wax combs in the hives. Honey smells of the flower source, sometimes exactly what you expected, and easily identifiable. Sometimes they are quite different. Citrus blossoms, orange in particular, provide delightful honey. If you live in a city, check around the health-food shops and larger department stores for varieties. Quite possibly an hour or two's drive from the centre of your town will reveal local, special honeys, and those beekeepers always know where another special source exists. Most of them are flavour enthusiasts. I managed years ago to gather together over twenty separate honeys for my family to taste as a single Sunday morning exercise. The range in Australia is vast; the eucalypt honeys provide a spectrum nearly impossible to cover in detail. Probably the best, and among the most delectable anywhere, is honey from the yellow box tree, for which the beautiful town of Mudgee is justly famous. Columella, the classic writer on agriculture and much else, tells us:

> Thyme yields honey with the best flavour; the next best are Greek savory, wild thyme and marjoram. In the third class, but still of high quality, are rosemary and our Italian savory. Next the flowers of the tamarisk and the jujube-tree and the other kind of forage which I suggest have only a mediocre flavour. The honey which is considered of the poorest quality is the woodland honey which comes from dirty feeding-grounds and is produced from broom-trees and strawberry-trees, and the farm-house honey which comes from vegetables.

The special herb honeys of the Mediterranean are ravishing; the thyme, savory and marjoram character of Hymettus, rosemary blossom honey, the myrtle honey of the wild bees of Sardinia, the list of the special flower fragrances of honeydew is endless. You will have much fun finding your own special ones – heather, mango, leatherwood of Tasmania, California sage, and so on.

They vary in colour virtually from white through yellow and brown to black. All but a few crystallise with age, but can be liquefied easily by gentle warming. (Don't overdo it and turn your honey to caramel.) These crystals are basically glucose. Honeys may be almost all sucrose or fructose (hence the more intense sweetness of some honeys high in the latter) or mixes of those and glucose. The food scholar Harold McGee calculates that a bee could do seven million miles on the energy produced in a gallon of honey. Nice one, Harold.

To taste honey, use small squares of bread or toast (multigrain bread enhances the flavour) and some butter or low-fat spread, line up spoons with the jars of honey, and away you go, sniffing and tasting and talking – Sunday morning fun.

Coffee

Professionals use their own coffee terms but anyone tasting a cup of black coffee will notice the aromas, the body of flavour, perhaps the acidity, and the bitterness of finish. There are over 400 identified components of coffee aroma. They are complicated by the results of the roasting process, much as happens with wine during fermentation and ageing. This is the alchemy that transforms the building blocks of 'roast' and 'caramel' flavours into coffee aroma. It may not be practicably possible to recreate this exactly, for the same reasons that apply to wine and other complex food flavours. Many *hope* it never will be.

Coffee aromatics are highly volatile, starting on their path to air even as the roast beans cool. They retain an acceptable degree of quality for a week or two at best, unless consigned at once to an airtight container, or to the freezer, which is where I keep my beans. It is difficult to imagine true coffeeholics buying ground coffee unless they live within a fast walk of a good coffee shop, or very quickly use up a vacuum-packed tin. The start of the art of enjoyment of coffee is to grind one's own supply of freshly roasted beans, with the risk, of course, of driving everyone crazy with the aroma within smelling range. Some true coffee freaks roast their own green beans, but that is another story. Be assured it is difficult to get an even roast with home gear.

The length of the roasting process is critical to

flavour. A light roast gives an almost 'milky cocoa' lightness. Various degrees of medium brown roast perform their Maillard and caramel magic to hit the apex of odour complexity. A little longer in the oven, and the oil starts to become apparent on the shiny dark beans. This is the start of the release of the acid, which is completed in the black over-roast, with not much except bitterness left. There may be a smoky tone to such coffee, especially if taken cold. It is rather similar to Lapsang Souchong tea, if you like that character. The oil sustains whatever sweetness exists in the berry, and when it goes, the bitterness is even more pronounced. That comes from the alkaloids of which caffeine forms the largest proportion.

One interesting character released by roasting was initially noted in some coffees exported from Rio de Janeiro; thus called Rioy. For want of a better description, I liken it to the halogens, iodine, bromine, and so on, the smell of the old-style hospital casualty department. It is not well regarded, but one finds traces of it in some of the top coffees, where it probably increases the complexity of flavour. That specific character is also rarely seen in red wine.

Aroma is actually what the daily enjoyer of coffee buys. The manufacturers of instant coffee know this; pull the airtight seal off the newly purchased container, and hey presto – all your expectations are fulfilled. But with the exception of the best freeze-dried instant coffees, that delicious honeymoon is followed by a boring awakening, as the aroma is rapidly lost once the container is open.

The acidity of any food is rarely thought about. Its influence is discussed at various points in this book, but its effect is perhaps more obvious in black coffee than most everyday foods. It gives briskness of flavour. As with wine, a high acid coffee is sharp and sprightly, and a low acid one, broad and flat-flavoured. The average pH (a measure of available acidity: pH7 is neutral) of coffee is 5.1, more acid than milk (6.6), less so than wine (3.3 ±) or lemon juice (2.3). Small-sized beans tend to show high acidity (remember the effect of roasting on acid), which is perhaps why medium and large beans are more popular as single-variety coffees, and why the small beans are used to such good effect to lift the flavour of blends.

Ethiopian mocha is a high-acid coffee. Costa Rica, and the eleven or so mochas of the Horn of Africa and the Yemen (perhaps the historical perfume kingdom of Punt), are the most important high-acid coffees. The Mocha region, divided by the Red Sea, is the cradle of the cult of coffee. Spread by medieval Islam throughout Europe, it has become perhaps the most important world trading commodity after oil. *Coffea Arabica* began there, and remains the most subtle and complex coffee. *Coffea Robusta*, a high-producing clone, has a broader flavour, and substantially more caffeine. It is very difficult to know precisely what you have purchased when setting up a tasting. You must buy from a trustworthy merchant. Coffee professionals are exactly as other mortals, good and bad, moral and immoral. A skilful forger can get very close to the real thing. Take care particularly with Jamaica Blue Mountain coffee, of which there is far more sold than the seventy tons produced annually. Price is some indication, particularly if it has come through Japan, which buys 98 per cent of the crop. It is by far the most expensive coffee in the world. Medium roasted, the true mountain coffee is less than full bodied, and may need up to twice the usual amount to make a 'good' cup. I searched for it over a period of years and on one occasion I bought a pricey tin of beans at a specialist shop in St Helena, California, of all places, only to leave it behind when I returned the car to Mr Avis on leaving the Napa valley. It was becoming increasingly obvious that I might never taste the stuff.

Years later, in Tokyo, I tried again. Sometimes, among the many carefully prepared cups of coffee, one might come up as rather special. When that particular one was also expensive, it seemed the trail was hot. The first certainty was a specialist coffee-shop in Shinjuku. They had Blue Mountain on the list of coffees available; it was five times the price of other excellent coffees on the list; the place was redolent of fresh-roasted, fresh-ground coffee; it was small; the omens were good. The tables around the wall of the sit-down section were occupied. The buzz of earnest conversation, the English of which occasionally drifted across, was punctured by the staccato of some high-powered technocrats, computer designers, fashion people. I sat alone at a table in the centre waiting for my so-expensive JBM. Naturally the coffee cups in the shop were part of the Japanese ceramic experience; all different, and any single set of them one would be proud to own.

My order arrived. It came in fluted, fine, almost transparent white porcelain of a delicacy not seen before outside a museum or an antique shop. Lovely to the lips, as we say. I sniffed, I sipped. 'That's it, now I know what all the fuss is about.' It was exactly the same reaction as that in a cellar at Beaune in 1977, when I tasted my first authentic Montrachet, reportedly the best white Burgundy wine in the world and certainly among the most rare and expensive.

I clicked back, aware of silence; the coffee shop was hushed, approving eyes on the foreigner in the process of acquiring an expensive education. My white porcelain set me aside, of course. How Japanese the subtlety to match the vessel to the contents. Not quite sure how to handle the situation, I debated between standing with fists clasped high above head, or perhaps remaining seated with a modest smile, eyes slightly to one side and downcast. The latter seemed appropriate. Conversation resumed, and I slowly enjoyed the coffee, and the cup. I have since had real JBM, as far as one can be certain, on less than half the occasions I have ordered it in coffee shops claiming to serve it.

Was it worth the effort? If you are among those who are ready to enjoy the best, and are prepared on rare occasions during your lifetime to spend an exorbitant amount to taste something even better, yes. Only a little bit better, but an experience. I can put together a coffee blend for daily use which I enjoy as much, for less than a fifth the cost of JBM. And as the Baron Philippe of Mouton Rothschild once said, 'It is important to drink other quality wines, because if I took Mouton every night, it would become ordinary.'

The actual flavour body, size, thickness, mouthfeel, varies in coffees of different regions. Andean coffees, like Colombian, are dominated by breadth of flavour with softness; African coffees, like Kenya AA, have a fairly broad flavour, with hardness. Lighter bodies are characteristic of coffees from the West Indies, Indonesia and New Guinea. All of these vary both in the time the beans are stored after fermentation, and in the cleaning of the raw beans, usually a year or two before sale. Flavour body improves during that period, to the extent that specially aged coffees of particular areas attract an unbelievable premium. They may be stored for up to eight years, in 'parchment' (with husks) and then hulled to order on sale.

There are some superb single coffees, besides Jamaica Blue Mountain; Kenya AA; Costa Rica and mocha, both of which suit those who prefer a lifted flavour; and the real Hawaiian Kona coffee, to name but four.

The last can be a problem. It is sold in the Honolulu airport departure lounge as packets of fresh roasted beans. I had one of the best cups of coffee in my life in a back street in Honolulu, and enthused to the proprietor. 'Could I get some?' He gave me the name of the San Francisco blender who flew him a fresh roasted coffee blend every morning.

When you are buying coffee, look at bean size, colour and oiliness; try to smell the beans themselves, if permitted. The sales people get used to it, and anyone with pride in their merchandise is usually delighted to find someone so involved. I avoid shopping where I can't smell things. A lot of people in my local fruit market are now converted and ardent sniffers.

To prepare good coffee for a comparative tasting you should observe three rules. 1. It should be freshly roasted. 2. It should be fresh ground, coarse, medium or fine depending on your method of making. Make it strong, up to two tablespoons per six-ounce cup. 3. Allow three to five minutes contact with good quality water just under boiling point (in an espresso machine, under one minute).

The water must be tasteless. Buy it in bottles if you have to, at least for this tasting. Start with cold water and ground coffee, and bring them to the boil over a few minutes. Watch the surface and, just as it starts to seethe, tip in about half an egg-cupful of cold water and stir as you take it off the heat. This is the 'campfire' method, than which there is none better. The coffee does not need straining, if you are using a medium to coarse grind. This method is suitable for our tasting, but if you have too many coffees for your pots, just pour the boiling water over the grounds in a cup. Wait five minutes, and spoon off any floaters. If you have made it too strong, it can be diluted to taste with hot water. Too weak and you can't taste much at all.

Each participant tastes from a spoon. Smell, taste and talk. If you can get an experienced taster to lead the discussion, so much the better.

Here are some of the descriptions professionals use (with thanks to the coffee broker, Smith's of Johannesburg).

Acidity:	A sharp and pleasing characteristic, particularly strong with certain origins, as opposed to a caustic over-fermented, sour or bitter flavour.
Body:	A strong, full, pleasant characteristic as opposed to being thin, not necessarily acid.
Bitter:	Usually caused by over-roasting.
Coarse:	A raspy, harsh flavour, lacking in finesse.
Grassy:	A grassy, or greenish flavour particularly strong with early crop Arabicas which have been picked prematurely.
Harsh:	A hard, raspy, often caustic flavour sometimes described as Rioy.
Musty:	A flavour often due to poor storage, especially with Robustas. Can be due to lack of sufficient drying and ageing or over-heating. Mustiness due to age is not undesirable.
Rich:	An overall lively, full-bodied flavour.
Rubbery:	Mainly prevalent in Robustas, especially Indonesians.
Soft:	A well-rounded flavour lacking any harshness or acidity.
Thin:	A flat, lifeless coffee lacking any body or acidity, caused by underbrewing.
Winey:	Rich, rounded, fullbodied, with a smoothness characteristic of well matured wine. Prevalent in Colombian coffee.

Now you have tasted and assessed several freshly ground coffees. Try for a blend that suits your preference, or perhaps even to refine your concept of coffee flavour, one for morning perhaps more aromatic, one for evening perhaps more bitter. I generally like to add a small amount, perhaps a tenth, of an over-roast, black bean, still oily, not dry (the latter is just charred wood). I like the lift, and interestingly enough that contribution is more obvious in cold coffee.

Finally, a demonstration of an important flavour principle: the absorption of aromas by fats, and the fall in aroma perception as the temperature approaches zero degrees. This is perhaps the most interesting coffee tasting of all; it needs only one variety and can be done at any time. You will need to make up two lots of coffee, fairly strong, both equally so. Make the first batch, add milk or cream (don't weaken the coffee too much) and allow to cool. Then make an identical batch, and taste the hot and cold coffees side by side; an instructive comparison of flavourings. Then continue intermittently to taste the hot cup till it is just warm, comparing the cold cup each time. An even more striking flavour comparison is possible sometimes when the cold cup gets very cold. Iced coffee improves in flavour as it warms in the mouth and the volatiles are picked up at the back of the nose. The 'coffee' flavour leads to 'fig' and 'walnut', perhaps through to 'chocolate'. Some coffees are so 'chocolate' that you are reminded of cocoa. You will have observed similar major flavour changes in hot and cold phases of the same food. The aromatics may be quite different in the cold dish, as for instance in sausage and meatloaf.

The Options Caper

Probably the most educational flavour exercise, and the most fun, is a food options dinner. This half-wild, exciting creation of the bubbling brain of Ted Davis is put together for one special night a year by the New South Wales branch of the Wine and Food Society of Australia. It takes weeks of work to organise; the cooking is done by the more skilled members of the Society and their amateur assistants. The dinner follows a normal menu pattern, but each course is the subject of one to five questions, more or less as follows:

Canapés	2 questions
Cold entrée	3 questions
Hot entrée	3 questions
Main course	
Vegetable	5 questions
Cheese selection	3 questions
Salad	2 questions
Dessert	2 questions
Coffee	1 question

Each dish offers a set of options. These range from fairly simple and straightforward ones to the more complicated. On cheese, for instance, the option may simply be 'There are three cheeses, one is Australian. Is it A, B or C?' Whereas those presented on the subject of the salad might be more complex: 'There are six greens in the salad. How many kinds of lettuce, one, two or three?' 'Is the oil in the dressing olive, walnut or grapeseed?' and so on. Each table group elects a fearless leader who establishes a consensus, and conveys it to a blackboard scribe at the front of the room.

The tables separate quite early into potential winners and obvious losers, and the competition gets heated; table to table, even spouse to spouse. A good chairman is obligatory. We, for example, have an excellent barrister, an accomplished Thespian like most of his profession. There is a good prize for the best table, and all the elements for bribery, corruption, mayhem and an entertaining night are there. You learn to be clear and accurate, or else. One night a year of that is all that anyone could stand. If you decide to have a go, don't take it too seriously. If it becomes a power thing, remember there is no absolute palate. Oh, and pride goeth before a fall ...

If you wish to pursue this subject, read Jennifer Harvey Lang's *Tastings* (food) and Michael Broadbent's *Pocket Guide to Wine Tasting* (wine). If you have any French, the *Noveau Guide Gault et Milau* tastings are pre-eminent.

17

The Flavour of Japan. One Western View Thereof

To find and enjoy a new flavour adds seventy-five days to your life.

Japanese folklore

The visit of a young Japanese honeymoon couple to Lake's Folly became the inspiration to delve more deeply into the flavours of Japan, to reassess the staples at the core of an important and, as yet, not widely known cuisine. As a would-be flavour professional, I was already aware that there are some obvious differences in the Japanese palate and approach to the pleasures of the table. *Umami* (oomarmi) is but one of these, a fifth perception of taste, in addition to the sweet, sour, salty, bitter notes we all recognise, and which is still something of an enigma outside of Japan. The simple reason is that there is no English word to identify it. A single sensation of 'deliciousness' seems to express it. This taste was first labelled early this century (1908–9) and now has many descriptions. It is that character in foods which produces similar effects to MSG on flavour recognition, seen for example in reduced protein and vegetable stocks, tomato purée, certain mushrooms, soy sauces, grated mature Parmesan etc.

There also seems to be a preference for a higher level of sweetness than is common in the West, perhaps a function of the fact that sugar was virtually unknown to ordinary Japanese until fairly recently. Another important racial difference is that some Japanese lack the enzyme alcohol dehydrogenase, socially useful in Western cultures to speed the metabolism of alcohol.

Previous experiences in Japan had given me a clear idea of both Japanese foods and the entrancing ceramic and lacquerware in which they were served. When Joy and I were able to offer two attractive young visitors an unplanned lunch of a jellied codfish tail, a few snow peas, a flower of broccoli, some unpolished rice, and a dab of green dynamite *wasabi* arranged on handmade tenmoku glazed stoneware (from a previous visit to a Tokyo folk potter), the nostalgia of such unexpected hospitality so far from their homeland opened the floodgates. This started a friendship, one demonstration of which was to be the ultimate manifestation of Japanese hospitality at a dinner at their apartment in Tokyo, when one particular course displayed over sixty different components. The evening concluded with an ambrosial liqueur made from dried ripe persimmon fruit by a grandmother of my young friends. How can you adequately thank anyone so generous?

There can be few ethnic cuisines where so much respect is paid to the primeval forces of nature. M.F.K. Fisher observes that the preparation and serving of fine as well as routine Japanese food is more obviously mixed, than is ours, with other things besides hunger, such as aesthetics, religion, tradition, history, seasonal changes, sea storms, a guest's birthplace, or one's childhood. Consider also the special wooden box to measure the fifteen to twenty gallons of soybeans which will be used to make the next day's *tofu.* It is beautifully formed in the typical fashion of Japanese woodwork, with fine dovetailing or precisely mitred corners. Burnt into one side are images of the deity of craftsmen, tradesmen and fishermen, symbolising hard workers who earn their living by honest toil; and the other, a happy god who is so well off that he does not mind rodents nibbling at his sacks of grain.

There is a north/south rivalry to which any nation can relate, but which is sometimes difficult to understand. The Kyoto locals are said by Dr Umesao to believe that the flavours of their dishes are subtler than anywhere else in Japan.

To get some idea of tradition as it is seen in today's Japan, let me quote from Soei Yoneda, Abbess of the Sanko-in Temple, introduced by Robert Farrar Capon.

> There is, for example, a small plate of assorted cooked vegetables, beautifully arranged: a slice of mashed yam roll in *nori* seaweed, an arrow feather made of burdock root, a slice of lotus root tempura, a piece of simmered *tofu* and three lightly cooked snow peas. There is *rōbai*, a delicious concoction of deep-fried wheat gluten, softened in a soy-flavored stock and dressed with hot Japanese mustard. There is mock *tofu* made of sesame 'milk' and a *nori* roll filled with flavour-simmered spinach and served with a lemon-soy sauce. There is an altogether remarkable steamed savory cup in which grated turnip, chopped rice, ginkgo nuts, *shiitake* mushrooms, carrot slices, snow peas, fried waterchestnut balls and thickened *dashi* stock are turned into a delicate 'custard' punctuated with an emphatic dot of *wasabi* horseradish. There is a starkly simple shredded ginger

tempura, served crisp with mustard-soy for dipping. And there are clear soups and miso soups, and bamboo rice, vinegared turnips and pickled Chinese cabbage ...

Every vegetable, however deftly or mysteriously sauced, tastes first of all like itself – even in dishes where several ingredients are combined. And every presentation, even the most artful (there isn't one that's not: even three bits of fried, shredded ginger on a plate are arranged so as to have a front and back) is worlds away from mere artiness. Everything looks like food meant to be relished by both eye and palate.

The flavour preferences of the ancient and formal culture of Nippon derive from the produce of islands that arise out of bountiful seas. It is rather a small landmass of mountains and fertile farmland to support the needs of many millions of the most diligent and selective individuals on the planet.

Japanese food was traditionally based on grains, sea produce, and greens. It is worth noting that while ever rice was a medium for local barter and payment for labour, the farmers had little or no idea of variety in regional flavours. This changed radically with the establishment of brand differences only a century ago. Rice tended to be eaten at home and *soba* buckwheat was consumed in noodle restaurants. *Tempura* could be bought from street wagons.

Cattle and dairy produce were virtually unknown to the majority of the population, because there was not enough space to farm them, and there were religious objections. Another good reason for the scarcity of cattle, however indelicate the subject, is the simple fact of life that the body odour from a diet of cattle meat and dairy based products, so common in the West, has been offensive, at a cultural level at least, to Japanese sensibilities. No nation in the world spends more time and effort to ensure a natural and almost neutral body smell, and the rancid odour of the unwashed Westerner in confined metropolitan transport (a turn-off even to their own ethnic group) is the pits, and the subject of coarse hunmour. So, no cheese at all, nor milk for adults, until the current adoption of Western foods.

Even as the rest of the world watches in fascination, the tastes of the Japanese people are now shifting from traditional to international, from local and homemade to mass production. Those of us who think about food and flavour and suchlike have much to learn, and perhaps even something to teach. I first visited Japan in 1968, and there have been major changes in a mere twenty years, but my personal experience is limited virtually to the seven towns which have now become modern Tokyo. Foreign food was uncommon, and as an example, an initial careful search of the big department stores turned up about six wines, all of which were less than promising. Prior to that period, I have been told that if any wine was enjoyed, it was as a form of port, a sweet, fortified, locally manufactured product, and the less said about that the better. At that time Western table wines were considered 'too tart, too sour'. A few years ago a similar exercise revealed forty-four local wines, some of which were quite good. Beef was now 'in' to the extent of McDonald's hamburgers, and even Aussie meat pies. Cheese is still not widely found in any but the largest supermarkets, and then mainly where the wealthy, and foreigners, do their shopping.

The waves of Western influence on the austere culture that derived from the imperial court of ancient Tokyo began around the turn of the seventeenth century, with the second late last century. Neither did much to Japanese food preferences, and certainly nothing like the third wave that took place after 1945. It is quite fascinating to learn from Shizuo Tsuji of a reverse thrust: that the secret seasoning of the ceremonial banquets of Louis XIV of France was soy sauce imported to Europe from Nagasaki by Dutch traders! To many Japanese today, Western food has been synonymous with French, with little inspiration from anywhere else. But this is changing rapidly.

Paradoxically, at the same time as English-speaking peoples are turning to leaner meats, the Japanese import and market at centres like Kobe lot-fed beef heavily marbled with fat for extra flavour. (I can never work out what *rubbing* the cattle with beer does. It is probably a bit of foreign leg-pulling.) With the astronomical prices that a fine steak fetches on the restaurant plate in Japan, there is probably not much risk to national health.

Geography is the natural arbiter of flavour. Broadly speaking, intense stimulation from curries, chilli, spices, and suchlike are Equatorial. The milder flavours of animal fats, fish, and herbage derive from cooler zones, with striking exceptions like Szechuan and Korea. Today's commercial transport has blurred the distinctions, and nowhere is this becoming more apparent than in the Japanese islands.

The traditional staples are still to be seen in the flood of Japanese restaurants which now exist world-wide: rice, wheat, and buckwheat noodles; the bounty of the soybean in the form of miso paste, more than three thousand different brands of soy sauces (at one time there were five thousand!), wet (*tofu*) and dried curd, and soybean oil. Japanese food is happily fried in any light, fresh oil, stopping short of olive, which is considered too heavy and flavoursome for the subtlety of traditional dishes. *Tofu* has developed its own circle of connoisseurs, as knowledgeable and devoted as any group of winelovers in the West. Fish leads the vast range of seafoods, either wriggling fresh, barbecued, flaked and smoked, fried, or dumplings. Various kelps and seaweeds head the list of a vast collection of green and growing things.

Freshness of ingredients is a special feature of Japanese food. The only way to appreciate what I mean is to grow one's own vegetables. And as far as seafood is concerned, one should have the privilege of eating at places like Wheelers in London or the Grand Central Station in New York to clearly understand the Japanese pursuit of freshness. Their use of fish is classified by time out of the water. An early morning visit to the Tsukiji fish markets in Tokyo is a relevation, and among the most striking of the market visits I have made. For example, fish to be served as *sashimi* must be absolutely fresh. Any older and it is consigned to various cooking methods that relate to the time since it was landed. The skill and sensitivities of a chef may be judged solely on the care in the selection of the primary ingredients at the market. And this assessment applies equally in the home. You will see the celebrated *fugu*, Pacific puffer fish, auctioned for service later in the day by those licensed to prepare it to those adrenalin junkies who take the risk of dying fairly smartly if any quantity of the neurotoxins remain. The last known death was in 1975. Martin Franc reports that seven thousand tonnes of it are consumed yearly!

The large white *Daikon* radish would be near the top of the vegetable list, along with yams and a fascinating collection of mushrooms, shiso leaves (which have tones of mint, aniseed and 'Dr Pepper'-type sarsaparilla), the spice the Chinese call Szechuan pepper (whose pungency lies in the marjoram/sage/thyme area rather than black pepper), *wasabi*, horseradish, garlic, and other members of the onion clan, and ginger. Plenty of flavour interest, but more compact than the range available to equatorial cultures.

Some inquiring Westerners, used to stronger flavours in meat stocks, sauces and so on, may find the natural foods and drinks of Japan tend to be rather low key (the standard stock for noodles is made of shaved flakes of dried bonito fish and kelp). After weeks of a Japanese diet, I find many of the flavours tend to be less assertive than one is used to. I started to see the difference in terms of the colours of the spectrum. The flavours available to the Western kitchen run the gamut from red to purple. The traditional flavours of Japan lie in the more central yellow/green/blue range.

For those who argue they had the best Indian curry of their life in Roppongi, or that the best French food in the world is available on top of the Okura Hotel, look at it this way: where else could you start a meal with five kinds of seaweed on a plate? They all have a common marine flavour, so what is the attraction? They all have a different form, their colours are different, and when you chew them they have a different 'mouthfeel' from slimy to brisk crunch ... that's the attraction. This texture difference is another part of my thesis. Much of the interest and excitement of Japanese flavour lies in the variety of textures available, and it is here that the West has much to learn. This subtlety is one facet of Japanese aesthetics, like the possibilities of *ikebana* based on a single twig, or the curving strokes left by a rake in the white pebbles of an indoor courtyard. And nowhere else will you see such exquisite presentation of food, the zenith of Japanese style. It verges on vandalism to disrupt some of the creations, for which I sometimes try to atone by a flash photo beforehand to serve as a permanent reminder of such inspiration. How many plates in good restaurants and homes around the world acknowledge their debt to the perfection that is inspiring in much everyday Japanese food?

It has been well said, 'show me what you eat, and I'll tell you what you are'. Can the same be true of drink? From Kyushu to Hokkaido (the Nipponese equivalent of from Lands End to John O'Groats), the foreigner gets the impression that an awful lot of *sake* is being consumed. Anyone in a Japanese subway late in the evening, or having a midnight snack of *yakitori*, believes this. But the figures show that there is four times more beer drunk, no doubt because it is very good. Increased wine production from grapes has paralleled their appreciation of its nuances, and I believe this will continue because table wine has about two-thirds of the alcohol of *sake*, and has a far more complex flavour profile. Quite a lot of domestic and imported whisky is taken, and a distilled spirit called *shochu* is a popular tipple because people tend to forget its revolting hangover.

Sake is likely to hold its position while ever tradition and culture retain their importance in Japan. The enjoyment of wine from fruit may have begun by the accidental fermentation of its sugars by yeasts in the air. Monkeys are reputed to ferment grain and drink the result, and elephants are known to make pilgrimages to get tanked up on fermented berries, complete with hangover! *Sake* certainly was made by chewing rice and spitting it into a tub, just as *kava* is made today in the Pacific islands. In the case of *sake*, the enzyme ptyalin in saliva converts starch into fermentable sugars, after which yeasts take over to produce *sake*. In 300 AD *bijinshu* 'beautiful women's *sake*' was made by young virgins who did the chewing. The making of *sake* became part of certain festivals, doubtless fostering a marvellous community spirit. The gods took a special interest in the conversion of rice to *sake*, and it became the drink of choice at weddings, dedications, for special gifts, and to be enjoyed with friends. Today, at table, it is more than polite for your friend to pour your first *sake* cup and to keep it topped up, and for you to do the same. This delightful bit of neighbourliness seems to have translated to cans of beer.

One special evening, Naoya and Yuriko took me to an inn where a wide range of *sake* of different regions and ages was kept. I went through the lot, including one that was fourteen years old and another that either the host or some ancestor had made and treasured. My notes are not clear. Anyhow it was a great honour. As near as I can recall, it seemed to be intended as a tribute to my international reputation as a wine judge. It did not seem fitting to remonstrate that any such reputation was based on the fact that wines being assessed were rarely swallowed, and the substantially higher alcohol of the *sake* was no help. What did strike me was the fact that the range of flavours of even the greatest *sakes* was far less than that of our good creature of the West, wine, and thereby less likely to evoke the discussion and general interest that it does. Again, as with the traditional food, we seemed to come to rest in a limited part of the flavour spectrum. As a final comment on *sake*, its aroma, and that of other rice residuals, typifies, to this traveller, the smell of Japan, in the way, for example, that the aroma of garlic and Gauloises is an intrinsic part of the ambience of rural France.

The range of teas, green and black, is phenomenal. One shop in the maze of independent food stalls under the Ginza has over two hundred. But it is in exploring the coffees in Japan that the keen Western palate experiences its greatest shock. The best coffee is imported and drunk in Japan, without a doubt. They take 98 per cent of the seventy-ton annual production of the rare mountain coffee of the island of Jamaica, and it is available in Japanese specialty shops at about three times the price of lesser coffees, both in an exquisite white shell porcelain cupful of perfectly filtered bliss, or by the kilo of beans.

Which brings us to the current flavour of Japan, in such a state of flux that the observant visitor becomes aware of turbulent transition. The nation's traditional foods, which include the staple grains, greens, and fruits of the seas around the home islands, are meticulously selected for freshness and visual impact, to be presented in a unique style, which individualises flavour and delights the eye. A marvellous mélange with their favoured Western goodies is occurring. And perhaps the best French food in the world is to be found there. As they say in Japan, 'Let little seem like much, as long as it is fresh and beautiful'.

My warmest thanks for the help of Tak Nishizawa, who has absolutely no responsibility for any error or malapropism. Then, perhaps, neither have I. 'I was out of the country at the time.'

18

The Cola Wars

Coca Cola is the sublimated essence of all that America stands for. A decent thing, honestly made, universally distributed.

William Allen Winter in 1938, partaking of Coke on his seventieth birthday.

In 1885, a pharmacist, John Pemberton, registered a trademark for 'French Wine Cola – Ideal Nerve and Tonic Stimulant'. It was widely reputed, at that time, to contain cocaine. A year or so later, caffeine was added; plus an extract of kola nut to improve the flavour. The amount of caffeine in the average cola is about the same as a cup of tea – fifty milligrammes. A cup of coffee is double that. Coca Cola was born, initially to be peddled as a cure for hangovers and headaches. Cocaine was removed from the formula many years ago and the Stepan Company produced a narcotic-free coca flavouring for specific use in the Coca Cola recipe. The popularity of 'Coke' and its rivals and the history of their successes and reverses form one of the most remarkable case histories in the study of flavour.

In 1919, the Coca Cola Company was bought by Ernest Woodruff of Atlanta, Georgia, who has merited his own historians. He is recognised here for his undeviating pursuit of perfection. By rigorous quality control he made certain there was only one genuine Coke taste throughout the world, even though the syrup was bottled in vastly differing conditions. Imagine the variations, for example, in water quality. If you don't understand the size of the problem, any Scotch whisky distiller will tell you about water and product flavour.

During and after the Second World War, Coke was bottled in 155 countries and drunk 3.3 million times a day. Each year, the hypothetical average American drinks fifty gallons, and advertising runs to the tune of hundreds of millions of dollars. The formula of Coke syrup is more carefully guarded than Fort Knox. No more than three people, at any one time, know the accurate ingredient mix. The care taken in its formulation sequence is legendary. Essential oils are of the highest concentration and most expensive quality – 'the real essence'. The code for the classic formula, 7X, was held to be so inviolable, that when the Indian Government, perhaps on the advice of their food standards authority, demanded to know the formula, Coke simply closed down and quit India completely.

In the 1890s, Pepsi Cola was created by another pharmacist from further south, in North Carolina, as a remedy for dyspepsia. After two bankruptcies, the company was bought by Charles Gurth in 1931. The flavour was not to his liking, and he changed the formulation of the concentrate. This is a feature of the Pepsi taste philosophy *vis-à-vis* Coke, who unswervingly maintained consistency of flavour until the centennial débâcle described later.

Pepsi's progress had been impressive in more recent years, but a problem remained. For complicated reasons, the brand image carried a suggestion of hard times. An 'in' joke had it that one drank Pepsi in the kitchen, but served Coke to visitors. If you were to put Coke in a Pepsi bottle, you would starve to death. If you put Pepsi in a Coke bottle, you would get rich quick. When the soft drink TAB was put in a new can labelled 'Diet Coke', there was a meteoric rise in preference, such is the power of the Coke name.

This 'label drinking' is akin to wine snobbery. In blind consumer tests, the public actually preferred Pepsi by a small margin. Big money is involved. A one-point difference in their rating sale means something like two hundred and fifty million dollars in retail sales. Rigorous studies of consumer tastes and preferences were undertaken by both companies. Were palates changing? Market research came up with some of the answers.

Pepsi offered a *choice* in many areas where previously only Coke had been available. It was skilfully targeted on the generation who followed after the 'Cola-colonisation' of the Second World War, and who had not been exposed to logistic marvels like the availability of iced Coke in the impossible conditions of jungle warfare. In a century of increasing expansion, despite advances in flavour technology and changing tastes in the populace, Coke spared no effort to sustain uniformity. In this period Pepsi flavour was altered on at least two occasions, but it was only in 1983, with Pepsi's continued challenge, that taste superiority became the central issue in the battle of the two giants. Coke decided to develop a new formula in an attempt to burnish their image.

In the first taste trials of new Coke, 70 per cent of the children liked it better than the old. Within a few weeks, however, their preference was seen to change, approximating to that of adults, whose assessment had been broadly negative. It is interesting that surveys undertaken by NASA showed that neither Pepsi nor Coke was popular with the astronauts. This took some working out until it was realised the reason was that the samples were drunk *warm.* (Flavour and fragrance in space deserves its own book.) If you think about it, a considerable part of the charm of these drinks, for their addicts, is that they are best drunk chilled. That becomes a further factor in their flavour assessment.

A dispassionate test of Coke and Pepsi is an instructive exercise, to be undertaken with children if possible, and following the general guidelines in the chapter 'Start to Taste'. How do the two look, smell, taste? See the tasting notes on the next page. They have similarities. I would have had difficulty in separating them and stating why, as I did when I first started looking at large numbers of similar new red wines thirty years ago. It is not easy, but if you persevere some differences become apparent. They certainly did so to the professionals, in the run-up to the decisive battle between the two brands. The other table in this chapter (p. 198) is the guess of one small private group of individuals pondering the typical 'cola' flavour (of which, incidentally, there are thirty-two different, but comparable, brands in the United States).

The sweetness factor of diet drinks was to be the key and occupied the chemists' attention for a considerable period. Coke sweetness in the early years was based on sugar, sucrose from cane or beet. Sugar costs became an insurmountable economic problem, which resulted in the use of substantially cheaper high-fructose corn syrup. But there was a problem with fructose – its extra sweetness on the palate.

The question of sweetness opened the question of the huge, critical market of diabetics and weight-watchers. Diet drinks became enormously popular, one of them, Tresca, containing saccharin as its only sweetener. Saccharin's disadvantage is that it has a bitter aftertaste to some, and being re-examined by the American Food and Drug Administration as a

Cola Tasting Notes

	Cola A	Cola B
pH	2.41	2.39
Aroma	—	More aromatic than A
	Orange ++	Fragrant, floral +++
	Kola, perceptible	—
	Spice ++	Spice +++
	Cinnamon, ?clove	Cinnamon
Sweetness	Similar to B	Similar to A, perhaps a touch drier
Acidity	More perceptible than B	—
Mouthfeel	Good, 'full'	Less than A
Finish	Astringent, hard	Smoother than A

potential carcinogen did not help its popularity either. Cyclamates, too, were scrutinised and it was only in 1983 that aspartame, under the brand name 'Nutrasweet', became available. Aspartame and saccharin interact. In a mix, less of each is needed to produce a level of sweetness than would be expected, adding up the quantities of each singly. Simply 1 + 1 = 3. Less of each gave added benefits, both economically and in flavour. The Coke organisation concluded that people cared more about calories than taste. In fact, in a diet-conscious population, as for instance in New York City, low-calorie drinks are twice as popular as in the rest of the United States. This consumer group is very supportive to manufacturers and if calories were the issue, once the problem was solved, it seemed that only the flavours of the different beverages would separate them and they would then be back to square one – *taste.*

The Coca Cola chemists continued their experiments until a product evolved which managed to equal the consumer acceptance of Pepsi, and was therefore considered to be an improvement. By September 1984, the Coca Cola specialists triumphantly, but secretly, reported that there was a 'swing of up to eighteen points'. New Coke rated six clear points better than Pepsi. The swing included results of the previous tests with classic Coke – so Pepsi was being compared to a choice of two Cokes. This fact is worth a closer look. At one level it eliminated the gap between what people said they drank and what they actually did drink, a true preference, formed by different age groups all over the country. But the questionnaire had never made clear to the consumer that classic Coke was not to remain as a *choice*.

As the day of the public launch approached, flavour descriptions were honed. The chief executive officer of Coca Cola, a flavour chemist by training, described the new Coke as 'smoother, rounder, bolder, a more harmonious flavour'. On the other hand, the competition described their drink as follows: 'Pepsi has a more complex and delicate flavour than Coke. It is more aromatic. It tastes a lot smoother. In a harsher cola like Coke you didn't notice the difference between sugar, and half fructose-half sugar. In tests of Pepsi sweetened with the fructose available in 1980, you did.' (Fructose quality improved in the years following, to such a degree that the Pepsi containing it came to be preferred.)

The difference between the two in the amount of sweetness is 'infinitesimal', according to the President of Coca Cola. The sensation of sweet taste became the biggest issue. Compared to classic Coke, the 'bite' of the new Coke was 'smoother'.

This brings the focus on to acidity, the sensation of sourness. 'Smoother' the new Coke may be, *flat* it is, relatively. The flavour chemists had been tinkering with phosphoric acid levels and carbonation. Carbon dioxide makes a weak acid in water, as you will recall from the taste of soda water. Any lowering of the fizz, and therefore the acid level, could have a perceptible

What Actually Is in a Cola?

(This is an inspired guess at cola ingredients and, as they say in the movies, any resemblance to any beverage living or dead is not intended and is purely coincidental.)

Kola nut		
Vanilla	Oleoresin	
Citrus	Essential oil	Orange
		Lemon
		Lime
Spice	Essential oils	Cinnamon
		Cassia
		Nutmeg
		Mace
		Coriander
		Possibly ginger root
		Fenugreek
Acids		Phosphoric
		Citric in use at times
Sweeteners		Sucrose sugar
		Sucrose, fructose mix
		Saccharin
		Cyclamate
		Aspartame, Nutrasweet (B)
		Caramel (for colour)
Others		Prune juice and coca leaf extract with cocaine removed are among the rumours. The list on the side of the can may be informative.

influence on the liveliness of flavour, apart from the bubbles. This led to the joke, 'It used to take just seven days to dissolve a tooth in Coke. Now it takes just seven weeks.'

As a student I first encountered the relatively high levels of phosphoric acid in Coke after a copper coin left in a glass of it became shiny. (It was supposed to dissolve eventually, but I did not wait to see it.) Coke of that era had its own lore and it achieved some reputation in pre-Pill days as a contraceptive douche. I never had occasion to try that either, but the acidity could certainly be effective – a kind of *ex vitro* sterilisation.

On 23 April 1985, the centenary of the beginning of Coca Cola, the new Coke was officially launched. Within forty-eight hours, 80 per cent of people in the United States had heard about the new taste of Coke, according to independent research organisations. It became available, virtually simultaneously, at two million outlets. The result was chaos. Outraged telephone calls to the Coke organisation became a torrent, protests running to thousands daily. They peaked at about eight thousand a day. An 'official' protest group formed.

On the day a few months later when the President of Coca Cola announced publicly that classic Coke would be reintroduced, there were eighteen thousand telephone calls of approval. Choice was restored and peace descended on the landscape, the fizz landscape anyhow.

What can we learn from this? There are many principles of flavour and philosophy involved. There are some simple, clear ones such as that children prefer sweetness, because of their higher energy needs. Cold lowers the perception of flavours in general, sweetness in particular. Aside from that, sweetness lifts fragrance. Flavours may add or subtract to or from each other. And acidity, sourness, lifts middle flavour; its apparent lessening or absence produces a dullness and flattening of flavour. Less simply, we are, all of us, label drinkers, for one reason or another. The only way to be certain to avoid this problem is to taste the subject 'blind' and without fuss, as is done professionally. Finally, the huge development of the human frontal brain separates us from other animals in many ways. All demonstrate a strong emotional response to flavour but our intelligence gives us a free *choice*, one of the ultimate human distinctions. Deprived of it, we languish or become irate. People will always insist, in a free society, on choice.*

> Cola wars are interesting to the public because it is 'war' without victims, and battle without blood, and it's easier to choose sides.
>
> Joe McCann, Vice-President of Public Affairs
> Pepsi Cola, USA

*This chapter has drawn heavily on *The Real Coke, the Real Story* by Thomas Oliver, and *The Other Guy Blinked* by Roger Enrico and Jesse Kornbluth.

3

STYLE, TASTE AND FLAVOUR

19

Evolution and Eve

Life began in the sea, and the element still exerts a powerful influence on us. We continue to receive our flavour information by means of a watery medium bathing the nose, mouth and throat. Smell and taste, at the core of the essence of excitement, stimulate through the molecules that carry this information, dissolving, but rarely entering into chemical combination. Several body fluids correspond fairly closely to the composition of the sea during the period when life forms left it to inhabit the earth; the brain itself is afloat in one such medium, a sophisticated internal hydraulic cushion, or waterbed, if you like, in which the brain hormones circulate.

The moon influences the tides, and times the female reproductive cycle. There are many such rhythms in our body chemistry, of which one of the most important is called the alkaline tide. While we sleep, carbon dioxide accumulates in the blood from energy metabolism, raising the acid content. When we get up and start our morning activities, this excess acid is blown off as we breathe. The products of digestion, the activities of the liver and kidneys ensure a regular rise and fall every twenty-four hours. This tide affects our perceptions of flavour – for example, how we react to an acid wine or a fruit juice.

The rise and set of the sun make the light/dark cycle that control circadian rhythms. Thus, blind people may not exhibit the normal pituitary high from 6 to 9 a.m. Many other hormones – the chemical messengers of the body – show a similar rhythm. The hormones of the steroid miracle (see page 253), those that control the sexual surge and the protection of life itself, have a morning tidal peak.

In the beginning, in the water, there was a single cell, with the ability to pass molecules back and forth through its wall. For survival, the cell needed to differentiate between 'good' and 'not good' particles, which is not so different from the no-go/go binary sensing of the modern computer. By analogy, I would equal 'go' with survival or growth, and 'no-go' with deterioration or death. We have a negative response to 80 per cent of our odour input, probably a remnant of those early 'tastings' when most of the offerings were toxic. Those cells best able to recognise the difference thrived and grouped together at the same time as they developed the ability to move around, avoiding and seeking out particles. From this we can discern the basis of the sensory and motor components of a nervous system, and of the beginnings of memory. In the healthy human today these faculties are huge, but use perhaps a tenth of the available brain under ordinary circumstances.

In fairly primitive crawling things we find something which might be called a 'taste brain'. This has survived in humans as the nucleus of the solitary tract in the brainstem, the first central relay station for those tastes we perceive as sweet, sour, salty, bitter and *umami* (delicious). It is thought to be one of the two principal central nervous system sources of the beta endorphin which we will later refer to as a happy hormone.

The early brain, for example in worms, was involved mainly in chemical sensing. Later in evolution, in addition to the taste brain, there developed what has aptly been called the 'smell brain', or by scientists with a classical education, the rhinencephalon. It comprised the amygdala (almond), hippocampus (seahorse) and their higher brain associations. The smell and taste brains are now considered to be part of a wider system, the components of which are connected to the hypothalamus, and the conception of which remains under review as new knowledge of these complex and deeply hidden structures comes to light. 'Smell brain' will do for the time being.

It may seem a purely philosophical point but, as it is of interest in evolutionary terms, I mention here that the early development of the brain may be a response to information received from the outside world. This idea has an important contemporary application: we can produce the optimum human by tender loving, touching and smelling care of the newborn child, and dare it be said, we can do the same sometimes much later, for example when brain-damaged patients, or even the lonely and alienated, can be caressed and massaged back into everyday life.

We have a smell brain and a taste brain, developed at an early stage in our marine evolution. What came next? Parallel with their development and continuing after they had reached what is nearly their final form, is the 'intelligent' brain.

As we look at the animal world around us we can get some idea of the blossoming of choice and discrimination as the new 'intelligent' brain has increased in size relative to the old brain concerned with more basic matters. Of course, old and new work together and cannot be separated: an instance of this is that dogs, whose wet noses may recall our marine origins, have a superior sense of smell and may hunt their prey, an 'intelligent' activity, by scent. Similarly, cattle

The smell brain in evolution

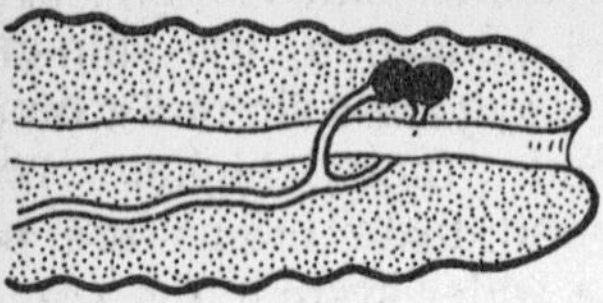

Taste ganglia in a worm, virtually its taste brain

Smell and taste in the fish

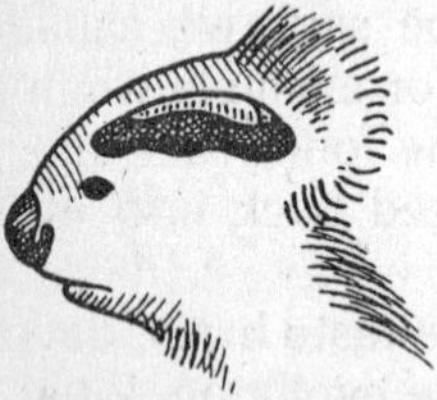

The koala has, relatively, a huge smell brain

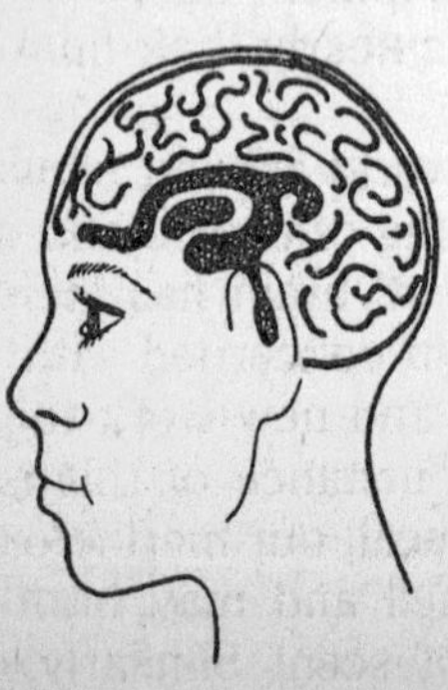

Eve and her limbic system

will graze with their wet noses to the wind so that they can catch the first scent of danger. Dry-nosed cats tend to hunt by sight, relying on stealth and patience to secure their prey. A lot higher off the ground, but also using vision, dry-nosed horses graze with their tails to the wind, watching out for signs and sounds of approaching danger in the same way as humans. Over the ages, humans may have come to use sight and hearing as tools of survival in place of smell, and in developed cultures perhaps the only moments when we use all our senses together are in the acts of eating and drinking and in intimate contact with our mates and children.

As smell, taste, memory and intelligence have become integrated, an accompanying intimate emotional dimension has emerged. It is difficult to conceive of the tender emotions applying to worms or fish. Have the bee, which emasculates its partner during the nuptial flight, or the spider or mantis, which enjoy their slow mates as a protein-rich post-coital snack, an evolutionary vestige in the human love-bite? Perhaps not.

Pair bonding in animals, appears, initially at least, to be odour driven, and smell also plays a most significant part in quite different kinds of emotional reactions and even immune responses. For example, R.H. Wright describes a police dog in training. Most misdemeanours are met with a simple reprimand and the incident then forgotten. But incidents involving smell are exceptions; then for some reason a rebuke is followed by a long sulk or worse. (On the other hand smell is not always a sensitive matter: we don't suspect any emotional upset when a female rat aborts as a pheromonal response to the arrival of a new male rat in the cage.) We refer to animals that get all their food and sex cues in the 'all-fours' position as 'lower' in the evolutionary scale, and we should realise that this also applies to their level of perception. The relatively bigger brain results from standing up, using hearing and vision and developing a forelimb with the opposing thumb which allows its owner to use a precision tool, strike an adversary with a weapon, play the violin or make love. We rely less now on odour than at any other previous evolutionary stage. This fact, and the uncomfortable comparisons which can be made with some animal behaviour, has helped to bring about the relative neglect of our capacity to smell and taste – neglected this century, that is, outside those groups who explore the worlds of flavour and taste for commercial reasons. Few modern women would care to have their sexual behaviour compared with that of the mating sow, nor would most sensitive men see themselves in the guise of a bull standing, neck extended, downwind of a young heifer.

We still have a substantially developed smell brain, which we employ to a greater or lesser extent according to our circumstances and training. Few of us make enough of its powers. It begs for more use, more experience, to provide even greater rewards. If we do not take this path, who knows if a quarter of a million years down the evolutionary track, the smell brain might not have atrophied to the size of an apple pip. And we would be bored out of our brains.

20

The Three R's: Reception, Recognition and Reaction

We assess pungency, texture, mouthfeel and all the nuances of taste and smell by second nature, as a totality. The human brain can, with a lot of effort, separate flavour input into the half a hundred bits which are the backbone of this chapter. Let us examine how we are able to say 'Ah, that smells (or tastes) good!'

Those who study flavour restrict the term taste to mouth and throat sensation. Smell arises in the nose. Flavour becomes the total of both. Around the dining-table, and elsewhere in this book, the words taste and flavour tend to be used interchangeably, but there is no need for confusion if the scientific meanings of the terms are remembered. Taste with the mouth, smell with the nose.

After a time lapse dictated by our readiness to perceive, our brain, like a computer, delivers its verdict on the sensory messages it receives from mouth, throat and nose. We will later see a fascinating demonstration in the story of the airline pilot. The memory bank has a record of thousands of external smells. These are assessed against about three hundred of the body's own odour molecules on the expired breath twelve or more times a minute. Those blood-borne odours also charge one of the skin's three odour systems – the skin itself (the others are the two forms of sweat). There are dozens of odour blindnesses to these, which inevitably create differences in perception. Another problem is that people may claim to have not smelt something, yet demonstrate a measurable brain and body response. Such are the factors that go to make it so difficult to know if you are perceiving the same scent as your neighbour. What you smell is unique, probably as unique as your immune response to the insults of the outside world, and likewise genetically determined.

There is a patch of yellow-brown lining at the top of the roof of the nose, covering the deep cleft on either side over an area of about five square centimetres. This is the olfactory epithelium, and it contains up to fifty million odour receptor cells, which are constantly changing, maturing and degenerating every moon month. There is still no accepted explanation of how we detect smells. It helps to understand the differences in the olfactory performance to know that a German shepherd (Alsatian) dog has perhaps forty times this number. In addition the whole of the inside of the nose has a myriad of free nerve endings which perceive pain and irritation, plus sensors for hot and cold, all of which contribute to our idea of 'smell'.

Odours have been classified, by quality, into as many as thirty groups. Each cell may respond to several odours, and it seems that the brain recognises a particularly quality not in the activity of one cell but in the pattern or code from the activity of many. Even more interestingly, as they change and regenerate, cells may change the odours to which they respond. This could have a bearing on the excellent result we see from training and experience; not to mention the baffling alterations in flavour that we perceive from time to time. We usually smell with one side of the nose at a time, cycling between twenty minutes and four hours. We sniff with both nostrils, unaware that one is often 'out'.

Normal quiet breathing does not give the exposure to smells of the outside world that a good sniff does as it presents turbulent airstreams of warmed air for examination. What is known about the actual mechanism of olfaction is that the smell molecules dissolve in the fluid around the olfactory cell 'whiskers', which are stimulated to fire off messages to the brain by the shape of the odour molecule, by the vibrations it sets up, by a pattern of particles presenting themselves at different times during the sniff, by differing intensities of odour, or conceivably by a combination of all these. Quite a lot of verbal heat has been generated in the back rooms of this science by those working on the different theories. None of them seem mutually exclusive.

> The truth is not mine alone.
>
> St Augustine

From the pickup area in the roof of the nose, the first relay station is in the olfactory bulb inside the skull directly over the nose. The fibres pass through fine holes in a thin plate of bone and are easily damaged by injuries to the face and base of the skull, with major loss of olfactory function the sad result. The next relay station is the smell brain itself, a beautiful thing of graceful curves and extraordinary complexity. The reason for its shape can only be guessed at. It may be the most economical way of relaying to and from the hypothalamus, where the sex hormone release mechanism is fired off. It enfolds the hypothalamus like some creature of the deep guarding exquisite treasure in a hidden grotto. There are several areas and parts of the body that are equally stunning in the beauty of their design. Some are midline like the smell brain, and some are bilateral like the whirling cochlear shell of the inner ear, itself next door to the incredible little hammer and anvil of the middle ear.

The olfactory cortex is the oldest section of the limbic system, explored more fully by Carl Sagan in *The Dragons of Eden.* Because of their intimate anatomical association, the components are usually described as a unit, comprising in large part, amygdala, hippocampus and associated cortex, thalamus and hypothalamus-pituitary complex.

The hippocampus is the library of long memory. It is not really developed until the last third of pregnancy when any toxic influence will interfere with the infant's capacity to learn and store impressions. The amygdala is another vital portion of the smell brain from which pass direct links to control the release of the hormones governing all sexual development and activity, not to mention beta endorphin.

There is also an accessory olfactory system. Lower animals have a supplementary organ of smell which perceives pheromonal scents that keep them sexually tuned. It is to be found at the apex of the nose at the junction of the vomeronasal bones, from which it derives its cumbersome name. Did you know the male house mouse sings an ultrasonic ditty just before he goes into the act of love? He does this as a response to the scent of his lady friend. You may find this difficult to believe, but if there is any problem with his vomeronasal organ, his lyre is broken. No song! This secondary system picks up and deciphers the information available from large molecules which are not very volatile, and tend not to stimulate the ordinary receptors. They may be what I have called the close-up pheromones. If so, they could still have their own receiver. It is a unique type of chemical sense, neither taste nor true smell, but it is the basis for discrimination of male and female scent cues. The information travels centrally by its own nerve, a special slip of the olfactory nerve to the amygdala, and thence to the hypothalamus. This secondary olfactory system was thought to be absent or to have no function in humans, but that opinion is shifting. In fact, the system does seem to respond to sexual chemical messages in some individuals, at least. What do you think?

The Pleasure Principle

Freud lingered at some length over the pleasure principle, but nowhere is it more important than in smell and taste. There is a pleasure value (positive or negative) in smelling and tasting that is absolutely intrinsic to the act. Emotion is the holograph of flavour and gives it a dimension akin to the feeling of 'space' in stereo sound. Does one ever really smell or taste anything without a like/neutral/dislike reaction? Complete loss of smell is often accompanied by a depressed outlook, and if corrected suddenly, for instance by surgery, there is a remarkable emotional lift. I think a new word is needed that combines taste, emotion and fragrance, and accordingly have coined 'temavour'. This word crystallises an important value of flavour that can only be described now by several words: an 'emotional value which is an inextricable part of a particular smell or taste and thus an intrinsic part of the action of smelling or tasting'.

The concept is supported by anatomy. Part of the amygdala receives odour input, but the basal part is involved in the expression of emotion. The amygdala and its neighbour the hypothalamus, together with the solitary tract nucleus (taste input) are among the principle repositories of beta endorphin in the central nervous system. When the effects and widespread action of this happy substance are considered, it surely seems reasonable to give the flavour/emotion relationship a short, easy handle. If the word becomes accepted, temavour could be assigned a numerical value, 0 to 10, positive or negative. Those who have delved as deeply as I have *have* to be impressed by the association. Time will tell if it needs temavour.

Imagine living in an odourless world. Some people try to, for fear of sending or receiving the wrong messages. They may be emotionally unable to handle the input that they do perceive. Every human has an individual scent signature. It should not become a cause of alienation and inhibition.

Odours can be easily separated into qualities, such as fragrant, putrid, burnt and so on. Classifications of this nature have been going on for hundreds of years, but recently it has become clear that related odours frequently have molecules of similar configuration, even though they may be quite different chemically. This approach makes it likely that there must be at least thirteen or fourteen primary odours, and perhaps thirty or more. By primary odours I mean those that cannot be made up by mixing other odours. Of course not everyone may be able to smell all of the primaries. There are as many as seventy recorded odour blindnesses to primaries or combinations of them, of quite a specific nature. An individual can be more certainly identified by his odour blindness than by his fingerprints. These are a few:

Fruitiness generally; citrus fruit
Camphor, mothballs
Cinnamon, cloves
Almonds

Vanilla
Garlic, leeks, onions
Jasmine, geraniums, violets
Fish
Cat urine, musk, stale urine, blood, sweat, faeces, putrefaction
Crushed ant
Mouldiness
Grassiness, cooked vegetables, mint
The burnt smell

Some people have a very acute sense of smell. It may be so sharp as to catapult them into a feeling of disgust while their companions have no problem. Trygg Engen makes the point that children getting such information learn to keep out of trouble by keeping their mouths shut. They may become isolated, even rebellious.

Because the tongue is so accessible a good deal is known about taste at the peripheral level. The tongue used to be said to pick up the sensation of sweetness at the tip, bitterness at the back, and sourness and saltiness at the sides and top. Of course nothing remains unchallenged in this science, and the current idea is that all four are perceived all over the tongue, but are concentrated in the traditional zones. More to the point, the whole mouth and throat are well supplied with taste sensors of various kinds and they regenerate at more than twice the rate of the smell receivers. As Dr Morley Kare says, two weeks from now you will have a fresh set. An infant begins with twenty thousand, but these have dwindled to two thousand by adult life. Taste sensations are transmitted by four separate cranial nerves, bundles of individual nerve cells, to an area of grey matter in the brainstem, the nucleus of the solitary tract. The path the nerves take through tortuous tunnels in solid bone in the skull is little short of miraculous, and a permanent record of the stages of evolution of this sense can be traced back and compared to the simple, uncomplicated route in, for example, the lizard.

Other sensations that travel by the fifth cranial nerve make substantial contributions to taste. The first of them is mouthfeel, here recognised as the sensation of 'body', thickness, slipperiness, and its temavour varies from delight to disgust. Some flavours cannot be adequately defined without including this feeling. Nerve endings in the mouth and nose communicate pain to the brain along the same path. To a somewhat lesser degree, the pungency of chilli is part of this sensation. Hot and cold also travel by this nerve, so that something like menthol cannot only be smelt but is accompanied by a sensation of coolness and even pain. This is an example of a secondary nerve besides the first, strictly olfactory, nerve contributing to the 'smell' of something. All voluntary muscles have tension receptors among their fibres, and when the jaw and facial muscles are in action, texture information is also added to the flavour computer. These fifth cranial nerve impulses travel to the thalamus, sitting on top of the hypothalamus at the front of the base of the brain.

Umami is the fifth important component of taste (the others are sweet, sour, salty and bitter). Defined around 1909 by Professor Kikunae Ikeda, it is the Japanese word for a delicious or savoury quality, something the Western palate still finds difficult to distinguish from the other elements of taste simply because there has been no word for it. It is perceived at the back of the tongue, and 'brothy', perhaps 'salty', 'meat stock', come to mind in describing it. Babies like it. It certainly increases satisfaction in the taste of meats, in fact it even diminishes the desire for salt by a third. There is a high degree of *umami* in the stocks of fish, and meats, in mushrooms, cheese, and some vegetables like celery, carrot, seaweed, cauliflower, and of course monosodium glutamate. The temavour of cooked white rice is slightly better than zero if it is merely boiled. A pinch of salt or MSG registers some improvement, but nothing to compare with frying it in one of the ordinary cooking oils. If you add soy sauce there is a quantum leap from that level to nearly double, an excellent demonstration of synergism, here $(1 + 1 + 1 = 8)$.

Cross-culture differences in flavour are remarkable, and they are exaggerated by problems of communication. There are many examples in this book of how putting a word to a tantalising phantom flavour gives it form and flesh. It is worthwhile giving such attention to *umami*. It is able to stand on its own, possibly of equal value to all the other taste sensations combined.

There is substantial overlap between sweet and bitter, and were it not for the fact that bitter and astringent probably travel by separate routes to different areas of flavour registration (nucleus of the solitary tract and thalamus respectively), they would be more difficult to separate than they are now.

Salt and sweet can evoke warm and pleasant feelings at the right concentrations. Sweet can actually be relaxing, and salt exhilarating. As an energy marker sweetness cuts off appetite, hence it is an efficient closure to a meal. It also has the remarkable ability to increase the perception of fragrances, for instance in table wines. Minor additions of sugar as a flavour enhancer were discussed in Chapter 12, 'Flavour Power'.

The relatively high energy requirements of children drive their love of sweet things. The problems arise later in life when temavour is divorced from calorie needs. An hour's hard physical exercise might burn up a candy bar. Bitter is an evolutionary toxin marker, but with advancing age it is well appreciated for its ability to provoke digestive juices and lessen thirst.

Anosmia and impotence could have been co-titled fragrance and frigidity, except that such problems appear to be more common in male. In view of the complete integration of taste and smell reception with the hypothalamic centre that controls such basic drives as sex, plus most of the major hormone mechanisms outside the brain, when alterations in odour and taste perception do occur they may be expected to have a hypothalamic response.

One of the most striking of these is Kallman's syndrome: small genitals, loss of smell, and delayed social development. Here is that syndrome described by N.A. Bobrow and his colleagues:

> Patients associated the lack of visible signs of male puberty with their delayed sociosexual maturation. However, the evidence of physical maturation after treatment did not have the ameliorative effect on their social behaviour one would have liked to predict. Dating behaviour was limited before and after treatment for all the patients, and sexual interest was low even for the three married ones. The experience of falling in love was notably absent in the relationships described. Two characteristic social reaction patterns were social introversion and hostile rejection of agemates. Intellectual functioning and the incidence of personality pathology were not diagnostically noteworthy. None of the patients had any problems with gender identity except for erotic apathy which extended to masturbation. There was an absence of homosexuality.

What a bottomless well of human misery lies hidden

behind this clinical report. Kallman described the problem in 1944, but as Trygg Engen drily observes, 'people with the anomaly do not readily talk about it or submit to examination' to explain their neglect.

People with a poor sense of smell may show loss of weight and appetite. This is common, but in a severe case, the weight loss and depression can be formidable.

Food smells found to be pleasant when hungry can be unpleasant when appetite is satisfied. The olfactory bulbs contain more of the hormones insulin and CCK than elsewhere in the brain, and are thought to influence the selection of the more palatable and tasty food.

Threshold is the word for the minimum level of flavour that an individual can detect: the first 'yes I can smell it' in a test using a series of dilutions of a flavour starting from nothing and working up. (Or threshold can be determined by the reverse procedure.) Once above the threshold, each individual has a range of perception from that point which includes a level of preference, then indifference, and finally

Thresholds (First Perception)

Substance	Taste	Threshold Percentage (as proportion of tasteless substance)
Alcohol (ethyl)	Burning	15–25
	Sweet	11–14
Sucrose	Sweet	0.5
Salt	Salty	0.2
MSG	*Umami*	0.03
Acetic Acid	Sour	0.012
Quinine	Bitter	0.00005

Some of the 50 per cent of people who can smell androstenone can pick it up at 200 parts per trillion in the air (exquisitely sensitive!)

Another Way of Looking at Thresholds

Substance	Odour	Addition to Olympic-size Pool
Alcohol (Ethyl)	Sweetish	50 gallons
Benzaldehyde	Almond	2 gallons
DMS	Stink	12 drops
Geosmin	Beetroot, Pinot	1 drop
IMP*	Capsicum Bell Pepper Cabernet Sauvignon	1/10 drop
Thiamin† (impure)	Cooked Brown Rice	1/50 drop

*IMP – The strength of this odour, in green vegetables and so on, may be a marker for Vitamin C.

†The extraordinary potency of thiamin may be involved in its importance to survival in evolution. It is the vitamin which preserves the integrity of nerve sheath insulations.

aversion. Looking at thresholds of various substances gives an indication of their intensity of flavour.

Threshold may vary between individuals by a factor of up to a billion, and people themselves vary during their lifetimes. For example, various studies, reinforced by the most recent one by *National Geographic Magazine*/Monell in 1986, show a substantial rise in threshold for combined sulphur smells in the aged. There is a good practical reason why this matters: a smelly compound has been added to odourless natural gas for safety reasons, and apparently this is not being detected by a substantial number of the very age group at the highest risk.

Some simple sums: there are several possibilities when two odours are perceived together.

The effect may be additive	$1 + 1 = 2$
One may mask the other	$1 + 1 = 1.5$
There may be synergism	$1 + 1 = 3$

A light stays bright, but an odour does not. Once it is registered it dwindles to nothing, needing to be smelt again. It takes far longer to register than light;

in fact pain is the only slower sensation.

Violet is quite remarkable in this respect. In fact people are inclined to say that the flower has lost its perfume, only to find twenty minutes later that it has 'returned'. We adapt to this refractory period by continuing to sniff, for varying periods, as long as it takes to resume the computation.

The effect of smoking on flavour perception continues to be warmly debated. Non-smokers know that any strong odour, particularly if introduced without warning, interferes with the efficiency of smell. The negative temavour is an additional disadvantage. Careful wine-tasters experience the same reaction to a noticeable perfumed companion. There is a difference of opinion about the effect of smoking on the palate. I have lived on both sides of the fence. I have judged wine internationally as a heavy smoker, in the company of similar degenerates, and did not note any difference in sensitivity compared to non-smokers. When I stopped smoking some years ago, there was a difference, 'everything tasted better'. Not more but better. My guess is that smokers learn to accommodate to the odour of the smoke, in much the same way that a colour filter on a camera lens influences the final picture without altering the focus. In fact one of my teachers found his threshold for metal in wine was lower by the power of six when he smoked than when he abstained. All this has been thrown open again by the *National Geographic*/Monell survey. In five of the six test 'scratch and sniffs' the perception of five of them was lowered in smokers, but not musk. The temavour of smokers was down.

Age is said to diminish odour acuity. The decline starts in early adult life and steadily continues thereafter, with a sharp drop in the last decades of the century. Individuals vary tremendously, and I suspect like most human skills, olfaction works in a most satisfactory way with continual use, enhanced by training and expansion of the range of experience. Use it or lose it. Perfumers and wine professionals work till they die. Dr Morley Kare agrees with me that with a little luck, you will have good taste and smell ability all your life, if you can avoid being malnourished or being on medication, and keep your marbles.

The most recently developed intelligent brain is perched on top of the limbic system. There are huge connections between them resulting, as far as flavour is concerned, in two relevant functions, choice and computation. The newest brain is a fine-tuner; inputs are stored in the smell brain memory bank, they are then integrated, to become subjected to acts of will by the new brain. This is the genesis of choice.

Perhaps the most human of qualities, free choice is first clearly and consistently encountered in primates. For example, in a test with monkeys, brain activity was found to relate to the 'goodness' of food, while at the same time behaviour related to sweetness – not to nutritive value at all. In other words, a choice is made, which is beyond 'lower' animals with less developed brains, whose selection of food is virtually automatic, according to physiological drive alone.

In the early fifties, a team of Japanese scientists began a study of a troop of macaques on an isolated island. They developed rapport by leaving sweet potatoes out to entice the monkeys. In 1953 'Imo', a young female, initiated a change in the routine. On this particular occasion she took a potato down to a pool, dipped it, and proceeded to clean the dirt off with her hand. A new idea had occurred in the animal's brain and a choice had been made. So what? She continued and next month another monkey followed suit. Four months afterwards, Imo's mother started. It became a group activity and they widened their options by moving from fresh water to the sea. That community to this day are said universally to wash their sweet potatoes in sea water and the only monkeys who never made the transition were old when Imo first got her idea.

This event is worth a treatise on its own. There are several possibilities. The food could taste better. Or there could be a net improvement in the nutritional status. This would confer an evolutionary bonus, in the form of more efficient reproduction, on an individual or group possessing such knowledge. So in this simple piece of monkey business we get a glimmer of 'natural selection', we see a hint of 'ethnic culture', and the application of many of the principles discussed in this book.

When the new brain overrides, the results can sometimes be counter-productive. Trygg Engen reports that the effect of psychological variables on sensory experience has in fact been appreciated for a long time. In 1899 a scientist by the name of Slosson reported in the *Psychological Review* a classroom demonstration on *odour hallucinations*:

> I had prepared a bottle filled with distilled water carefully wrapped in cotton and packed in a box. After some other experiments I stated that I wished to see how rapidly an odour would be diffused through air and requested that as soon as anyone perceived the odour he should raise his hand. I then unpacked the bottle in the front of the hall, poured the water over the cotton, holding my head away during the operation, and started a stopwatch. While awaiting results I explained that I was quite sure that no one in the audience had ever smelled the chemical compound which I had poured out, and expressed the hope that, while they might find the odour strong and peculiar, it would not be too disagreeable to anyone. In fifteen seconds most of those in the front row had raised their hands, and in forty seconds 'the odour' had

> spread to the back of the hall, keeping a pretty regular 'wave front' as it passed. About three-fourths of the audience claimed to perceive the smell ... More would probably have succumbed to the suggestion, but at the end of a minute I was obliged to stop the experiment, for some of those in the front seats were being unpleasantly affected and were about to leave the room.

We all share the experience of forcing a taste or scent into a preconceived 'box' without the slightest problem. Connoisseurs of wine know this as *label drinking*, interpreting the flavour according to the name or description of the wine rather than what is actually in the mouth. In truth, the most difficult aspect of professional judging is the absolute necessity to focus only on the sample; not to be influenced by all the other input that might be offered, such as who made it, whether they are kind to their relatives, what someone else thinks about it, and so on. On one occasion a friend, a respected and therefore influential wine authority, described in glowing terms the flavour of a glass of wine in front of him. It was great theatre, smooth, vastly impressive, eloquent jargon that should have precisely fitted the classic wine of a great year. It was so incongruous as to be funny because the glass of wine itself was in fact a flavour disaster, a bad bottle, something that can happen at any time. I suspect his problem was jetlag compounded by boredom and a lack of readiness to perceive which I discuss elsewhere. Every one of us is capable of making a similar mistake.

I do not know enough to become embroiled in artificial intelligence, real-time pattern recognition, and related problems but in my view, the analogy between flavour recognition and the workings of a computer memory bank is persuasive. The long-term memory for the association of smell with the events or surroundings of a particular event is amazing. I am not going to repeat yet again Proust's account of the memory of the madeleines of his childhood if only because everyone has a far more immediate recollection of his or her own.

A curious difference between olfaction from other senses is the inability that most people have actually to summon a particular scent to mind, to smell it on recall. Sight or sound provide laser-sharp examples at will. Smell gives the most vivid associations but not the actual smell. Not to most of us anyway. This provides some indication of the method of operation of the memory bank of the computer, and also gives a hint on improving our performance. If it is non-linear and works by association, it is best trained and expanded by association. This can be achieved by learning the techniques of comparative tasting (Chapter 16, 'Start to Taste'). The pleasure hormones are rewards for the activities demanded by Nature, to eat and reproduce. Few, if any, can recall the quality of the pleasure, just that it was so special as to be compelling. How clever! Smell is the subtle sense in more ways than one.

There must be a readiness to perceive. Without it, literally nothing happens, and smell and taste will be completely ignored. Or apparently so. Some stimuli override all the other sensory inputs. The late Professor R.H. Wright some years ago gave an example of which the following is an adaptation.

A passenger aircraft is on its landing approach, pilot communication with the control tower at the airport in full flood. The door to the flight deck is opened by an attractive stewardess, retrieving a cup of coffee. The pilot does not even smell the coffee. He is aware of the fragrances of the attendant, not actively so but filed away for future reference. What makes him turn around is the smoke of a cigarette just put out by a passenger in the compartment behind. The three priorities of odour, determined by evolution and survival, are well expressed here. The threat to life, burning, overrides all others. Danger smells are usually very small molecules, fast moving, very volatile, and perceived at the start of the enquiring sniff, demanding most urgent action.

In all these computations, before the answer is forthcoming the result of the memory search has to be balanced, as I note earlier, against internal odours. These are produced in normal metabolism, and diffuse into the air in the lungs to mix with volatiles from food and drink, such as those obviously present in garlic and wine. There may be as many as three hundred of these in one outgoing breath, to be received by the olfactory sensors at the back of the roof of the nose. For example, a person may not detect garlic or onion on the incoming airstream, if his or her expired air is loaded with garlic volatiles from the meal of the previous evening. In fact, he is less likely to pick up most combined sulphur smells, in comparison with someone without this overload. So garlic should be shared with companions. Don't eat it before occasions where the flavours might clash or dominate. These remarks apply to all powerful odorants.

A substantial part of our response to the molecules of flavour is inherited. It is common to encounter someone who does not like the smell capsicum, bell pepper, and find that one or both of his parents also did not. One of the earliest and best studied taste blindnesses was discovered in the following way, and reported by Dr Boyd in his *Genetics and the Races of Man*.

> In 1932 Dr A.L. Fox had occasion to prepare a quantity of phenyl-thio-carbamide (usually abbreviated PTC). As he was placing this compound in a bottle some of it was dispersed into the air as

> dust. Thereupon another occupant of the laboratory complained of the bitter taste of the dust. This surprised Fox, who, being much closer to the scene of operations, had of course inhaled more of the dust, but had perceived no taste. He was so positive that the stuff was tasteless that he went so far as to taste some of the crystals directly, finding them as tasteless as chalk. Nevertheless the other chemist was convinced the substance was bitter and was confirmed in this impression when he in turn tasted the crystals and found them to be intensely bitter. Naturally a lively argument arose. In an attempt to settle it, the two chemists called in various other laboratory workers, friends and other people with whom they could establish contact. It was supposed that the verdict of these people would establish beyond question which of the two chemists was peculiar in taste reaction. Some people declared the substance was tasteless and some again found it bitter. The latter were in the majority.

The racial distribution of 'blindness' for this bitterness is interesting: pure Negro people (Shillacs) 4 per cent, North American whites 30 per cent, Arabs 37 per cent. This defect is specifically genetic. The inferences from the latest mass survey are less clear, because of the racial mix and because no information is included on familial background. This table is adapted from the *National Geographic* survey. Many odours are more easily detected on repeated exposure. Androstenone is, but the PTC bitterness described above does not vary.

Some people are odour blind to danger signals, an inherited fault. Surprisingly, 10 per cent of the population cannot detect the almond odour of cyanide gas, one of the most immediately lethal gases on the planet. Fire may be the gift of the sun, but to be

Odour Blindness to Androstenone

Country	Percentage of Males	Percentage of Females
Africa	21.6	14.7
Latin America	24.6	17.7
Europe	24.1	15.8
Australia	24.2	17.9
Asia	25.5	17.2
Caribbean	29.2	17.5
United Kingdom	30	20.9
United States of America	37.2	29.5

unable to perceive 'burnt' is a hazard in everyday living. It is amusing how often Nature seems to be attempting to redress the balance in a marriage by having only one of the partners being 'burnt'-blind (usually a toast and pot burner of some frequency).

21

Babies

> Variety and contrast give pleasure to taste, sex, sound and sight.
>
> Epicurus (*his order of importance*)

At the instant of birth, the baby is switched on by contrast, the universal teacher, and learning speeds from that most magic of moments. Beforehand, the baby is afloat in warm fluid, in the dark, able to taste perhaps, but nourished in an odourless environment, and relatively silent except for the beat of the mother's heart. Within one pass of the sun, an incredible series of contrasts has occurred. The newborn baby is cold, hungry, dry, unsupported and with its limbs unconfined, in a bright, noisy, chaotic world, full of smells and tastes.

What can it really taste or smell? Embryos of seven months respond to sweetness in the amniotic fluid. A three-month-old baby has already developed strong odour choices.

Despite our most vivid imaginings, and what we are told by writers of creative science fiction, an actuality of another being's sensations cannot yet be shared. The detection of them is often open to question, such feelings remaining in the most private human domain at whatever age. So how can we be certain what conclusion a baby reaches when tasting or smelling?

'Earth mothers' will find the question irrelevant, perhaps amusing. They dwelt in the domain of body language long before the term was invented by a man. They seem to use extrasensory perception and certainly do recognise and understand the newborn baby's responses, its facial reactions clearly in line with the classic pleasure response – 'like, indifferent, don't like'. Even those unfortunate infants born with most of the brain missing or out of action respond to the primary tastes, and to the amount of each.

The actual taste apparatus is defined in the foetus at twelve weeks. After reading *Brave New World* by Aldous Huxley, I decided it was a good idea to play Joy's and my developing twins a lot of Baroque music because it is my own favourite personal stimulus. I wonder what new fields of endeavour have opened up to creative parents, following Huxley? As far as the newborn baby's palate is concerned, my guess is that the simplest, freshest, and most varied diet for the nursing mother would produce the best results. The baby will have plenty of time to explore the rest of the taste world later. Of course, the opposite may be true. Confront it with every possibility, thereby increasing its discrimination. Or the truth may lie in between.

We can easily surmise that a baby likes 'sweet' because it is a high energy consumer, it recognises a supply of energy (sugar) with pleasure. It dislikes 'sour' and 'bitter' because neither will do it much good and in the case of 'bitter' could be seriously toxic. Generally speaking, *umami* has been put forward as a preferred taste among babies, perhaps because it is a marker for good, body-building protein. In the first year of infancy, babies have little or no aversion to faeces. On occasion, some even appear to enjoy it, which is just as well, they lie in it often enough!

There is a lot more to breast feeding than meets

How Does Age Influence Odour Preference?
(suggested by the work of R.W. Moncrieff)

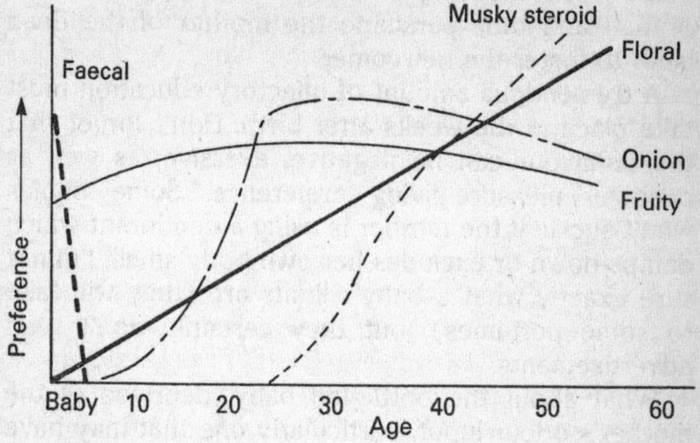

the eye. Digestion of breast milk produces a newly discovered happy hormone, casomorphin, which helps explain the bliss of suckling. We know also that other endorphins are released by the simple acts of cuddling and fondling. On the subject, very little has been said about the role smell plays in both mother and baby. Watch an infant struggle to reach the nipple – it is probably attracted by the pheromone IBA and the mother's body smell. Some odour is absolutely critical for the suckling of blind and almost helpless newborn marsupials and mice. Indeed it has recently been found to relate very closely to the immune system of the male mouse's choice of future mate (see the Epilogue for the extraordinary reason for this). The suckling human baby comes to recognise its mother's scent quite clearly within a fortnight of birth, as she recognises the infant's. This is vital to the survival of some species where, for example, the mother sheep will reject an orphaned lamb seeking milk, unless something is done by the farmer to persuade the mother of kinship with the new arrival.

There is a commercial pheromone-type spray available for this purpose; earlier generations of shepherds used the skin of a dead lamb to cover an orphan and thus persuade the mother of the dead lamb to foster the newcomer.

A tremendous amount of olfactory education must take place in the weeks after birth. Don't forget that the temavour can be negative, aversive, as well as positive, pleasure-giving preference. Some babies won't suckle if the mother is using a deodorant which damps down or excludes her own body smell. I'm not sure exactly what a baby's limits are (they will take to some perfumes), but they certainly don't read advertisements.

What about the bottle-fed baby, deprived of the mother's odour input, particularly one that may have spent many weeks of early life in the closed and controlled world of a hospital nursery? What sort of memory bank and responses, what sort of development takes place in the apparatus of smell and taste of such a child? It would be no surprise if a lot of human odour and taste variations have their origin in an early absence of breast feeding. My wife Joy has the most acute sense of smell I have encountered, and she was a miraculous survivor of premature birth. It could be worthwhile to set up a register of such infants for flavour testing later in life.

Watch a baby suckling. One cannot but feel astonished by the amount of nipple, areola and sometimes actual breast it crams in in the process; and the way it pummels the breast. Is it to stir up the circulation? Perhaps it lifts the odour as well. During suckling, the milk is being tasted at the back of the tongue and in the throat. The sweet sensors, mainly at the tip of the tongue, are but a fraction of the twenty thousand taste buds located in a baby's mouth, cheeks and throat. This tallies with the suggestion that *umami* sensors are well back in the mouth.

22

Highs and the Happy Hormones

Tune in, turn on . . .

The body produces several chemicals that alter mood and emotion. The whole study of neurobiology is in a state of excitement because no matter how much has been discovered, it is becoming increasingly clear that we are only at the beginning. These marvellous molecules may be manufactured by glands, or be part of the actual transmission of nerve impulses, inside the brain to work their magic there. Richard Bergland sees the brain as a giant gland in addition to its traditional functions.

The term hormone used to apply to a substance secreted in a gland which lacked an outlet pipe. It soaked into the circulation and triggered a response from a particular body target. It was a chemical messenger. The pituitary was the 'conductor of the endocrine orchestra' of these ductless glands. About a thumbnail in diameter, it hangs from the brain by a short stalk which transmits a substantial exchange of chemical and electric messages with the automatic nervous system control centre perched above it. This circulation with the hypothalamus is busier than the Straits of Dover. But the conception of a hormone has now widened to encompass other molecules, including many of those formed during nerve impulse transmission, which have been found to have remarkable effects on our feelings.

It is well known now from studies of the effects of morphia and heroin that there are natural equivalents inside the brain. Pain relief, feelings of well being, and even of infinite pleasure, are gifts of the 'opium' afloat in the brain fluid cushion. The enkephalins were the first group to be named, followed by endorphins and dynorphin. They have a drastic influence on our emotions and daily activities. They show a tidal waxing and waning like so many other functions and play a substantial role in daily body rhythms.

There is a very strict control of the chemicals allowed in and out of the brain. This blood-brain barrier has hindered investigation for lack of easy access to the deep areas of the brain, but some opioids, for example, have been found widely scattered in distant parts of the body. Research into tissue responses has come up with some fascinating results.

Casomorphin is another enkephalin, produced during the digestion of the mother's milk. It is thought to have a significant influence on the baby's emotions, physical actions and even immune response. We have already seen that tender loving touching releases beta endorphins. The tears of joy and sorrow are chemically different. There is the celebrated example of Norman Cousins who, in his own book *The Anatomy of an Illness*, describes how he was cured of a severe chronic disease by the 'rejuvenating power of belly laughter'. Ten minutes of it from watching the Marx Brothers would give him two hours of pain-free sleep, among other benefits. As far afield as the adrenal gland, a hefty molecule, named 50K for its weight, has been discovered to contain enkephalin in one of its segments. The vas deferens connecting the testicle to the ejaculatory mechanism has opiate receptors that cause it to contract rhythmically under their influence. The response is so constant that strips of mouse vas have been used to assay the amounts of these hormones. And why would it not be part of the mechanics of orgasm? There seems to be a dearth of volunteers to be needled (or whatever) during these particularly private seconds of life on earth.

It is an over-simplification, but in the present state of knowledge it seems fair to state that the beta endorphins appear to be the happiest of the opioid collection. Again, it may not be the last word, but John Holaday's report includes the information that the cells with large amounts of beta endorphins are to be found in the hypothalamus and the solitary nucleus in the brainstem. This nucleus of grey matter and its tract are the first central relay centre for all the events that happen in the mouth and throat that we call taste. The smell brain, and the amygdala in particular, abuts directly on the hypothalamus. The limbic system (in effect that part of the brain connected to the hypothalamus) and its adjacent areas of the interbrain modulate bliss, rage, lust, hunger, thirst and sleep. From here springs the pulsatile secretion of hormones that result in ovulation and the gonadotropin release thought to be part of genital erection.

This all seems to add up to an answer as to why things smell or taste good or feel marvellous. We are becoming aware of another bonus. Some neurotransmitters (and this chapter abounds with them) and brain hormones have been found to switch on the immune system responses. Nature intends the wheel of life to turn, and rewards us handsomely for following her dictates, as we see in the highs of love and orgasm, which have their own chapter.

Soon after cortisone was used to assist the

treatment of disordered responses of the immune system, some interesting side effects were noticed. Apart from the serious bad ones, there were two that some patients did not seem to mind. Sometimes there was a heightening of mood verging on euphoria, and some people experienced a startling and occasionally embarrassing increase of sexual drive. The adrenal gland has an outer shell or cortex which makes stress response hormones analogous to cortisone, and these share the incredible family relationships of the 'steroid miracle' described in the sixth day of Genesis (Chapter 24).

Glutamate has been well known as an excitatory neurotransmitter. It now has other fascinations. Solomon Snyder, in 1973, developed a 'grind and bind' technique using rat brains and chemicals with radioactive tags, and thereby identified the opioid receivers (and producers of endorphins). We are now aware of the analogy with glutamates, supported by the finding that the street drug 'angel dust' (which is said to make one feel pretty good) acts on glutamate receivers. Glutamate is in the spotlight now. It does not cross the blood-brain barrier, which is just as well, as it is universally found in complete protein foods. Glutamate receptors are widely distributed in the brain, and also on the tongue, where the 'tastiness' (*umami*) of food is the immediate reward. Any positive temavour is probably an evolutionary bonus for eating protein. It has been observed in mother's milk and probably does something nice for the baby. Its presence in ordinary diet is explored in Chapter 12, 'Flavour Power'.

Happy hormones are released by the act of eating and by what is eaten and, as we have seen, appear to be activated by the smell and taste sequences. There is a further group that might well be called the excitement hormones, which are skimmed from the fight-or-flight danger response of the adrenal gland, which sits on top of the kidney. An activity that gets the best of both worlds is the Japanese cult of eating the *fugu* or Pacific puffer fish. Some of its organs and membranes contain one of the most potent toxins known. Several years of intense study and practical experience are necessary for a chef to achieve certified proficiency in the removal of the dangerous tissues, of which the otherwise attractive and delicious roe is the worst. Japanese friends took me to a *fugu* restaurant in Tokyo where every dish featured a preparation of the fish, *sashimi* (strips of raw fish), soup, crunchy charred fins and so on, without any ill effects. Connoisseurs seek out those chefs who are sufficiently skilled to leave enough toxin behind to produce some tingling and numbness of the lips, among other symptoms. It has also been served as a 'dip'. Not surprisingly, deaths are not unknown, and in 1975 Mitsugoro Bando, a Kabuki theatre superstar, perished from *fugu.*

I have taken the liberty of using the word adrenalin as a generic term for a whole group of the excitement hormones because most people have come across the evocative phrase 'adrenalin junkie' for someone who is hooked on excitement. The natural 'high' of excitement is almost a taste in the mouth for many who enjoy dangerous sports such as fast driving, free-fall parachuting and the like. Completely addicted and out of control, the condition may be terminal. Could the earliest response of this kind, and the most socially acceptable, be the pleasure of the pungency of chilli and incandescent curries?

On the negative side there are many who profess indifference or even hostility to several of the subjects of this book. Those who have substantial 'blindnesses' of smell or taste suffer a lack of pleasure from simple lack of input. Then there are the thin-lipped, guilt-ridden individuals who nonetheless have a latent capability for liberation. Sexual impotence, frigidity and anorexia nervosa are other possible associations. Many men, confused about the social penalties of instinctive pheromonal response, shut off for their own protection. It *is* possible to fine tune.

Despite what you read about ecstasy-inducing drugs like MDMA ('Speed' and 'XTZ' are the street names for related or equivalent drugs), something as reliable and harmless as the Soma of Aldous Huxley's *Brave New World* is some years away yet. In any case, is it really needed? Dr Field of Miami has shown that beta endorphins are produced in newborn babies who are massaged, cuddled and stroked, and that such infants thrive better and secrete more pituitary growth hormone than those who have the minimum of handling. The happy hormones are free on a do-it-yourself basis, whenever you achieve a terrific result from hard mental or physical effort or are deeply moved by natural beauty or art and music. The line between these simple highs, and the spiritual and sexual kinds, is not all that clear-cut. And the simplest and most natural highs can come from a good laugh, or perhaps 'a loaf of bread, a jug of wine and thou beside me singing in the wilderness'.

23

Time and the Measure of Flavour

Time is a measure not a force

The internal forces that make up the particles of which all matter is composed resonate to a measurable rhythm, divisions of time. A collection of molecules at the top of the right atrium of our mother's heart beats three billion pulses in her lifetime and sets our first standard of rhythm. The rise and fall of the sun and moon, Baroque, Beatles and Boogie, modify life's rhythms. Smooth muscle waves are intrinsic to digestion, and the acts of love and birth; we smell with one or other side of the nose on a rhythmic basis. Like a classical sonata form, or cycles of the Buddha if you wish, flavour is stated with emotional harmonics, to be restated and subside, ready for another loop. The feedback controls of emotional hormone activities initiated by taste and smell are a bewildering complex, the more so the greater the development of the brain, and the further research advances. Some of these loops are described in a brief attempt to relate function and structure. Even more difficult to grasp is the fact that immune response is now known to be part of the loop.

The measure of these activities is a fascinating study in itself. Molecules jump around at different rates, in some relation to their weight. They move in a stream of air or water, in the same relationship. On this apparently simple fact are based a number of marvellous machines for the analysis of flavour. Olfactometers and chromatographs, coupled to specially programmed computers, are giving answers to questions which we are in the process of acquiring enough knowledge to ask. Take comfort in the fact that humans, unassisted, come up with inimitable information, and none of these mighty machines has yet yelled *Eureka!* in the bathtub, like Archimedes did after he lost the soap.

There is excitement in the rhythm of atoms. The forces that make up their particles resonate and their molecules can be seen under the microscope causing a dance, described first by Mr Brown, Brownian movement.

Few human activities in everyday life release more happy hormones than the rhythms we see and hear. As we have learnt our first standard in the womb, the closer musical rhythms are to the harmonics of the beating heart, the greater their instinctive appeal. The brain rhythms tend to synchronise and *voilà*, more endorphins. Superlearning (a speed-learning technique) takes advantage of this by utilising the wonderful rhythms of music of the Baroque period. The regular missed beat of syncopation is especially exciting because it invites the listener to contribute his/her own beat to the silent gap.

Buddha's conception of the Wheel of Life has a basis in science. We are part of a cycle, created in rhythm, entering the world by regular contractions of the womb; and when breathing and pulse beats cease the natural cycle still continues. Everything we enjoy eating results from interrupting some cycle. Our daily bread, ripe cheese, good wine, are all the result of the skilful interruption of a natural cycle.

The breathing of all cells is fuelled by a cycle of three linked carbon molecules which transfer oxygen around and around, air to plants to animals and man, to air, to plants. Virtually every living cell uses this cycle or would if not prevented. During these revolutions of the wheel of life, aromatics are being taken in, and volatiles given off, so that we smell of the things we eat, which taste of the things they eat.

We use the light of the sun to measure time. Light is the force. Flowers are at their most fragrant in the early morning. Most flowers, that is; some, such as the night-blooming jasmine, attract nocturnal insects for their reproductive purposes, as do some orchids. Early-morning milk is used exclusively for certain cheeses. International air travellers soon learn the importance of circadian rhythms to the harmony of their body physiology. Some poets believe the air and the sea smell differently when the moon waxes. During the lunar cycle, the body clock works over a broad compass of body chemistry, most obviously in the female, who experiences cyclic changes in response to odours, and in the production of her own attractant body scents. Deprived of the cycle of daylight, in dark caves on an experimental basis, menstrual cycles go awry, but will tend to synchronise with other females present.

The pleasure loop is one of the most common and obvious cycles of response to odour, like an endless tape on a machine. Switch on, play message, switch off, and so on. The pleasure of certain smells when the appetite for food (bliss point) or sexual activity is aroused, is followed by indifference when the appetite is satisfied and the tape switches off.

There are upwards of five brain hormones involved in this cycle. On the basis of the fact that they are spelt with ten letters or more and they are only mentioned once in this book, you may be grateful to be spared them. Anticipation, the pleasure of a reward, the motor processes to get it, and some less specific qualities like awareness, learning, and knowing, each have feedback systems that work on the hypothalamus and smell brain to result in *opioid*, happy hormone, release. That event completes the loop by influencing the first lot of hormones. I told you it was complicated, and that is not all. Consider the temavour, the emotional component. Unpleasant smells are generally the most effective in the arousal of awareness. Exposure to pleasant aromas inclines people to remember good experiences, and unpleasant smells tend to recall unhappy situations, of which more in the Epilogue.

In monkeys and more advanced species, the grey matter of the solitary tract (first relay of the primary taste quintet), extends right up the brainstem to the thalamus. The interbrain is the box seat to centralise all the loops concerned with eating, pleasure and other emotions. Serial processing of the input becomes possible, and the higher the level of integration, the more precise the fine tuning and the more flexible the response. The final bonus of these loops is to allow independent judgments of pleasure and other qualities, for example, food value. *Choice* is one of the characteristic traits of intelligence, a benefit, as we have seen, of the huge new brain.

Every science needs tools of trade to formulate and measure. Quite apart from social barriers, the science of olfaction has been held back by the lack of precise, clear standards. Long ago there was general agreement on a theoretical length of a man's foot, and how to split up the time it takes for the earth to revolve. Odour has been different. Apart from most people feeling good about the smell of a rose, no standard 'rose' could ever be agreed upon. No longer. Even the vast variation in the ability of individuals to pick up a particular smell or taste has been by-passed by new techniques, so that at last we are on solid ground. The last century has seen a watershed, starting with the synthesis of carbon chain compounds to provide, among other things, constant, reproducible odour standards. The fact that the fragrance of a rose alters during the day, or that the bouquet of a wine changes every ten minutes, as does the sniffer, is no longer an obstacle.

Enter chromatography. Have you ever walked along the shore at ebb tide? Or gazed tranquilly at the quiet flow of clear water in a shallow stream? Ask those who fossick for sapphires, gold particles, whatever, in river beds, where they have their easiest finds? Shells, stones, fragments slow and settle from a steady flow, according to their weight and size, in fairly constant positions. This applies from the smallest molecules up to the largest that will move in a flow. The principle has become the basis of some striking investigatory tools. It was first applied in Russia in 1906 for the separation of coloured plant pigments flowing down a column of chalk powder, where they separated into bands at different levels, later to be washed out individually. Mikhail Semenovitch Tswett called it *chromatography*, colour writing. I wish he had not, because the principle has since been applied in so many media, and with so many different kinds of particles, few of which have much to do with colour, that the title is cumbersome and confusing. We need a punchy two-syllable word meaning 'measuring particles by flow rate', to be used as a group name for other machines advancing our knowledge of taste and smell in this manner. Not the least of the benefits of the principle has been the development of equipment to exchange ions from seawater to produce fresh, and to soften hard, water.

The spectrum of electromagnetic radiation is the *ostinato* base of the harmony of the universe of which we are infinitesimal particles. Electromagnetic radiation is due to waves of energy caused by the acceleration of charged particles, electric and magnetic fields vibrating at right angles to each other, and to the direction of motion, if you wish to know. It is possible to measure the vibration rates that take place in different parts of this spectrum. Many of them yield valuable information to advance our knowledge of flavour.

The spectro(photo)meter measures the amount of light of particular wavelengths. It measures the difference between one beam of light that has passed through a colour and another going straight through the machine. Suppose then that the beam under investigation is passed through light of successively longer wavelengths. This provides an absorption spectrum, characteristic of each atomic group. The principle has been extended. Infra-red and ultra-violet spectrometry are ordinary tools now. Machines are able to perform non-destructive analysis by absorption of radiowaves, by scattering of light and so forth. Electrophoresis is separation in an electrical field, in liquid or gas.

Paper chromatography took off in the 1930s. If you dip a blotter into fluid in a vessel, the fluid creeps up the blotter. A drop of solution X on the blotter will show a similar banding of its constituents as first seen by Tswett. Gas (liquid) chromatography (GLC or GC) does precisely this, to separate gases, vapours, and odorants to be studied, in the medium of an inert warm courier gas blown over the aromatic compound under investigation. The separation is delicate and precise and gives answers not previously possible, as in the legend to the figure.

All the volatiles of the scents and stinks of food and drink, of the body and the land, show up in these examinations. In one small food group there are over seventy GC peaks in the carbon chain compounds present from C-1 to C-14. Such complexity is general for foods which have more than a hundred volatile compounds. Many of the same occur in different foods, wines and flowers. Then they differ in peak amounts, and times of presentation along the flow, to the odour computer in the smell brain. Only a few are unique, like the cut green grass of IMP or the clove of eugenol. The resolving power of gas chromatography is phenomenal. It can detect minute amounts in a complex mixture, of the hundred compounds in petrol, for example.

While on this subject, there is evidence that there may be a separation of odour molecules in the airstream in the nose, so that small, light particles register early and forward in the receiving patch at the roof of the nose between the eyes, and the big, heavier ones are perceived last. There may be a good reason for this difference. The molecules of the most dangerous threats to life tend to be smaller, as do some of the most arresting (female) pheromones. The most complex odour molecules are rather big and heavy, and suggest contemplation rather than urgent action. Androstenone is one of these.

The olfactometer is the oldest tool still in use in this science. From people sniffing measured odorants in a closed space, the method now has a very modern look about it. Trained rodents, who show the same intimidating variation in performance as humans, perform in plastic boxes, breathing controlled air, and make flavour choices; the new factor is that these are recorded and collated in an individual computer for immediate observation and action by the observer, if indicated. It is quite extraordinary to look at the screen reeling off the results of the day's testing alongside previous performance and be able to say 'Fred's not quite on his top form today.'

The bottom line remains encouraging to those who feel threatened with redundancy. Two to four boxes

A Marvellous Sniffing Machine, the Gas Chromatograph (GC)

(These particular examples are taken from the work of M.J. Eyles and R.F. Adams)

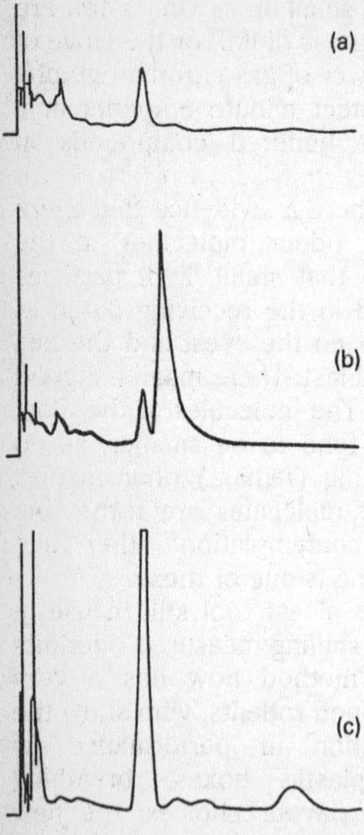

GC profiles of canned (a) mushrooms, (b) tuna, (c) tomato

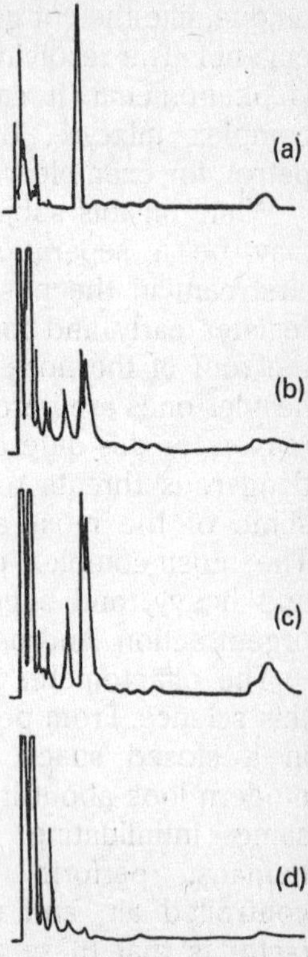

GC profiles of UHT cream: (a) unspoiled. (b, c, d) spoiled

of microchips coupled together provide an impeccable 'fingerprint' of the smell, but not yet the smell itself, nor the quality of recognition that the living, loving, sniffer can achieve. More of this in the Epilogue.

4

THE MOLECULES OF ATTRACTION

24

Genesis: The Seven Days of Flavour Creation

> Reality is not only more fantastic than we think but more fantastic than we imagine.
>
> J.B.S. Haldane

The biblical seven days of creation seem an excellent model for a pilgrim to progress to an understanding of the actual building blocks of the smells and tastes in Nature. This new concept, of the essence of excitement, explores the sequence from a single ion, through simple and volatile, to complex and ponderous. Almost all 'natural' odours and tastes are mixtures compounded sometimes of hundreds of different molecules. We have seen in Chapter 19, 'The Three R's', that they are perceived and identified as a unity by smell and taste working together.

Less than a billion years ago, algae and worms appeared. Billions of years before that the energy of all matter may have appeared in a single flash of light and heat. Even now cosmic particles sound the 'song of hydrogen' on our radiotelescopes. Out there in the dust clouds that are thickening to form new stars, as many as eleven carbon atoms have been found linked together. The linking of carbon atoms signals the beginning of life.

New light may be shed on the origins of life through a recent discovery by Australian researchers of the most complex chemical molecules known to exist in space. They were found in fragments of the Murchison meteorite which crashed in Victoria in 1969, and the discovery suggests that the first living things could have arisen through a combination of chemical building blocks derived both from space and from Earth. The meteorite is believed to be about 4.6 billion years old, slightly older than the Earth itself.

Dr Richard Pashley of the Australian National University believes that the polymers among those building blocks have the potential to form cellular membranes, and they are thought to be precursors of living cells. Earlier analysis of the same meteorite had previously yielded amino acids and other complex molecules which make up other chemical building blocks of life. These molecules could have found their way to Earth, and in contact with water could have formed cellular structures.

This seems a fitting prelude to the few examples I have assembled for this book, of the logic of the carbon chain and its beautiful and predictable harmonic sequences. And at the conclusion, how better to describe the intimate chemistry of human sex and survival than as a steroid miracle?

> It makes good sense to revere the sun and the stars because we are all their children.
>
> Carl Sagan, *The Cosmos*

Ancient cultures worshipped the sun as the giver of life. This echoes the fact that everything we are, or perceive, derives from the matter and energy of the universe, and in particular from the hydrogen atoms identical to those issuing from a solar flare even as you read this.

Creation, day one, starts with a hydrogen atom. The outer shell of this atom has a single electron on point duty ready for action. The solitary atom of hydrogen carries a positive electrical charge which in solution acts as an acid, so that the first taste in evolution may well be sour. Perhaps its positive electrical charge is the primary trigger of the go/no-go response that is the basis of survival of the primitive cell and is much later to become the working language of the flavour computer.

Day two sees other electrons joining the outer shell. Depending on their number, atoms of carbon, nitrogen, oxygen, and later sulphur materialise. Oxygen, nitrogen and carbon dioxide make up the loose mix called air. Water exists as clouds of steam.

Things really start to move on the third day, when hydrogen, carbon, nitrogen and sulphur form marsh gas (methane), ammonia and rotten-egg gas (H_2S), in a primordial soup. None of them supports life and a fourth gas, cyanide (hydrogen, carbon nitrogen) is instantly toxic. It smells of almond and it is also bitter, one of the first warnings of danger in the genesis of flavour. Ammonia is very pungent and H_2S and methane verge on the putrid. What a paradox that what are to become the foundations of life itself first appear in so noxious a form. Sodium and chlorine will be around now to form salt. A soupçon of iron, copper, magnesium, cobalt and a few other atoms also appear.

Day four ushers in the dawn of the carbon chain, the linking carbon atoms without which the chemistry of living cells cannot exist. The most informed science fiction writers tell of life forms in other galaxies which are silicon-based and able to thrive in a kind of heat we can only guess at. Why not?

The atom of carbon has its own unique set of reactions. It can link with another to start to make a chain. It can combine with oxygen, i.e. oxidise. It can

Flavours of the Carbon Chain

-C- crushed ants
-C-C- vinegar
-C-C-C- similar but different
-C-C-C-C- rancid buttery
-C-C-C-C-C- sweaty, 'scenty', sour
-C-C-C-C-C-C- intense, rancid, less sour
-C-C-C-C-C-C-C less sour
-C-C-C-C-C-C-C-C- fatty oil, less sour
-C-C-C-C-C-C-C-C-C- mildly nutty, fatty
-C-C-C-C-C-C-C-C-C-C- rancid, cheesy

Odours of the first ten fatty acids in the carbon chain

unite with two atoms of oxygen and one of hydrogen to form the remarkable family of carbon or organic acids, which can do just about anything except ionise like an inorganic acid. Those ending with =O are called aldehydes and far into the future will be made in a laboratory to give the top notes in the world's most popular perfume. Sweetness appears now in the three-carbon compound, glycerol. Three-carbon compounds are at the centre of the fuel/energy cycles of plant and animal cells. Our 'sugar' is made from two of them and chains of these sweeteners provide the energy reservoirs, starch and glycogen, long lines of sugars (polymers) which paradoxically have lost their flavour. Conversely to the delights of our everyday 'sugar' and 'alcohol', some of the first molecules in the various carbon series can be rather negative. The one-carbon acid (they are often called 'fatty acids' because of their role in the make-up of fats) is pungent and very corrosive. Its alcohol is selectively poisonous, with the capacity to destroy the optic nerves (methylated spirits really can send you blind). Immediately after this, matters improve. Many consider the two-carbon alcohol (as in wine) and its acid (the acetic of vinegar) to be benedictions. Much of the flavour of the various milks and cheeses of different animals resides in the first ten fatty acids. The former is our first food, teaching template of human smell and taste. The latter is one of the most ancient and nutritious foods of human social groups.

Umami, deliciousness, is the last primary taste to be created, having had to await the formation of glutamic acid from nitrogen joining up with the carbon acids. These amino acids are the building blocks of the proteins of cells and genes, at the centre of life itself. Pheromones are the most compelling of all the excitements of flavour, and some of the female scents IVA, TMA and dodecanol appear now, to continue through evolution. The lighter fragrances are starting to make their appearance, to reach their acme in the coming day.

The sun is eternal, incandescent heat. Its offspring on earth is fire, terrifying master or marvellous servant. On the fifth day the primal markers of smoke and 'burnt' appear with the closure of the links in the carbon chain to make a ring. This flash of enlightenment appeared as a snake, coiling head to tail, during a reverie enjoyed by Friedrich August Kekulè von Stradonitz on top of a Clapham bus. These rings may consist of five or more atoms, thereby giving the myriad possibilities of flavour. All the Maillard toast and roast delights, the greens of IMP, the essences of spices, flowers, surely now entitle us to a biblical 'behold and it was good'.

Day six starts with the squalene molecule, key to the steroid miracle, crowning achievement of the chemistry of creation. It is an unwieldy long-chain carbon molecule first found in ray-type fish and now known to be a substantial part of the skin surface lipids. Dr Amos Smith at the Monell Centre has shown it is also among the major volatiles in the scent signals of some monkeys and some moths.

Cyclic closures of parts of the chain take place, and from here a series of logical steps through cholesterol ends with the production of androstenone, the pheromone that is the essence of excitement. The related flavour of musk is a surprising addition to the food and drink of many cultures. The hormones involved with stress, survival and sex are formed along the way.

The seventh day, by all that is holy, should see a day of rest. It does seem a good time to ponder the progress made by human hands in the past hundred years. The actual synthesis of an organic carbon compound first occurred in 1845 in the laboratory of Adolph Kolbe. It was the -C-C- fatty acid, the acetic acid of vinegar by any other name. The subsequent construction of the first molecule that had never existed before has been attributed to Pierre Bethelot. This is the promise of human genius, and its application to the genesis of flavour has resulted in substances that some consider on occasion to be an improvement on the natural thing.

25

IMP and Family

To start, the name of the subject presents a problem. For years I have been referring to it as MIP. I wouldn't presume to give anything so important a nickname like IMP. Its given name, that which is now preferred by most professionals, is isobutyl methoxy pyrazine. We have to call it something less cumbersome because it will be mentioned frequently, and it is a very important compound in flavour. So IMP it is. To keep in touch with reality, the smell of a cut capsicum (bell pepper) drifts over as I write. You might just possibly munch one as you read, to establish a mood.

IMP is the smell of cut green grass and bell pepper, a note shared by many green vegetables, perfumes, and some very special wine grapes. Several outstanding scientists have devoted much of their careers to the examination of this seminal flavour group: to name two, Dr Ron Buttery, an Australian in the United States Department of Agriculture at Berkeley, and my very tolerant friend and deeply wise teacher the late Jack Shipton, member of a group working on pyrazines at the Council for Scientific and Industrial Research.

This subject is about pea flavour as much as anything. It is a subject of great economic importance, emphasised by remarkable observations on the preference of American urban children for 'round' peas, against the 'square' ones. Round peas are from a can, and the square ones are natural and fresh. The children reacted in this way because they had never tasted fresh peas before the test, but that belongs in 'Start to Taste'.

An Australian research team spent some years on the project. Its leader, Dr Frank Whitfield, became severely afflicted by sinus trouble as a direct result. To complete the research he was forced to wear a respirator. One of the first major problems the team encountered was the absence of a reliable chemical comparative standard for IMP (nowadays available at a phone call) and a considerable delay ensued while it was synthesised. Nearly twenty years ago that particular diversion ended up as just a few lines in their trail-blazing paper. A small note here hardly seems sufficient recognition for such devotion to the scientific method.

It all started with a truckload, a mountain of just-picked green peas, which were chemically winnowed down to a small stoppered phial of the ultimate heart scent of Pea. With the stopper out the aroma of fresh peas 'could be smelt in Canberra'. Sometimes Jack would carry it from room to room in his lab coat pocket with a handkerchief over it. If he pulled the handkerchief out, someone was sure to exclaim about fresh peas in the room. This little bottle became the precious focus of the research, and as the conclusion of the project came into view, safe-guarding the extract became a matter of the utmost caution. On one occasion, it was safely laid to rest in his desk, with the strongest warning not to touch it. A while later he recognised the strong green odour he had come to know so well. His quick accusation that the phial had been interfered with was halted by the sight of his blameless wife sitting in the kitchen shelling some really fresh peas.

The work has become a classic. They found 119 distinct flavour compounds in fresh peas. Peas, hand-picked and put straight into the cooking pot, had a mild and characteristic flavour. Harvested by machine, there is unavoidable damage, which releases enzymes that stimulate the production of more of our compounds. Much the same process occurs when an onion is cut or garlic is crushed. Some prefer the flavour of peas one to two hours after picking. Longer delays induce a characteristic flavour change, comparable to the smell of old hay.

My own interest in IMP dates from a meeting with Dr Richard Peterson at Monterey in the mid-1970s, after I had been growing cabernet sauvignon grapes for about ten years and was attempting a book on the variety which I wanted to make as complete as I could. Our discussion was on the green note present in the aroma of cabernet sauvignon, especially if grown in cool conditions or from vines cultivated without understanding. This note can dominate the young wine, with a suggestion of Hungarian goulash rather than the lovely blackcurrant which is its noble birthright. Work was in progress at that time at the University of California at Davis, which had tracked this grassy flavour to IMP (or MIP as it then was).

We now cut to an evening in 1981, to the Chemistry School at the University of New South Wales. It is a spellbinding experience to hear the master of a subject, Ron Buttery, expounding with deceptive simplicity. This was such a night. As the lecture progressed, quite suddenly I was riveted at the words 'and when a methyl [one-carbon] group is added to the ring, the bell pepper capsicum green note is replaced by a minty odour. Add another, and you have a suggestion of camphor.' I felt the hair on the back of my neck rise with excitement. The lecture theatre was crammed to the roof with my betters. (I had little right to be there, a gatecrashing ex-surgeon, with an unspecified interest in hearing a world-class researcher discourse on food flavour.) No one seemed particularly moved at that moment, no intake of breath, no hushed silence, nor any buzz of comment. Didn't they realise that here, now, they might well be learning why the green grass aroma of some cabernet sauvignon wines later develops a bouquet with mint overtones? The lecture proceeded without interruption to its brilliant conclusion.

Someone was watching over me. I have since found that it is in the range of alchemy to try and tack one or two methyls on to that side of a carbon ring – highly improbable, if not impossible. Furthermore, there are numerous other aromas available in the flavour bag of tricks possessed by the mighty cabernet sauvignon to create a minty note.

IMP is also present in sauvignon blanc. It may dominate that grape's wine flavour in an unpleasant way (to many) unless the vines have been carefully tended, or grown in a relatively hospitable climate. With delicate additions some perfumes hint of a 'green' note, but it must be done with restraint.

The substance IMP is in the vanguard of the most powerful smells in existence. Dr Buttery described the threshold (first notice of it), as being at the strength of one-tenth of a drop of the pure compound to an Olympic-sized swimming pool. Why is the smell of IMP so potent? It could well be an evolutionary survival marker. Capsicum, the IMP smell, is very high in Vitamin C, and we all know how important that is. That is a simple answer. It just may be true.

Other pyrazines turn up in the wider investigation of food flavour. Potato and beetroot don't surprise, but what about twelve different members of the family in cocoa? Heat develops the appreciation and quantity of pyrazine flavour. Boiled potatoes are very bland with an earthy pyrazine-based flavour. Jacket-baked, without oil, a whole new range of the family appears – the alkyl pyrazines, with a vast increase in flavour, especially in the lovely peanutty skin, where they are concentrated. Frying chips, in fact, to 170 degrees C/338 degrees F brings up 170 flavour volatiles! Annie Gallois describes a similar transfiguration of pyrazine flavours by various bacteria, for example, the nutty note of some great cheeses, even part of the flavour of soya sauce and chocolate.

I don't wish to tire your patience by wandering any further into the pyrazine business, but it was important to open the door a fraction, to introduce an aspect of flavour you might not otherwise encounter.

5

UNTIL NOW

26

Eden and After

Be not the first by whom the new is tried
Nor yet the last to cast the old aside

Sir William Osler

This capsule of the history of flavour and fragrance embraces the lightest and darkest areas of the human experience. Records and hard evidence only cover a fraction of it and we are left to guess at much of what might have been. We begin this retrospect with fragrance. The woman of the Sahara, wrapped only in a woollen shawl, who squats over spices and herbs on coals in a hole dug in the sand and whose ancestors performed the same ritual for thousands of years, is separated by less than half a century from the user of the perfumed and flavoured douches touted by Madison Avenue. Both pay tribute to the kind of behaviour you may have observed in your own dog, given that opportunity. Straight out of a much-resented bath, probably smelling of soap it abhors, it rolls ecstatically in steaming manure or rotting seaweed, actions which demonstrate the instinctive attractions, masking capabilities, and repulsions of smell.

Imagine the first excited comment from the archaeologist lowered several metres down into a recently discovered chamber in the Egyptian desert, undisturbed for more than five thousand years, something like 'I can smell cedar!' The Egyptians believed that the wood was imperishable, and used it to make sarcophagi and funeral boats in which deceased VIPs were conveyed to the other world. It was burnt as incense at religious ceremonies and its exquisite oil was used in cosmetics and perfumes, alone or blended. The routine was to be rubbed down with a lesser oil, then to be scraped dry and finished with something more special. The practice was followed in the whole Mediterranean basin for several thousand years. It kept the skin supple in the dry and blinding heat, made a stunning contribution to the attractiveness of the wearer, and persisted long after water became more easily available. Military expeditions were mounted to ensure a stable supply of cedar wood. The final result today is that there are only miniscule areas of indigenous cedar forest remaining, in Lebanon, Cyprus, Spain and northern Africa. Sandalwood occupied a similar position in the fragrance hierarchy of India and China, possibly at a later date, and of course some of this beautiful timber and its perfume found its way to the Incense Road in response to the insatiable needs of Pharaonic Egypt.

The Kingdom of Punt was the fragrance centre of the ancient world. It is difficult to determine exactly where it was; somewhere near where present-day Yemen dents the Somali coast of Africa, and probably on the African side or even both sides of the Red Sea. Frances Kennet describes the publication of pictures in 1877 of the carved bas-reliefs showing the Egyptians trading with the King of the Puntites and 'his grotesquely fat wife', and how the wall depicting the latter and all the description disappeared. Perhaps it has become the 'before' image on the wall of some exclusive weight-reduction establishment (with luck to surface soon so that we can learn where these fabled ingredients came from).

The point of Arabia Felix on the Red Sea was the domain of the Queen of Sheba, she to whom was addressed that most erotic and pheromonal poem we appropriately call the *Song of Songs.* This remarkable business woman managed to have both herself and her bodyservant impregnated in the one evening. Solomon departed this mortal coil at forty to be remembered at the height, so to speak, of his awesome powers. More of this remarkable couple in 'Queens of Fragrance'.

It is difficult to give a balanced account of the use of fragrance in the Nile valley. Records go back five thousand years, of which the earliest describe lotions to prevent body odour. Food and drink were scented. Workers went on strike because no ointments were supplied. Cosmetics seem to have been used about as much as today, or possibly more.

> If thou art a man of standing thou should found thy house and love thy wife at home as is fitting. Fill her belly and clothe her back. Ointment is the prescription of her body.
>
> *Ptah-hotep* (translated by Frances Kennett)

The range of ingredients was really very extensive, seeming only to lack a few important animal fixative agents like musk and ambergris. The oils included almond, sesame, olive, safflower, radish, cedar and others. The resins and gums of shrubs and trees gave myrrh, pine, juniper, frankincense and liquid amber (storax). Among the spices were cinnamon, nutmeg and cassia. Plants and trees also produced citron, ginger, rosemary, myrtle, peppermint, various grasses and rushes, and a seemingly endless list of flowers and trees beginning with rose, mimosa and heliotrope, and of course the standard cedar and sandalwood. These are some of the common ones, mentioned as likely to be encountered somewhere in modern fragrance at least once in a lifetime. They used a pretty reliable fixative, despite the lack of the animal notes. Tutankhamen's tomb, opened in 1922, contained an ointment which was still fragrant.

Hatshepsut of the eighteenth dynasty (*c.* 1567–1320 BC), she who sent the expedition to Punt recorded above, was conceived after a visit by the god Amon, according to a wall inscription quoted by Frances Kennett (compare the *Song of Songs*, written a few hundred years later):

> He found her as she slept in the beauty of her palace. She awakened at the fragrance of the god, which she smelled in the presence of his majesty. When he came before her, she rejoiced in the sight of his beauty. His love passed into her limbs, which the fragrance of god flooded. All his odours were from Punt.

Male gods smelt rather special. Those from India were depicted with mangoes, still known for their aphrodisiac powers in India and elsewhere although the all-night mango parties are less common beyond the subcontinent.

Myrrh and frankincense were at least as valuable as gold. Recall the gifts of the three Magi to the baby Jesus. Eleven centuries before this Ranses III ceremoniously gave one of the three great gods of Egypt over nine thousand jars of incense ingredients, plus nearly a ton of myrrh. The scale of the perfume trade is difficult to encompass. Roy Genders tells of Herodotus (300–200 BC) discussing the delivery of thirty tons of frankincense to the king of Persia, by Arab traders, on a yearly basis. When one considers the labour of gathering the myrrh resin from the beards of goats who grazed this inaccessible shrub, compressing it into little cakes, and then transporting it by camel caravan over long waterless desert to the perfumers, the importance of the product to the users becomes apparent.

The magnificent perfume Kyphi, Khepri, perhaps the forerunner of 'Chypre', is first encountered as a gift from the gods used by the Egyptian priestly class. Plutarch's version is from his *Lives*, ten centuries or so later.

> Acorus calamus, andropogon, schoenanthus, cassia, cinnannomum, peppermint, pistacis and convolvulus scoparius, which were dried and powdered and then mixed together. Saffron and dbellium were added. Equal quantities of juniper, acacia, henna and cyperus longus were macerated in wine and added to honey, resin, myrrh and raisins steeped in wine. The whole concoction was beaten up, made into a paste and allowed to solidify. It was then ready to be placed in the burner as an offering.

Plutarch also records that it is 'made of those things that delight most in the night', a fascinating comment from a conservative old scold.

It took a few centuries for the Greek and Roman conquests to destroy the Egyptian legacy to civilisation, leaving but a message in stone of what had gone before. The newer cultures were partly derivative, but there were some developments, especially in personal hygiene. Bathing, followed by the massage of scented oils, became general. Anyone visiting the ruins of Pompeii cannot fail to be impressed by the scale of the private baths and the plumbing that must have been involved. The next time that such highly organised arrangements are encountered, after the thousands of public baths in Constantinople of Justinian's era, is the 'stews' of the European eighteenth century, all-day baths (doubling as brothels if required). Sydney has at least one such at the time of writing, and I am sure it is not alone. In Japan, extensive attention is still given to cleanliness at public baths, but here it is traditional for the family group to take part in a wholesale ritual. Young and old are soaped and scrubbed immaculate, to finish with a swim or a hot soak.

Much more could be written on the use of fragrances by ancient civilisations, but to do them justice would require a book with a wheel at each corner.

A big book is a big nuisance

Callimachus

The use of fragrances was virtually universal in sweetening the passage of an ordinary day; for all manner of religious purposes such as thanking the gods for manifest blessings like perfume, or the ceremonies involved in a scented farewell to the dead, and in enhancing the art of love. Good smells were equated with good health, the converse being equally true. The use of odour-producing plants solely for health later became a separate profession from that of the perfumers.

Athenaeus, in *The Deipnosophists*, 'the philosophers at dinner' – written about two centuries into the present era – assembled a droll and wonderful catalogue of flavour and fragrance. We owe him the deepest gratitude for the details of his fantasy, an incredible epic of conversation and feasting during a binge that lasted for three days; fancied guests ranged over food, wine, cooking, perfumes and morals, with inimitable style and wit. He probably had an important classic from the previous century, the even longer work of Pliny, to draw on, but Pliny wrote it straight and it can be hard going. I have a frail hope that this comes across more like Athenaeus than Pliny.

The Romans adopted Greek fragrances wholesale. Everything in first-century Rome was scented with something, streets, sails of ships, walls, pets, whatever. As already mentioned, the special development of the Roman Empire was the popular use of special bathing centres where specialists ministered to the hygiene and fragrance preferences of their *clientèle.*

The Greek botanist of the fourth century BC, Theophrastus, in *De Odoribus* provides a complete and acceptable 'modern' view of the perfume industry of the period. The oil of the balanos tree, from East Africa and Egypt, was the preferred fixative, along with sesame oil and almond oil. Olive oil was thought too thick and greasy. He described *kypros,* whose predecesssors have already been mentioned, here compounded from fragrances grown on the hills of Cyprus, the forerunner of a whole perfume style, *Chypre.* Thus, the original Chypre was made from *calamus,* sweet rush (spicy and bitter), *styrax* (suggesting the fresh sweaty odour of love-making), and *labdanum* (fresh, clean hair), to give a fairly sensuous, even 'blissful' scent that would bring lasting distinction to Edmund Coty of Paris about two thousand years into the future – 1917, to be precise. Greek preference, influenced by a better water supply, and a more amenable climate, and fostered by the more delicate local fragrances, inclined towards floral notes. They contrast with the resins that oozed from vegetation of the parched regions of Africa and Asia, and the need for the heavy, spicy, clinging scents by dwellers of those arid lands.

Theophrastus made specific recommendations. 'Perfumes appear to be sweetest when the scent comes from the wrist.' The women of that period developed to a fine art the application of different perfumes to separate areas of the body. I have already mentioned my wine-tasting friend, who 'never applied perfume above her waist'. 'The lightest perfumes, rose, kypros and lily, seem best applied to men. For women, myrrh, sweet marjoram, spikenard, Megaleion and the Egyptian.' The latter two were extremely expensive (duty-free?), compounded of the rarest fragrances and needing long preparation.

Just as the Greek use of fragrance was taken up by the Romans, so also did the Muslim rulers of Baghdad assimilate the Persian culture, particularly the passion for flowers and gardens. Two centuries before, the founder of Islam is reputed to have himself spoken graphically of his own body smell, and lyrical descriptions of the scents of places and people in the hereafter were offered to all true believers. Solomon may have used the ravishing sandalwood for the pillars of his temple to perfume the devotions of worshippers, but Islam frequently incorporated musk and the most powerful and rarest of resins in the mortar of the walls of the great mosques. It is still perceptible.

A crude form of distillation may have existed about 3500 BC, but the Arabs perfected the still. This has been an incalculable influence on fragrance and flavour, quite apart from the revenues of governments, ancient and modern, and the health of the cultures which have over-enthusiastically adopted its products. Distillation of the essential oils of fruits, flowers, and various vegetable substances has subsequently provided one of the most direct paths to the essence of excitement. And how much gladder was the heart of man in so many peasant dwellings of the past as a result of the products of 'moonshine', *eaux de vie* of fruits and grains. It is a pleasure to acknowledge the debt I incurred to an ancient and alien culture during my adolescent rustication, from the distillation of the little, red, intensely sweet apples that grew abundantly in the farm's orchard. Pleasure was only marred by the need to be back at the diary at sun-up in time for milking.

A considerable body of information was transmitted throughout Europe by the Islamic occupation. The Greek, Persian and Hindu were combined with new Arabic influences in encyclopaedic works, to be enthusiastically used by scientists, apothecaries, and perfumers. Distant England learned of these advances from the returning crusaders.

The sixteenth century was the golden age of Venice. The popular use of perfumes and spices compares with Rome's and Egypt's most extravagant exhibitions. Money, toothpicks and hairpins were all scented, to name only a few less obvious things. Rival Florence excelled as well. A noble Roman family created a perfume still known by their family name, Frangipani; it was made from just about every known spice, ground iris root (violet note) and a dash of civet or musk, the powder to be digested in rectified spirits of wine. The result was an extremely long-lasting perfume. The lovely West Indian flower of the same name has a similar bouquet. The French connection of the Florentine Renaissance and its perfumes is discussed in Chapter 8, 'Queens of Fragrance'.

Fear of the plague had much to do with the formal beginnings of French perfumery. Herb and flower gardens were planted as a source of herbal remedies more than for any other reason. Later on, musk, ambergris and civet dominated popular preference, together with Italian 'Chypre' and orange-flower water. Catherine de Medici established a domestic fragrance industry at Grasse, not far from Nice, today a paradise to visit at the flowering times of the various plants.

The English were quick to enjoy all that was happening in fragrance across the Channel, at least until the Commonwealth, when the use of fragrance was abolished by edict, and pleasure became shame. It is difficult to guess which was the most potent source of the guilt that permeates modern Western mores, the Essenes in the desert of the Holy Land of the last century before Christ or the Puritans of northern and central Europe. They are gone, but unfortunately not forgotten.

The art of perfumery reached its modern climax in nineteenth-century Paris. The little Corsican and his perfumer Houbigant were as responsible as any. Napoleon daily doused himself with *eau de toilette.* His beloved Josephine was actually christened Rose, and among her manifest virtues was the breeder of a delightful tea rose at Malmaison, itself a treasure trove of the most fragrant blooms. Her own scent can only be imagined, three days unwashed at the express command of the Emperor: '*Je reviens en trois jours, ne te laves pas!*' – a remark made even more famous as the name of a perfume 'Je reviens' by Worth. Perfectly unforgettable, she was in Napoleon's dying thoughts, despite his having divorced her in order to breed an heir. Now *that* is a lingering fragrance!

Paul Parquet of Houbigant added synthetics to natural components to produce classics like 'Fougère Royale' in 1882 (with its green fern note) and 'Parfum Ideal', with synthetics coumarin (fresh straw), musk ketone, eugenol (clove), and ionone (violet). This was a quarter of a century before 'Chanel No. 5' was created in 1921. Another Houbigant perfume led the trend away from the heavier 'Chypre' style to the lighter florals, which reached their acme in Nina Ricci's 'L'Air du Temps' even later. The fundamental reason for the alteration in direction was a vast improvement in standards of personal and public cleanliness, with a diminished need to mask body and other odours. Guerlain's 'Jicky' has survived and thrived from 1889; it is basically lavender, with heliotrope and a soupçon of civet. Marcel Proust used it then, and other men do well with it now. It is an effective unisex perfume. It is no surprise that a number of the fragrances constructed for women work well on men.

So much for fragrance. What does history tell us of flavour? Biblical historians place the Garden of Eden in the fertile crescent of the Tigris and Euphrates rivers in Asia Minor, perhaps six thousand years ago. The apple of temptation might have been a pomegranate. The authors of the story clearly recognised the irresistible, instinctive drives of the limbic system, which can swamp intelligent choice as we all know.

What were the beginnings of the enjoyment and excitement at table, that we tend to take so much for granted today? As early as ten thousand years ago it seems mustard seeds were chewed with meat. Charles Lamb's droll view of the origin of roast pork must have some counterpart in reality: someone must have been the first human enjoyer of Professor Maillard's reaction. The sweetness of honey and salt licks were already enjoyed by mammalian forebears, as well as the products of fermentation if elephant's present-day splurges on fermenting berries in the African bush are any hint.

Many people pursue wine for the excitement of its flavour and complexity, as much as for the pleasures of moderate alcohol shared at meals. Some are even called connoisseurs. They had their counterparts in the civilisations of the Egyptian kingdoms and the Mesopotamian river valleys where fermentation became an exact science. Reay Tannahill considers that 40 per cent of Sumerian grain was used for beer, which was brewed by women. Honey converted to mead, palm sap to toddy, rice to *sake*, and dates and numerous other fruits to wine. The refined grape varieties appeared quite early in history to make wines which generated a degree of 'connoisseurship' contemporary wine buffs would clearly relate to.

Parallel to this developing expertise in fermented beverage flavours, bread and cheese reflected the continued search for improvement, and variety is one of the hallmarks of a highly developed brain. A few thousand years later, we have acquired the ability to vibrate the molecules of our daily bread at the rate of thirty-three million times a second to freshen it up in a microwave oven. It is likely to have in it several substances which did not even exist last century, all added in the pursuit of flavour.

Just as fire was carried by our ancestors fifty thousand years ago, later on when a good leaven of yeast was discovered, some of it was shared with neighbours, or kept or carried to start the next lot of bread, as a sourdough. We like the taste of fermentation, and the flavours that result from the by-products of lactobacilli are an additional dimension. Of these, cheese and yoghurt are the most obvious, and wine, pickles and other fascinating tastes and smells are influenced by this family of organisms.

After salt, fish sauce could well be the most generally used flavour enhancer in history, and certainly the oldest. Factories were set up, and the products of certain cities achieved special recognition. Here is a classical preparation of *liquamen*, or *garum*, from Bithynia on the Black Sea taken from Reay Tannahill's *Food in History*:

> It is best to take large or small sprats, or, failing them, take anchovies, or horse-mackerel, or mackerel, make a mixture of all and put into a baking trough. Take two pints of salt to the peck of fish and mix well to have the fish impregnated with salt. Leave it for one night, and then put it in an earthenware vessel which you place open in the sun for two or three months, stirring with a stick at intervals, then take it, cover it with a lid and store away.

(If the sauce were made with larger fish, the two to three months' exposure might stretch to as much as eighteen months.)

Some people add old wine, two pints to a pint of fish. If the sauce were made from especially fine fish, or from shellfish – shrimps, for example – the result was a refined, expensive, gourmet product. But whatever the ingredients or fermentation time, the liquamen was usually a clear golden fluid which kept well in a bottle or jar, and added a distinctively salty, slightly fishy, slightly cheesy flavour to any dish.

Spices are seeds or their covering, bark or roots. They have been a major influence on food and perfume for most of recorded history. The Spice Islands of Ceylon and the East Indies and southern Asia were the earliest sources of cinnamon, nutmeg, cloves, and above all, pepper. Their supply to the great civilisations of the ancient world dominated transport and trade.

In AD 408 the barbarian Alaric demanded and received three thousand pounds weight of pepper as part of the ransom to be paid by vanquished Rome. There were salt, spice and incense roads, of which the Silk Road, travelled by Marco Polo, is best remembered today. Spices were the main cargo of the caravans which made the epic journeys from Han China to the Mediterranean traders, the more so after silkworms were smuggled out of Cathay to Byzantium and a silk industry established in the West.

Apart from the zip of flavour, spices preserve food. Their value in cultures without cold storage can be understood by their widespread use. From thousands of years BC, the market of a major centre carried cinnamon, mace, cassia (coarser than cinnamon), cloves, nutmeg, black and white pepper, cumin, fennel and other forms of anise flavour, and saffron;

meat and poultry staleness was easily concealed, and to a degree arrested, by one or more of these aromatics. Chinese records date from about 1100 BC and their famous five-spice mix comes to our notice after that.

A totally new set of flavours swept Europe from the New World in the sixteenth century. The pungency of chilli was already understood from experience with pepper, mustard, horseradish, and some of the green vegetables, but the rose floral note fired (in every sense) the palates of devotees. Bell peppers, capsicum, tomatoes, potatoes, maize and chocolate caused great interest, even alarm, and some pretty stupid rumours about their effects. Dark, bitter chocolate is a sensational melder of the tomato, carrot (with tops), potato and turnip flavours, simmered in a casserole of tongue in the style of Aragon.

The less fortunate may not have the flavour choice of the well-to-do, but they do have their excitements. At the olive harvest in one impoverished village in coastal southern Italy, on festival night, a primitive press is loaded with consecutive layers of ripe olives, cloth, sheets of iron, olives again and so on, up to the top of the press under a huge wooden log. The weight of this is slowly applied to the load of fruit, when the first pressing, truly virgin oil, starts to ooze down to be collected in a tray below the stack. Hot crusty hardwheat bread just out of the oven is dipped into the light oil subtly flavoured by IMP, sprinkled with salt gathered from the dried deposit in rock pools, and washed down with wine made last week or so behind the casa. All this to noisy singing and abandoned dancing, which lasts the entire night.

Peasant food in dynastic Egypt was based on bread, onions and beer. The poor of Rome ate pastes and porridge made from grains. In early years this was mainly millet. Olives, figs and cheese, with an occasional piece of roast meat or salt fish from the corner store, lent some variety. The upper class of that society indulged in the most excessive banquets in history. The monotony of the energy food of working people, be it rice, beans, bread, potatoes, grain or pastes, has often been broken by some powerful, exciting note, however small the amount, such as curries, soya, chilli, curds, cheese, or sauces of meat and fish.

There are marked historic racial and ethnic flavour preferences. The fats and oils used for cooking tend to be strongly regional in origin and with a few exceptions have definite and often very attractive flavours. Some typical examples are, by region:

Mediterranean basin	Olive oil
Cold Europe	Butter, beef and pig fat, cream
India	Ghee (clarified butter)
Southern India	Sesame, coconut oils
Bengal	Mustardseed oil
South-east Asia	Peanut oil
China	Lard, peanut and soybean oils

Every nation has many individuals who cherish pungency in food to the point of pain, and beyond. The pretty green *wasabi* horseradish of Japan gives thermal punishment several dimensions greater than those of its European equivalent. Some forms of chilli and cayenne in Asia can become a near-religious experience for the uninitiated. Mustard sufficed for the English, and pepper is catholic. Regional tastes in something even as common as rice may vary widely. China and Japan prefer short grain. India likes a fluffy long grain with salt, Malaysia and her neighbours much the same but without salt, while Laotians, South-east Asians, adore sticky rice. Those I know about, anyhow.

Raw versus cooked is a striking contrast to the

taste traveller. Once wonders if those enjoying the current fad of *sashimi* fish realise that it was originally eaten raw (and wriggling fresh) in a Japan with meagre fuel resources. Conserving fuel has been the basis of other styles. Stir-frying in a wok produces the most delicious amalgam of flavours and textures. It also uses one container, and that quickly, for the principal part of the meal.

Besides *tartare*, a chopped raw beef (the Mongols started with horse), the Lebanese make a combination of chopped mutton, or lamb if you wish, with soaked, coarse-ground wheat called *kibbi*. Raw or cooked, it is delicious. There are an interesting number of variations, to the extent that some gourmets of Lebanese ancestry amuse themselves by guessing at the familial and geographical background of the cook.

There is little point in dwelling on the geography of fruit, mainly because now so many are available world-wide, either grown nearby or speedily transported by one means or another. Two that still somehow retain a secure local identity are the faecal, creamy, tropical durian of the Spice Islands, and the persimmon in Japan. Otherwise put, you only truly understand their unique flavours in their homeland. The persimmon liqueur made by a traditional Tokyo grandmother can be truly ambrosial.

Flavour has always benefited by national intercourse. Sometimes this has been peaceful, as it was after the marriage of the Florentine Renaissance and the court of France, but more often it has been the result of conquest or emigration, as it was with Islam's gift of coffee and distillation. But there is nothing in history to compare with the cross-fertilisation that has occurred during this century, by the migrations from persecutions and conflicts in Europe, the Middle East, India, and South-east Asia.

There is some soul of goodness in things evil
Would men observingly distil it out
Thus may we gather honey from the weed.

Henry V, William Shakespeare

EPILOGUE

27

Epilogue

It is very hard to make predictions, especially about the future.

Samuel Goldwyn

Quite recently, I read of a substantial public response to an advertisement in *Agricultural Digest* which featured the actual odour of the leather trim of a Rolls-Royce. Such exposure is becoming common. Morley Kare suspects that up to four hundred billion dollars are now spent each year world-wide to alter the smells and tastes of earthly existence. Are we getting value? We certainly are from institutes like Monell, the Warwick group, the Fragrance Foundation, and others around the world too numerous to mention here. We must supply more money and we must apply their findings with more despatch.

Who has heard of how Monell has developed 'scapegoat' management of that loss of appetite that is a part of the misery and deterioration of some forms of late cancer? The method works by focusing general aversion to food onto some preliminary item of little nutritional value such as diet soda. In some astonishing way that leaves the patient clear to eat a reasonable diet afterwards. The fizz seems to mop up all the dislike of food; has become a scapegoat. Of course, that patient will never like diet soda again!

A major Japanese company has a huge investment in a robot that monitors and manipulates fragrances in a closed environment, to be checked and changed on a frequent and regular basis during the month. The more we understand the workings of the smell brain, the better we will be able to make this odour Muzak work for us.

There are new applications of the role of memory of olfaction. Suppressed memories are being recalled and dealt with by odour association and good 'vibes' (happy hormones) encouraged by making attractive aromas an intrinsic part of the treatment. Miriam Rothschild has reported recent experiments that apply this potential to enhancing the learning process and conditioning at various ages. How many have already made use of this technique without realising it?

The relationship between pheromones, hormones and immunity has been mentioned in several places in this book. It is a hot topic of research. One private American organisation has spent a mint on it without releasing any details, yet. From Monell, Gary Beauchamp's mice area pointer to the future. Male mice prefer to mate with females whose collection of immune responses is as different from their own as they can be. The biological bonus of this is the widest possible immunity in the offspring. What is astonishing is how they acquire the ability to detect immune responses. They get it from the smell of their mother at suckling. If their odour perception is destroyed, they make random choices. In another experiment quoted by Stuart Berger, rats were given flavoured water containing a drug which knocked out their immune systems. Later, after they returned to normal health, the same flavour given without the drug repressed their immune response. Should these experiments have a human analogy, just ponder the ramifications.

The increasing application of computers to odour and taste is paralleled by the high-tech development of the machines themselves. On the one hand we are looking at the beginning of a multi-dimensional intelligence that will give today's children a future breadth of perception and response we can only guess at. On the other hand, the input from computer sensors is also in a state of flux. Enzyme-based biosensors already exist, and now bioengineering is designing molecules that will, among many functions, be able to detect and measure specific odours. Even as I write, the backroom think-tanks are dreaming up ways of incorporating living matter in silicon chips, a tertiary development of true biocomputers. These will probably exert their magic on 'natural' fragrances and flavours intentionally produced inside living bacteria, and harvested for our benefit.

We have been living in an era during which the incredible olfactory capacity we still have has been seriously neglected. We are nearly through that now. I believe we are on a curve; the future itself has become a part of the essence of excitement. The world has begun a new exploration of flavour and fragrance, with the potential to lift it into a fresh orbit of enjoyment. The other unique promise of our time is that there are now so many with the capacity to share it. Enjoy!

Glossary

ABSOLUTE. Perfume extraction tends to be a closely guarded secret. We have all had the experience of being given some special recipe only to find that the result leaves something to be desired. Some minute but essential detail has been 'forgotten'. In broad terms an absolute is obtained by extracting the concretes (q.v.) with alcohol and then evaporating the alcohol under reduced pressure, leaving a residue of honey consistency. Older methods involved initial extraction with the petals in, or on, some form of warm or cold fat (for example, lard, mutton), which was then treated with a solvent finally to yield an absolute coupled with the name of the solvent.

ACETYLATION. The transfer of -C-C- from one molecule to another, as in the breakdown of fatty acids.

ADRENALIN. In *Through the Looking Glass* Lewis Carroll had Humpty Dumpty sharply telling Alice that a word could mean anything he chose. Here I have given the word a rather broad application, as an excitement hormone, a representative of a special group of neurotransmitters, and an adrenal gland secretion. The meanings span several quite different molecules with functions that have some relation to each other.

ALCOHOL. A compound where -OH is attached to a -C-. Where this is in a ring it is called a phenol. Alcohols oxidise to aldehydes, and form esters with acids. The alcohol that is 'such a good and cheerful creature' (treated with proper respect) is ethyl alcohol, ethanol, -C-C-OH. See Chapter 15, 'The Flavour of Wine', and also the Index.

ALDEHYD. A carbon-chain molecule with a tail of H-C=O joined to another -C-. Aldehydes oxidise to acids and reduce to alcohols.

ALKALOID. An alkaline plant extractive with a nitrogen atom in the ring structure of the active molecule. Many important drugs and poisons are derived from alkaloids.

AMYGDALA. The almond-shaped part of the smell brain, also concerned with long-term memory and emotion. See Index.

ANDROSTENONE. Another grab-bag of a word, adopted in the interests of simplicity and prompted by the numbers of close relatives in the research literature. The principal male pheromone, it is produced by special glands (apocrine) that empty on the hairs. It is formed in both sexes by the influence of testosterone. It smells of musk among other things, and is the raw fuel of libido. It drives the female menstrual cycle. (See Chapter 2, 'Marine Venus'.) One-third of the general population can't smell it, which may be just as well, as it can provoke serious aggression in men. Because it is such a relatively heavy molecule for a volatile I have called it the close-up pheromone. It is discussed at length in Chapter 1, 'The Transfer of Excitement', and in Chapter 24, 'Genesis'. It may not be as important in human sexual activity as, for example, it is in pigs, because by the time it is perceived in sufficient strength to exert its effect the die may be cast, so to speak. See Index.

AUTONOMIC NERVOUS SYSTEM. Part of the nervous system that oversees the body's steady state. The central automatic control resides in the hypothalamus and has inputs from all over the body. The front of the hypothalamus has a parasympathetic orientation (for example, ejaculation, emptying of the bladder) and the rear half is concerned with the sympathetic responses like arousal, erection and 'goose pimples'. See Hypothalamus and the Index.

BETA ENDORPHIN. One of a substantial group of molecules found widely in the body, classed as brain hormones because they are produced in quantity in the brain at sites where the opium family of drugs act. They are eighteen to fifty times stronger than morphine (D.A. Fox). There is a gradual and phenomenal rise in placental levels as pregnancy advances. Some women experience a precipitous fall in the endorphin level after the event of birth which may be responsible for post-natal depression. See Chapter 22, 'Highs and Happy Hormones', and the Index. See also endorphin.

BROWNIAN MOVEMENT. The random dance of minute particles in suspension caused by the bombardment of surrounding molecules, named after Robert Brown and figured out by Albert Einstein.

CASOMORPHIN. An enkephalin (q.v.) found in milk.

CONCRETE. Concretes and absolutes are called 'natural flower oils'. They are made by a different process than the distillation and pressing of what the industry calls the essential oils. They all end with different and sometimes major fragrance variations from the original starting point of flowers, leaves, roots etc. The 'concrete' is extracted from early morning flowers under the coolest and most careful conditions by waxy solvents, which are evaporated without heat to leave a fairly thick wax. It takes up to a month to dissolve some of this concrete with alcohol, and the resulting tincture in many cases has a remarkable fidelity to its source that may be irreplaceable. If this alcohol is now evaporated, the absolute remains. Modern technological modifications of these ancient principles do not concern us here.

DMS. Dimethyl sulphide, a most unpleasant smell in the cabbage/radish area, except at less than one or two parts per million, when with other more attractive fragrances it gives a certain lift and attractive complexity to overall character, or at least some think so.

DODECANOL. A 12-carbon alcohol, one of the hundreds of natural odorants in human genital smells. It is fatty, soapy and sour in excess. Still within the intensity discussed in Chapter 7, 'To Choose a Fragrance', the normal rise at ovulation can be delicate and floral. Said to be found in some flowers and Mexican lime.

DYNORPHIN. The most powerful enkephalin (q.v.).

ENDORPHIN. Morphine-like substances produced by your body. They block pain signals and 'lift' mood. Dr Fox believes an hour's quiet thought may raise the level. There may be as many as twenty of them. They are 'protected' by phenylalanine, an essential amino acid present in normal diet. See also Beta endorphin, Casomorphin, Dynorphin, and Enkephalin.

ENKEPHALIN (or encephalin). An opium-like family of molecules distributed widely in the tissues. It was the first of the pain-blocking opioid brain hormones to be discovered and is the shortest of the family. See Chapter 22, 'Highs and Happy Hormones'.

ESTER. Formed by the combination of acid and alcohol. Many have characteristic fruity odours.

5-GMP (GUANYLATE), and IMP (INOSINATE). Flavour intensifiers. See Chapter 12, 'Flavour Power'.

FRUCTOSE. A 6-carbon carbohydrate that is twice as sweet as another 6-carbon sugar glucose. It is teamed with this to form sucrose, ordinary table sugar.

GLUTAMATE. Formed from the essential amino acid glutamic acid. It is a natural neurotransmitter, discussed in Chapter 22, 'Highs and Happy Hormones'. Its monosodium salt MSG (q.v.) is in the spotlight in Chapter 12, 'Flavour Power'. Also see Index.

GONADOTROPHIN. The group name for some of the pituitary sexual hormones, also formed by the placenta. Their functions include stimulation of the gonads (sexual organs), and the tuning of the emotions and actions of mother love.

HIPPOCAMPUS. That part of the limbic system (q.v.) which used to be more intelligibly called the smell brain. It has some known specific memory functions and with the amygdala is part of odour recognition. See Chapter 20, 'The Three R's'.

HOMEOSTASIS. A steady state of the body chemistry. There are numerous feedback loops and mechanisms which, in health, return body functions to this phase after any excursion above or below the line. This includes all normal activity up to and including extreme stress.

HYPOTHALAMUS. Sitting inside the skull rather where the pips of an apple are, it is the control station of the autonomic nervous system (q.v.). It influences fear, rage, lust, greed, sleep and thirst. It is in electronic contact, and also on a hormone freeway, with the pituitary gland which hangs below it. The connections with the smell brain and the newer intelligent cerebral cortex are so extensive I sometimes wonder which is the boss. The best neurological definition of the limbic system is any part of the brain which has a synaptic (q.v.) connection with the hypothalamus.

IBA. Isobutyraldehyde is a 4-carbon aldehyde that is thought to act as a pheromonal marker for the breast-seeking infant.

IMP. Isomethoxy propyl pyrazine. The butyl cousin does just as well. The high note of the smell of green vegetation, especially bell pepper or capsicum. See Chapter 25, 'IMP and Family'.

INDOLE. One of the disgusting smells of the rear end of animals and their waste products, without an infinitesimal amount of which an amazing number of our favourite fragrances don't smell of their 'natural goodness'. See Chapter 7, 'To Choose a Fragrance', and the Index.

INTERBRAIN. Seemed like a good idea fifty years ago when I was being seduced into the wonders of comparative neurology. It includes the thalamus and the brain immediately above and below it. As a concept it is out of fashion now.

ION. Chip the single orbiting electron away from the shell of an atom of hydrogen and it becomes electronically charged. A hydrogen ion in solution is positive and tastes acidic, and travels (ion is from the Greek for traveller) in the opposite direction from negative ions.

IVA. Isovaleric acid is a 5-carbon acid present in the healthy vagina as a result of the action of the lactic bacteria family. It peaks at ovulation and its aroma is one of the main constituents of intimate feminine attraction and some of the world's most popular cheeses. Because of its relative light weight and volatility it falls into the category of what I have called the distant pheromones. See Chapter 2, 'Marine Venus'.

LACTONE. Ring molecules with a -CO-C- link formed from acids. There are some delightful aromas in this family; for instance, peach has more than one. See 'whisky lactone' in the Index.

LIMBIC SYSTEM. Originally and simply called the smell brain. Broca 'improved' the name when he identified a complex ring of nerve cell centres around that part of the inside of the brain which deals with visceral activity (including sex), odour, including the computer memory bank, and a substantial part of their emotional and mood components. G.O. Watts in 1975 identified over fifty regions involved, extending from the midbrain into the base of the new cortex. The end is not in sight, because of the difficulties of investigating such a deep-seated area. To date much of our knowledge springs from careful observation of a few chance results of surgery for some quite unrelated indication or from an unfortunate accident like an ice pick up the nose. See Hypothalamus, Chapter 20, 'The Three R's', and the Index.

MAILLARD REACTION. A new range of flavours arising from the interaction of an amino acid and a sugar in the temperature range of a medium oven. The source of many of our most enticing flavours, for example, bread crust and toast, potato chips, beer, coffee. See Chapter 13, 'Fire, Smoke and Ice', and the Index.

MOLECULAR WEIGHT. Near enough to the sum of the weights of the atoms that make up the molecule and having a bearing on how easily it moves around. See Volatile.

MSG. A sodium salt of the essential amino acid, glutamic acid. Meaty, 'delicious', *umami*, flavour enhancer, present in a wide variety of everyday foods. It is quite harmless in recommended quantities except in those with a specific allergy which is not common. See Chapter 12, 'Flavour Power', and the Index.

NERVE. Five and possibly six cranial nerves carry smell and taste information to the brain. The first, olfactory, nerve is actually a projection of the smell brain that resides in the attic above the back of the nose. All the rest are concerned entirely with sending taste information. Apart from the quintet we call sweet, sour, salty, bitter and *umami*, the fifth or trigeminal nerve carries all the sensations of the rest of flavour. What is left? Texture (sound of crunch, and fizz, go via the eight or auditory nerve), hot/cold, pain/pungent, and mouthfeel as in oily, thin and so on. The taste quintet above (sweet etc.) travel by the seventh or facial nerve, the ninth or glossopharyngeal, and by the tenth or vagus nerves. If you think that is complicated, consider the calibre of the doctors around the turn of the century who worked it out from the riddles presented by patients, and by evolutionary studies of the animal hierarchy. There is more in Chapter 20, 'The Three R's'.

NEUROTRANSMITTER. The end fibre of a nerve cell does not connect directly to another nerve, muscle or secretory gland. Difficult as it is to believe, there is a microscopic gap and the electrical nerve impulse is ferried across the gap by a chemical, the neurotransmitter, of which a growing number have been found in this most fruitful area of current research. To help the reader through the maze of specific substances like epinephrine, norepinephrine, serotonin, dopamine, and so on, I have purposely blurred the picture and avoided these and some others in the text. This is sure to draw the fire of researchers denied this indulgence. So be it. Adrenalin, glutamates, enkephalins, PEA, are enough for now. Are you confused about hormones? I said a hormone was a chemical messenger, and isn't that what a neurotransmitter is? In earlier days hormones used to deliver their message to glands and neurotransmitters to nerves, but in the last ten years the lines have crossed. That is why you will see neurotransmitters floating free in the brain fluid called brain hormones, and the brain itself described as the thinking gland.

OPIOID. A substance with the actions of opium and its derivatives, acting through the same receptors to relieve pain, induce a state of euphoria and so on.

OXYTOCIN. A hormone secreted by the posterior part of the pituitary gland. Causes contraction of the uterus and ejection of milk. It happens to be the first protein to have been synthesised. See Chapter 10, 'Love and Orgasm'.

PEA. Phenylethylamine is a mood-altering chemical said to be an essential part of the tender emotion, specifically 'falling in love' and perhaps much more. Those who have confessed to going on chocolate binges, and especially if they have been crossed in love, are not surprised to learn that chocolate is rich in PEA.

PHENYLETHYLALCOHOL. Characteristic rose odour, a major part of natural rose fragrance, a role analagous with that of ionone in violet fragrance.

pH. A measure of the available acidity. The figure is actually the log of the hydrogen ion concentration. Zero is the most acid, 7 is neutral, and 14 the most alkaline. Small changes in the pH imply major changes in biological systems, because they are usually buffered and hold their pH constant or within narrow limits. See Index.

PHEROMONE. A volatile substance, the odour of which evokes a response in another member of the same species. It is often, but not necessarily, sexual. The more inhibited male scientists and editors appear still to have a problem in accommodating a human equivalent. See Chapter 1, 'The Transfer of Excitement', Chapter 2, 'Marine Venus', and the Index.

POLYMER. A molecule of linked repeats of a single original, or group of, molecules. Glucose polymerises to starch. See Index.

PYRAZINE. A six-atom -C- ring with two -N= atoms opposite each other in the circle. A major base of flavours.

SYNAPSE. A microscopic gap between two nerve ends across which the chemicals of nerve impulse transmission flow.

TEMAVOUR. A new word humbly offered to fill the need to indicate the emotional response some consider to be an inseparable and intrinsic part of smell and taste. I do not believe it is possible to smell or taste anything without registering a positive or negative value. If you agree, the word will take on. Discussed further in Chapter 20, 'The Three R's'. Also see the Index.

TERPENE C_5H_8. Molecules in single, treble, or more rows. Usually pleasant, very definite characters in the essential oils of peel, leaves, and so on.

TMA. Trimethylamine is the smell of rotting seafood. At subthreshold levels and just beyond (see Chapter 20, 'The Three R's'), it is a powerful flavour enhancer analogous to MSG. It is said to be a menstrual pheromone in some individuals. See Chapter 2, 'Marine Venus', Chapter 12, 'Flavour Power', and the Index.

VOLATILE. Capable of flying (*OED* 1626). Liable to evaporation or diffusion at ordinary temperatures. Discussed in the conception of distant and close-up attractants. See Chapter 1, 'The Transference of Excitement'. In wine jargon, it has also been used to mean the odour of a certain kind of spoilage, but in that case is qualified in the context.

Bibliography

Amerine, Maynard A., Pangborn, Rose Marie, and Roessler, Edward B., *Principles of Sensory Evaluation of Food* (Academic Press, New York, 1965).

—— and Roessler, Edward, *Wines, their Sensory Evaluation* (San Francisco, Freeman, 1976).

Amoore, J.E., 'Specific Anosmia, A Clue to the Olfactory Code', *Nature*, vol. 214, p. 1095, 1967.

—— 'A Plan to Identify Most of the Primary Odours', *Proc. III. Internat. Symp. Olfaction and Taste* (ed.), Pfaffman, Carl. (Rockefeller University Press, New York, 1969).

—— 'Specific Anosmia and the Concept of Primary Odours', *Chemical Senses and Flavour*, vol. 2, pp. 267–81, 1977.

Anon., *Sweet, Sour, Salty, Bitter and Umami* (Umami Information Centre, Tokyo, 1988).

Apicius, *The Art of Cooking*, trans. by Flower, Barbara, and Rosenbaum, Elisabeth (Harrap, London, 1958).

Arctander, Steffan, *Perfume and Flavor Material of Natural Origins* (Elizabeth, N.J., published by the author, 1960).

Arndt, Bettina, quoting Emily Jacobs, *Observer Fortnightly*, Sydney, 31 July 1987, p. 35.

Arnold, Sue, 'Scents and Sensibility', *Observer Magazine*, 27 July 1988, p. 66.

Asimov, Isaac, *Asimov's New Guide to Science* (Penguin Books, London, 1987).

Athenaeus, *The Deipnosophists*, trans. C.B. Gulisk, vol. 2, section 148 (William Heinemann, London, 1967).

Attenborough, David, *Life on Earth* (William Collins, London, 1979).

Auel, Jean, *The Mammoth Hunters* (Hodder & Stoughton, London, 1985).

Bacon, Francis, 'Of Gardens', *Essays* (Everyman's Library edition, Dent, London, 1972).

Bacon, Josephine, 'Search for the Sun and The Importance of the Citron', *Oxford Symposium on Taste* (Prospect Books, London, 1987), p. 21.

Bailey, Adrian, and Dowell, Phillip, *The Book of Ingredients* (Michael Joseph, London, 1980).

Baillen, Claude, *Chanel Solitaire* (Quadrangle/New York Times Book Co., New York, 1974).

Balogh, Esther, 'Tastes in and Tastes of Paprika', *Oxford Symposium on Taste* (Prospect Books, London, 1987), p. 25.

Barraclough, Geoffrey (ed.), *The Times Atlas of World History* (Times Books, London, 1978).

Beauchamp, Garry, quoted in: 'Mothers Will Choose All your Girlfriends for You', *New Scientist*, 23 June 1988, p. 42.

Beck, Simone, Bertholle, Louisette, and Child, Julia, *Mastering the Art of French Cooking* (Cassell, London, 1963).

Bedicheck, Roy, *The Sense of Smell* (Michael Joseph, London, 1960).

Beeton, Isabella, *Book of Household Management* (Ward Lock, London, new edition, 1906).

Bergland, Richard, *The Fabric of the Mind* (Penguin Books, London, 1985).

Besedovsky, Hugo O., del Rey, 'Immune-Neuroendocrine Network', *Progress in Immunology VI* (Academic Press, New York, 1986).

Bienfang, Ralph, *The Subtle Sense* (University of Oklahoma Press, USA, 1946).

Billot, M. and Wells, F.V., *Perfumery Technology. Art: Science: Industry* (Ellis Horwood, Chichester, 1975).

Birch, Martin, and Hefetz, Abraham, 'The Mating of Moths', *New Scientist*, October 1986, p. 48.

Bobrow, N.A., Money, J., and Lewis, V.G., 'Delayed Puberty, Eroticism, and the Sense of Smell, Kallmann's Syndrome', *1,329 Archives of Sexual Behaviour*, 1971.

Brillat-Savarin, Jean, *Gastonomy as a Fine Art*, trans. by R.E. Anderson (Chatto & Windus, London, 1976).

Broadbent, Michael, *Pocket Guide to Wine Tasting* (Christie's Wine Publications, Mitchell Beazley, London, 1982).

Buchner, Greet, *Cooking with Flowers*, trans. by Helena Brandt (Thorsons, Northamptonshire, 1978).
Burton, H.S., McWheeny, D.J. and Pandhi, P.N., 'Non Enzymatic Browning. Browning of phenols and its inhibition by sulphur dioxide', *Nature*, vol. 199, pp. 659–61.
Buttery, Ron, 'Chemistry of Vegetable Flavours. Origin of Food Flavours. Odour, Potency, Chemical Structure and Volatility'. Inaugural Jeffery Lectures, University of New South Wales, 1981.
Cain, W.S. 'History of Research on Smell', in Cartette, E.C., and Friedman, M.P., *Handbook of Perception, Volume IV: Tasting and Smelling* (Academic Press, New York, 1978).
Cameron, Paul (University of Louisville), quoted in Claire Spencer, 'Good Times', *Sydney Morning Herald*, 11 February 1986, p. 1.
Carr, Sandy, *Cheese* (Mitchell Beazley Pocket Guide, London, 1981).
Carter, Carla, 'Fragrance', *Vogue Australia*, October 1986, p. 148.
Castle, Tim, 'The Taste of Coffee, the Taste for Coffee, and the Attempt to Discuss Either', *Oxford Symposium on Taste* (Prospect Books, London, 1987), p. 43.
Charles-Roux, Edmonde, *Chanel* (Jonathan Cape, London, 1976).
Chemical Formulary (Chemical Publishing Company, 1939, and Forum Books, World Books, Cleveland, Ohio, 1942).
Clark, Tom, 'Human Pheromones and Olfaction', Numbers 1 and 2 in Numbers 80 and 81. *Pharmabulletin* (Health Commission of Victoria, 1983).
Cleugh, James, *The Medici* (Doubleday, New York, 1976).
Columella, Lucius, *On Agriculture*, trans. Harrison Boyd Ash (Harvard University Press/William Heinemann, London, 1977).
Cornforth, Monica, and Davidson, Gail, 'Palette', *Harper's Bazaar*, Australia, May 1986, p. 87.
Cousins, Norman, *The Anatomy of an Illness* (Norton, New York, 1978).
Cutler, Winnifred, B. *et al.* 'Sexual Behaviour Frequency and Biphasic Ovulatory Type Menstrual Cycles', *Physiology and Behaviour*, vol. 34, 1985, p. 805.
Darwin, Charles, *Autobiography*, quoted by Thomas Mallon, in *A Book of One's Own* (Penguin, London, 1987).
Davidson, Alan, 'Tastes, Aromas, Flavours', *Oxford Sympo-*

sium on Taste (Prospect Books, London, 1987), p. 9.
Diamond, Milton, *Sexwatching* (Macdonald, London, 1984).
Douek, Ellis, *The Sense of Smell and its Abnormalities* (Churchill Livingstone, Edinburgh and London, 1974).
Dravnieks, Andres, 'Atlas of Odor Character Profiles', *ASTM Data Series*, DS 61, Philadelphia, 1985.
Droscher, Vitus, *The Magic of the Senses* (Panther Books, London, 1971).
Durden-Smith, Jo, 'How to Win the Mating Game by a Nose', *Next*, November/December 1980, p. 85.
—— and De Simone, Diane, *Sex and the Brain* (Pan Books, London, 1983).
Edis, Geneviève, *Merde Encore!* (Angus and Robertson, Sydney, 1986).
Ellis, Havelock, *Studies in the Psychology of Sex, II, Smell* (Davis, Philadelphia, 1928).
Engen, T., *The Perception of Odors* (Academic Press, New York, 1982).
Enrico, Roger, and Kornbluth, Jesse, *The Other Guy Blinked* (Bantam Books, New York, 1986).
Everett, Mark, *Medical Biochemistry* (Paul Hoeber, New York, 1942).
Eyles, M.J., and Adams, R.F., 'Rapid Chromatographic Detection of Microbial Spoilage of Commercially Sterile Food', *CSIRO Research Quarterly*, vol. 46, 1986, p. 90.
Feibleman, Peter S., *The Cooking of Spain and Portugal* (Time Life Books, 1972).
Fenaroli, Giovanni, *et al.*, *Handbook of Flavour Ingredients* (Chemical Rubber Company, Ohio, USA, 1971).
Fitzgibbon, Carmel, 'Sexual Healing', *Observer*, London, June 1988.
Flemming, J.R.G., *Sensory Analysis* (Academic Press, London, 1986).
Fox, Arnold, and Barry, *D.L.P.A.**, *To end chronic pain and depression*. Pocket Books, Simon & Schuster, New York, 1986.
Fraser, J.T., *Time the Familiar Stranger* (University of Massachusetts Press, 1987).
Furia, Thomas E., *Handbook of Food Additives* (CRC Press, Ohio, USA, 1972).
Gallagher, Winifred, 'The Etiology of the Orgasm', *Discover*, February 1986, p. 51.
Gallois, Annie, 'Les Pyrazines Presentés dans les Aliments',

Sciences des Aliments, vol. 4, 1984, pp. 145–66.

Gay, Peter, *The Bourgeois Experience, Victoria to Freud*, vol. 11. *The Tender Passion.* (Oxford and New York, Oxford University Press, 1986).

Genders, Roy, *A History of Scent* (Hamish Hamilton, London, 1972).

Gilbert, Avery, and Wysocki, Charles, 'The Smell Survey Results', *National Geographic*, October 1987, p. 514.

Gilling, Dick, and Brightwell, Robin, *The Human Brain* (Orbis Publishing, London, 1982).

Gray, Patience, *Honey from a Weed* (Prospect Books, London, 1986).

Guy, Christian, *An Illustrated History of French Cuisine* (Bramhall House, New York, 1962).

Hahn, Emily, *The Cooking of China* (Time-Life Books, New York, 1973).

Hall, Rudiger, *et al.*, *Guide to Fragrance Ingredients* (Johnson Publications, London, 1985).

Harris, Marvin, *Good to Eat* (Allen and Unwin, London, 1986).

Herrick, C. Judson, *Introduction to Neurology* (W.B. Saunders, Philadelphia, 1934).

Holaday, John, *Endogenous Opioids and Their Receptors. Current Concepts* (Upjohn, Michigan, 1985).

Houliston, Victor, 'How Good were Miss Muffet's Curds and Whey?' *Oxford Symposium on Taste* (Prospect Books, London, 1987).

Huggins, George, and Preti, George, 'Vaginal Odours and Secretions', *Clinical Obstetrics and Gynaecology*, vol. 24.2, June 1981, p. 355.

Huxley, Aldous, *Brave New World* (Harper and Row, New York, 1969).

Jackson, Judith, *Aromatherapy* (Greenhouse Publications, Victoria, Australia, 1987).

Jacobs, Emily, *British Journal of Sexual Medicine*, quoted in *Medical Observer*, Sydney, 31 July 1987, p. 35.

Jacobs, Jay, *A History of Gastronomy* (Newsweek Books, New York, 1975).

Kare, Morley R., and Maller, Owen (eds.), *The Chemical Senses and Nutrition* (Academic Press, New York, 1977).

—— Address to the Society of Wine Educators Symposium, Stamford, Connecticut, 4 August 1988.

Kawamura, Yojiro, and Kare, Morley R. (eds.) *Umami, A*

Basic Taste (Marcel Dekker, New York, 1987).
Kennett, Frances, *History of Perfume* (George C. Harrap, London, 1975).
Kensington Ladies' Erotica Society, *Ladies' Own Erotica* (Arrow Books, London, 1986).
Kimura, Dorothy, 'Male and Female Brains are Different', *Psychology Today*, November 1985, p. 51.
Kinder, Herman, and Kilgemann, Werner, *The Penguin Atlas of World History*, vol. 1. (Penguin Books, London, 1977).
Klein, D.F., and Leibowitz, M., 'Affective Disorders. Special Clinical Forms', *Psychiatric Clinics of North America*, December 1979.
Kloek, J., 'The smell of some steroid sex hormones and their metabolites', *Psychiat. Neurol. Neurochir*, vol. 64, p. 309, 1961.
Klyne, W., and Buckingham, J., *Atlas of Stereochemistry*, vols. 1 & 2 (Chapman & Hall, London, second edition, 1978).
Koestler, Arthur, *The Act of Creation* (Pan Books, London, 1970).
Kosikowski, Frank V., 'Cheese', *Scientific American* vol. 252, May 1985, p. 66.
Kuno, Yas, *Human Perspiration* (Charles C. Thomas, Springfield, Illinois, USA, 1956).
Labows, John N., 'Odorants as Chemical Messengers', *ACS Symposium Series*, No. 148, 1981, p. 197.
Lacoste, Beatrice, 'Smells Make the World Go Around', *Weekend Australian*, 24 January 1987, p. 11.
Laing, David, 'Nasal Molecular Polarity and Air Flow Rates', Lecture to Australian Society of Perfumers and Flavourists, Sydney, 1986.
Lake, Max, *The Flavour of Wine*, Address to the Australian Institute of Food Science and Technology (Jacaranda Press, Brisbane, 1969).
—— *Start to Taste*, Series: People, Food, Wine (published by author, Sydney, 1984–5).
—— 'The Hypothalamus', *Journal of the Sydney University Medical Society*, 1943.
Lamb, Charles, *The Essays of Elia* (1833).
Lambert, Joseph R. 'Shapes of Organic Molecules', *Scientific American*, No. 58, vol. 222, January 1970; and *Scientific American*, No. 46, vol. 225, August 1971.
Law, Mark, 'Ah the Sweet Smell of Success', *Mail on*

Sunday, London 1985, p. 9.

Legman, G., *Analysis of Sexual Humour. The Rationale of the Dirty Joke* (Grove Press, New York, 1971).

Leo, John, 'The Hidden Power of Body Odours', *Time Magazine*, 1 December 1986, p. 73.

McClintock, Martha K., 'Menstrual Synchrony and Suppression', *Nature*, vol. 229, pp. 224–5, 1971.

McDermott, Sandra, *A British Survey of Female Sexuality* (Corgi Books, London, 1970).

McEachern, Barbara, 'Sushi', *Kikkoman Taste*, vol. 2, 1988, p. 6.

McGee, H., *On Food & Cooking. The Science and Lore of the Kitchen* (Charles Scribner & Sons, New York, 1984).

—— 'Osmazome, the Maillard Reaction and the Triumph of the Cooked', *Oxford Symposium on Taste* (Prospect Books, London, 1987), p. 133.

McKay-Sim, Alan, and Laing, David, 'The Sources of Odours from Stressed Rats', *Physiology and Behaviour*, vol. 27, 1981, p. 551.

McLaughlin, Terence, *The Gilded Lily* (Cassell, London, 1971).

Mailer, Norman, *Ancient Evenings* (Picador, London, 1984).

Maruniak, J.A., and Mackay-Sim, A., 'The Sense of Smell', in Piggott, J.R., *Sensory Analysis of Foods* (Elsevier Applied Science Publishers, London and New York, 1984).

Mazrui, Ali, *The Africans* (BBC Television, 1986).

Michael, Richard P., *et al.*, 'Primate Sexual Pheromones' in Denton, Derek, and Coghlan, John, (eds.), *Olfaction and Taste*, V, (Academic Press, New York, 1975, p. 417).

Millen, James Knox, *Your Nose Knows* (The Cunningham Press, Los Angeles, 1960).

Mohs, Mayo, 'Where Has All the Fragrance Gone?' *Discover*, vol. 8, No. 6, 1987.

Moncrieff, R.W., *The Chemical Senses* (Leonard Hill, London, third edition, 1967).

Morris, Desmond, *The Naked Ape* (Triad Grafton Books, London, 1986).

Morris, Edwin, *Fragrance. The Story of Perfume from Cleopatra to Chanel* (Charles Scribner & Sons, New York, 1984).

Moscowitz, H., *New Directions for Product Testing and Sensory Analysis of Foods* (Food and Nutrition Press, Newport, Connecticut, USA, 1985).

Muller, Julia, *et al.*, *The H & R Book of Perfume* (Johnson Publications, London, 1984).
Nauta Walle, J.H., and Feirtag, Michael, *Fundamental Neuroanatomy* (W.H. Freeman & Co., New York, 1986).
Nickles, Harry G., *The Cooking of the Middle-East* (Time Life Books, Netherlands, 1969).
Norris, R.C., *Annual Review, Australian Government Analytical Laboratories* (Canberra Publishing and Printing Co., 1986).
NHK, Staff, *The Silk Road Photo Collection*, vol. 3 (Japan Broadcast Publishing Company, 1981).
Ohloff, G., *Olfaction and Taste* 4 (Wissenschaftliche Verlag, Stuttgart, 1972).
Oliver, Thomas, *The Real Coke, the Real Story* (Elm Tree Books/Hamish Hamilton, London, 1986).
Ostrander, Sheila and Lynn, *Superlearning* (Sphere Books, London, 1981).
Pearsall, Paul, *Super Marital Sex* (Ebury Press, London, 1988).
Pebeyre, Pierre-Jean et Jacques and Langlois Guy, *Le Grand Livre de la Truffe* (Daniel Briand, Robert Laffout, Paris, 1987).
Peterson, Vicki, 'Aromatherapy', *Harper's Bazaar*, Australia, 3 July 1987, p. 80.
Peynaud, Émile, *Le Gout de Vin* (Dunod, Paris, 1980).
—— *The Taste of Wine*, trans. Michael Schuster (Macdonald, London, 1987).
Pietras, R.J., and Moulton, D.G., 'Effects of Gonadal Steroids on Odour Detection etc.', in Denton, Derek A., and Coghlan, John P. (eds.) *Olfaction and Taste* V. (Academic Press, New York, 1975).
Piggott, J.R., *Sensory Analysis of Foods* (Elsevier Applied Science Publishers, London and New York, 1984).
Pitt, Valerie (ed.), *Dictionary of Physics* (Penguin Books, London, 1986).
Pfaff, Donald W. (ed.), *Taste Olfaction and the CNS* (Rockefeller University Press, New York, 1985).
Pliny the Elder, *Natural History*, in ten volumes, trans. H. Rackham (Harvard University Press/William Heinemann, London, 1974).
Plutarch, *The Lives of the Noble Grecians and Romans*, trans. John Dryden (Modern Library, New York).
Powell, Gareth, 'Learning Spanish, Artificial Intelligence',

Sydney Morning Herald, 28 September 1987.

Preti, G. *et al.*, *Chemical Studies on Human Vaginal Volatiles* (Monell Chemical Senses Center, Philadelphia, Scientific Program, 1981), p. 23.

Rhode, Irma, *The Viennese Cookery Book* (John Lehmann, London, 1952).

Rietz, Carl A., *A Guide to the Selection, Combination and Cooking of Foods* (AVI Publishing Company, Connecticut, 1976).

Roberts, Marjory, 'MDMA: Madness, Not Ecstasy', *Psychology Today*, June 1986, p. 14.

Rolls, Eric, *Celebration of the Senses* (Penguin Books, Australia, 1985).

Root, Waverley, *Food* (Simon and Schuster, Fireside Books, New York, 1986).

—— *The Cooking of Italy* (Time Life Books, Netherlands, 1969).

Rothschild, Miriam, 'The Red Smell of Danger', *New Scientist*, 4 September 1986, p. 34.

—— 'Hot on the Scent of Knowledge', *The Times*, London, 29 June 1988, p. 12.

Routh, Shelagh and Jonathan, *Leonardo's Kitchen Note Books* (William Collins, London, 1987).

Russell, Michael, Switz, Genevieve, and Thompson, Kate, 'Sweat Synchronises Menstrual Cycles', quoted in *New Scientist*, 8 January 1981, p. 71.

Sacks, Oliver, *The Man Who Mistook His Wife for a Hat* (Picador, London, 1986).

Sagan, Carl, *The Dragons of Eden* (Hodder & Stoughton, London, 1977).

—— *Broca's Brain* (Hodder & Stoughton, London, 1979).

Schiffman, Susan, 'Taste and Smell in Disease', *New England J. Med.*, vol. 308, No. 21, 1983, p. 1275.

Schultz, H.W. (ed.), *The Chemistry and Physiology of Flavors* (AVI Publishing, Connecticut, 1967).

Seely, James, *Great Bordeaux Wines* (Secker and Warburg, London, 1986).

Sharp, D.W.A., *Dictionary of Chemistry* (Penguin Books, London, 1983).

Shipton, Jack, Murray, Keith, Whitfield, Frank, and Last, John, 'In Volatiles of Off-flavoured Unblanched Green Peas', *J. Sci. Fd. Agric.*, vol. 27, p. 1093, 1976.

Smith, Emil L., *et al.*, 'Principals of Biochemistry', *Mam-*

malian Biochemistry (McGraw-Hill, New York, 1985).
Shnitzer, Rita, *The Mystery of Perfume* (Orbis, London, 1985).
Sokolov, Raymond, 'Of Curds and Whey', *Oxford Symposium on Taste* (Prospect Books, London, 1987), p. 195.
Solomon, Charmaine, *The Complete Asian Cookbook* (Summit Books, Sydney, 1976).
Steiner, Jacob, 'What the Neonate can Tell Us about Umami', In Kawamura, Yojiro, and Kare, Morley R. (eds.), *Umami, A Basic Taste* (Marcel Jekker, New York, 1987).
Stirling, John (ed.), *The Bible for Today* (Oxford University Press, New York, 1941).
Symons, Donald, *The Evolution of Human Sexuality* (Oxford University Press, New York, 1979).
Tannahill, Reay, *Food in History* (Eyre Methuen, London, 1973).
Toohey, Michael, 'Nasal Sex. The Odour of Love', p. 25, August 1977, *Hustler Magazine*, Columbus, Ohio. And letters in reply, October 1977.
Trimmer, Eric, J. (ed.), *The Visual Dictionary of Sex* (Macmillan, London, 1978).
Turk, A. *et al.*, *Human Responses to Environmental Odors* (Academic Press, New York, 1974).
Ubarov, E.B., and Isaacs, Alan, *Dictionary of Science* (Penguin Books, London, 1986).
Van Toller, S., Dood, G.H., and Billing, Anne, *Ageing and the Sense of Smell* (Charles C. Thomas, Springfield, Illinois, USA, 1985).
Van Toller, S., Dodd, G.H., and Billing, Anne, *Ageing and the Psychology and Biology of Fragrance* (Chapman and Hall, London, 1988).
Wallace, Irving and family, *The Intimate Sex Lives of Famous People* (Arrow Books, London, 1981).
Walter, Erich, *Manual for the Essence Industry* (John Wiley and Sons, New York, 1916).
Webb, Peter, *The Erotic Arts* (Secker and Warburg, London, 1975).
Weber, Joseph, and Smith, Emily T., 'The Scientist Who is Turning Nova into a Star', *Business Weekly*, 25 July 1988, p. 67.
Wechsberg, Joseph, *Blue Trout and Black Truffles* (Gollancz, London, 1953).

Weintraub, Pamela, 'Scentimental Journals', *Omni*, p. 48, 8 April 1986.

Wessels, Norman K. 'How Living Cells Change Shape', *Scientific American*, No. 77, vol. 225, July 1971.

Whitten, W.K., 'Modification of the Oestrus Cycle of the Mouse by External Stimuli Associated with the Male', *Journal of Endocrinology* vol. 13, pp. 399–404, 1956.

Wills, Ron, *et al.*, *Postharvest. An Introduction to the Physiology and Handling of Fruit and Vegetables* (New South Wales University Press, Sydney, 1982).

Williams, Roger, 'How Do You Smell?' *Sunday Times Supplement*, 14 June 1987, p. 24.

Wood, Jones F., *Buchanan's Manual of Anatomy*, (Ballière, Tindall & Cox, London, seventh edition 1946).

—— and Porteus, S.D., *Matrix of the Mind* (University Press of Hawaii, 1928).

Wright, R.H., *The Science of Smell* (Basic Books, New York, 1964).

—— *The Sense of Smell* (CRC Press, Florida, USA, 1982).

—— 'Odor and Molecular Vibration: Optical Isomers', *Chemical Senses and Flavour*, vol. 35, No. 3, 1978.

Wysocki, C.J., *Non-olfactory Nasal Chemoreception* (Monell Chemical Senses Center, Philadelphia, 1982).

Yen Hung Fen, Doreen, *The Joy of Chinese Cooking* (Faber and Faber, London, 1952).

Index

Also see Glossary